W9-BWJ-644

This
GLORIOUS
Struggle

ALSO BY EDWARD G. LENGEL

General George Washington: A Military Life

 Smithsonian Books

Collins
An Imprint of HarperCollinsPublishers

This GLORIOUS *Struggle*

GEORGE WASHINGTON'S
Revolutionary War Letters

EDITED BY
EDWARD G. LENGEL

All photo insert images are in the public domain. Those marked "DLC" were down-loaded from images at the Library of Congress and Photographs Collection online.

Maps © Rick Britton

HarperCollins books may be purchased for educational, business, or sales promotional use. For information, please write: Special Markets Department, Harper-Collins Publishers, 10 East 53rd Street, New York, NY 10022.

FIRST EDITION

Designed by Cassandra J. Pappas

Library of Congress Cataloging-in-Publication Data

Washington, George, 1732–1799.
 This glorious struggle : George Washington's Revolutionary War letters / edited by Edward G. Lengel.—1st ed.
    p. cm.
 Includes bibliographical references.
 ISBN 978-0-06-125131-3
 1. Washington, George, 1732–1799—Correspondence. 2. Generals—United States—Correspondence. 3. United States—History—Revolution, 1775–1783—Personal narratives. I. Lengel, Edward G. II. Title.

 E203.W298 2008
 973.4'3092—dc22

2007040079

08 09 10 11 12 OV/RRD 10 9 8 7 6 5 4 3 2 1

To my brother, Eric B. Lengel:

Teacher Extraordinaire

Acknowledgments

My debt to the Papers of George Washington documentary editing project, where I have worked since 1996, is enormous and can never be repaid. It begins with three former editors in chief, Bill Abbot, Dorothy Twohig, and Philander Chase; and continues with the current editor in chief, Ted Crackel, and his distinguished staff of editors: Beverly Runge, Christine Patrick, David Hoth, Bill Ferraro, Jennifer Stertzer, and Tom Dulan. It is worth mentioning that the letter transcriptions in this book are my own, and that I—not the Papers of George Washington—bear sole responsibility for any errors of transcription or interpretation.

I am particularly grateful to all of the wonderful people at Mount Vernon, who have laid out the welcome mat for me so many times over the past three years that I am feeling rather like a part-time resident at the Grand Old Man's estate: the director, Jim Rees; the regent of the Ladies' Association, Gay Gaines; Ann Bay; Nancy Hayward; and Wendy Van Woerkom. For too many reasons to list, my thanks also (in no particular order) to Don Higginbotham, John Ferling, Caroline Cox, John B. Hattendorf, Peter Henriques, Wayne Bodle, David Hackett Fischer, Henry Wiencek, David McCullough, and Professor Olivier Chaline of the Sorbonne, France. Thanks especially to Joe Ellis for his ongoing inspiration and support, and for his foreword to this book; my superb editor at Smithsonian Books, Elisabeth Dyssegaard, and my agent, Peter Matson. And, as always, to my wife, Laima; my children, Mike, Laura, and Tomas; my parents, Alan and Shelbia; and my brother, Eric.

Contents

Preface

Soon after the American victory in the War for Independence, George Washington predicted that historians would have a difficult time explaining the triumph:

> If Historiographers should be hardy enough to fill the page of History with the advantages that have been gained with unequal numbers (on the part of America) in the cause of this contest ..., it is more than probably that Posterity will bestow on their labors the epithet and marks of fiction; for it will not be believed that such a force as Great Britain has employed for eight years in Country could be baffled ... by numbers infinitely less, composed of Men oftentimes half starved; always in Rags, without pay, and experiencing, at times, every species of distress which human nature is capable of undergoing.

Washington's prediction has proven prophetic. In the first century, the emphasis was placed on the bottomless resolve of the citizen-soldiers, most especially the militia, in conjunction with the brilliant generalship of Washington himself. Neither of these patriotic interpretations has stood the test of time, as the documentary evidence has gathered to undermine the military effectiveness of the state-based militia, the waning support for the war in the countryside after it became a protracted war of attrition, and to expose Washington's multiple blunders—both tactical and strategic—in engagements against the British army. (Indeed, no successful commander in American history lost more battles than George Washington.) That said, unlike several military geniuses who won more battles—Hannibal, Napoleon, and Robert E. Lee come to mind—Washington won the war. How did he do it?

If you are serious about finding an answer to that question, this selective and judicious edition of Washington's wartime correspondence by Edward G. Lengel is the best place to begin. The full wartime correspondence, currently being edited by the staff of the *Washington Papers* at the University of Virginia, is the ultimate source, to be sure, but it remains a work in progress, likely to run to forty volumes, and is littered with battle orders, memoranda composed in haste and confusion, and logistical and administrative directives of little historical importance. Lengel has extracted the nuggets from this cavernous gold mine based on his knowledge and judgment as the member of the staff of the *Washington Papers* most responsible for the war years.

The net result is a double-barreled perspective that, on the one hand, immerses the reader in quite specific and palpable military actions—the Boston siege, the calamity at Long Island, the risky expedition across the Delaware, the fog at Germantown, the culmination at Yorktown. You are there for these times that tried men's souls, experiencing the contingency of it all as only the primary sources can convey.

On the other hand, Lengel affords a glimpse at the more panoramic perspectives, or perhaps has selected documents that allow us to see the larger picture that formed in Washington's mind as this eight-year war swung and swayed. For make no mistake about it: right up until the decisive victory at Yorktown, the outcome was very much in doubt.

At this more panoramic level, three overlapping questions get raised. First, how did Washington's understanding of the war he was fighting grow with time? Second, when and why did Washington come to the realization that he was leading, if you will, an insurgency as well as an army, which transformed the conflict from a contest he could not win, to a struggle the British could not win? Third, why did the lessons Washington learned in this roller-coaster ride make him such an outspoken advocate of a fully empowered federal government long before that idea was palatable to most Americans?

These are huge questions, and readers are unlikely to agree on all the answers. But Lengel has collected the documents here that permit the most informed dialogue we are likely to possess in order to launch this argument without end. History is happening in these pages, and Lengel's selection of sources takes you along for one of the most thrilling, topsy-turvy rides in the American experience.

Joseph J. Ellis

Editor's Note

I have transcribed the letters in this volume so as to make them correspond as literally as possible with the original manuscripts. The original format, punctuation, grammar, style, and spelling, even when in error, have almost always been retained. For ease of reading, I have made some exceptions to this rule by expanding contractions, and inserting letters and short words that the original writer (either Washington or one of his aides) had inadvertently omitted.

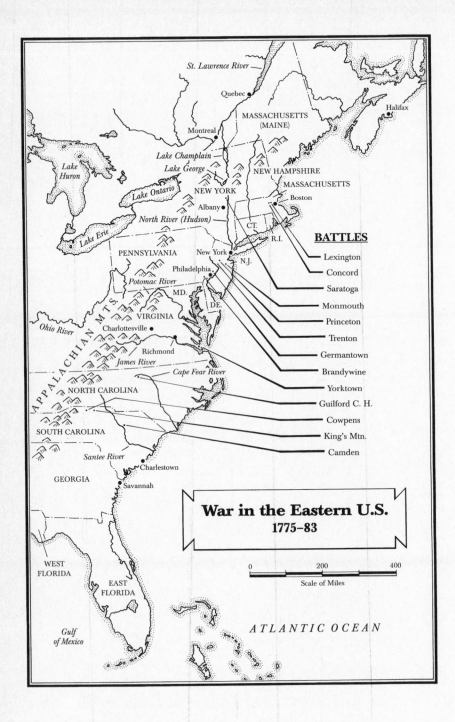

St. Lawrence River

Quebec

MASSACHUSETTS
(MAINE)

Halifax

Montreal

Lake
Huron

Lake Champlain
Lake George

NEW HAMPSHIRE
MASSACHUSETTS

Lake Ontario

NEW YORK

Boston

Lake Erie

Albany

North River (Hudson)

CT.

R.I.

BATTLES

PENNSYLVANIA

New York

N.J.

Lexington

Philadelphia

Concord

Potomac River

MD.

Saratoga

DE.

Monmouth

Ohio River

VIRGINIA

Charlottesville

Princeton

Trenton

Richmond

Germantown

James River

Brandywine

Cape Fear River

Yorktown

NORTH CAROLINA

Guilford C. H.

SOUTH CAROLINA

Cowpens

King's Mtn.

Santee River

Camden

APPALACHIAN MTS.

Charlestown

GEORGIA

Savannah

WEST
FLORIDA

EAST
FLORIDA

War in the Eastern U.S.
1775–83

0   200   400

Scale of Miles

Gulf
of Mexico

ATLANTIC OCEAN

1775

JUNE 16
ADDRESS TO CONGRESS

On May 9, 1775, George Washington arrived in Philadelphia to attend the Second Continental Congress, to which he had been elected as a delegate from Virginia. He found the city abuzz with talk of war. On April 19, American militiamen and British redcoats had fought a series of skirmishes near Lexington and Concord in Massachusetts; and now a swarm of Yankee minutemen was assembling to besiege the British garrison in Boston. Congress, hitherto preoccupied with political matters, now had to contemplate and prepare for a full-scale war with Great Britain—America's erstwhile imperial master, and the most powerful country in the world. The delegates debated how to recruit and equip an American army, and wondered who they could find to lead it. Washington, a French and Indian War hero, was the only truly military man in Congress; but although he wore his old uniform from time to time, he made no overt attempt to seek command of the army.

On June 14, John Adams brought the debates to a head by announcing that the time had come for Congress to appoint a commander in chief of the army. Adams declared "that I had but one Gentleman in my Mind for that important command, and that was a Gentleman from Virginia who was among Us and very well known to all of Us, a Gentleman whose Skill and Experience as an Officer, whose independent fortune, great Talents and excellent universal Character, would command the Ap-

probation of all America, and unite the cordial Exertions of all the Colonies better than any other Person in the Union." Washington, sitting near the door, fled the room as soon as he realized that Adams was alluding to him. On June 15, the delegates nevertheless unanimously selected him by ballot.

Washington's acceptance speech, delivered to Congress on June 16, struck some delegates as a little "too modest." Yet Washington's self-doubt was sincere. After the speech ended, choked by tears, he told Patrick Henry that "From the day I enter upon the command of the American armies, I date my fall, and the ruin of my reputation."[1]

Mr President, Tho' I am truly sensible of the high Honour done me in this Appointment, yet I feel great distress, from a consciousness that my abilities & Military experience may not be equal to the extensive & important Trust: However, as the Congress desire it I will enter upon the momentous duty, & exert every power I Possess In their service & for the Support of the glorious Cause: I beg they will accept my most cordial thanks for this distinguished testimony of their Approbation.

But lest some unlucky event should happen unfavourable to my reputation, I beg it may be remembered by every Gentleman in the room, that I this day declare with the utmost sincerity, I do not think my self equal to the Command I am honoured with.

As to pay, Sir, I beg leave to Assure the Congress that as no pecuniary consideration could have tempted me to have accepted this Arduous emploiment at the expence of my domestick ease & happiness I do not wish to make any proffit from it: I will keep an exact Account of my expences; those I doubt not they will discharge & that is all I desire.[2]

———

JUNE 18

TO MARTHA WASHINGTON

Martha Washington burned almost all of her correspondence with her husband shortly after his death. Among the few letters that survived—either because she had misplaced them, or because they held a particularly special place in her heart—were the two letters that George wrote to her just before departing to take command of the army in Massachusetts.

Philadelphia June 18th 1775.

My Dearest,

I am now set down to write to you on a subject which fills me with inexpressable concern—and this concern is greatly aggravated and Increased when I reflect on the uneasiness I know it will give you—It has been determined in Congress, that the whole Army raised for the defence of the American Cause shall be put under my care, and that it is necessary for me to proceed immediately to Boston to take upon me the Command of it. You may beleive me my dear Patcy, when I assure you, in the most solemn manner, that, so far from seeking this appointment I have used every endeavour in my power to avoid it, not only from my unwillingness to part with you and the Family, but from a consciousness of its being a trust too great for my Capacity and that I should enjoy more real happiness and felicity in one month with you, at home, than I have the most distant prospect of reaping abroad, if my stay was to be Seven times Seven years. But, as it has been a kind of destiny that has thrown me upon this Service, I shall hope that my undertaking of it, is designed to answer some good purpose—You might, and I suppose did perceive, from the Tenor of my letters, that I was apprehensive I could not avoid this appointment, as I did not even pretend to intimate when I should return—that was the case—it was utterly out of my power to refuse this appointment without exposing my Character to such censures as would have reflected dishonour upon myself, and given pain to my friends—this I am sure could not, and ought not to be pleasing to you, & must have lessened me considerably in my own esteem. I shall rely therefore, confidently, on that Providence which has heretofore preserved, & been bountiful to me, not doubting but that I shall return safe to you in the fall—I shall feel no pain from the Toil, or the danger of the Campaign—My unhappiness will flow, from the uneasiness I know you will feel at being left alone—I therefore beg of you to summon your whole fortitude & Resolution, and pass your time as agreeably as possible—nothing will give me so much sincere satisfaction as to hear this, and to hear it from your own Pen.

If it should be your desire to remove into Alexandria (as you once mentioned upon an occasion of this sort) I am quite pleased that you should put it in practice, & Lund Washington may be directed, by you, to build a Kitchen and other Houses there proper for your reception—if on the other hand you should rather Incline to spend good part of your time among your Friends below, I wish you to do so—In short, my earnest, & ardent desire is, that you would pursue any Plan that is most likely to produce content, and a tolerable degree of Tranquility as it must add greatly to my uneasy feelings to hear that you are dissatisfied, and complaining at what I really could not avoid.

As Life is always uncertain, and common prudence dictates to every Man the necessity of settling his temporal Concerns whilst it is in his power—and whilst the Mind is calm and undisturbed, I have, since I came to this place (for I had not time to do it before I left home) got Colo. Pendleton to Draft a Will for me by the directions which I gave him, which Will I now Inclose—The Provision made for you, in case of my death, will, I hope, be agreeable . . .

I shall add nothing more at present as I have several Letters to write, but to desire you will remember me to Milly & all Friends, and to assure you that I am with most unfeigned regard, My dear Patcy Your Affectionate

Go: Washington

P.S. Since writing the above I have received your Letter of the 15th and have got two suits of what I was told was the prettiest Muslin. I wish it may please you—it cost 50/. a suit that is 20/. a yard.[3]

———

JUNE 19
WASHINGTON'S COMMISSION FROM CONGRESS

In Congress
THE delegates of the United Colonies of New-hampshire, Massachusetts bay, Rhode-island, Connecticut, New-York, New-Jersey, Pennsylvania, New Castle Kent & Sussex on Delaware, Maryland, Virginia, North Carolina & South Carolina

To George Washington Esquire
WE reposing especial trust and confidence in your patriotism, conduct and fidelity Do by these presents constitute and appoint you to be GENERAL AND COMMANDER IN CHIEF of the army of the United Colonies and

of all the forces raised or to be raised by them and of all others who shall voluntarily offer their service and join the said army for the defence of American Liberty and for repelling every hostile invasion thereof And you are hereby vested with full power and authority to act as you shall think for the good and Welfare of the service.

AND we do hereby strictly charge and require all officers and soldiers under your command to be obedient to your orders & diligent in the exercise of their several duties. AND we do also enjoin and require you to be careful in executing the great trust reposed in you, by causing strict discipline and order to be observed in the army and that the soldiers are duly exercised and provided with all convenient necessaries.

AND you are to regulate your conduct in every respect by the rules and discipline of war (as herewith given you) and punctually to observe and follow such orders and directions from time to time as you shall receive from this or a future Congress of the said United Colonies or a committee of Congress for that purpose appointed.

This Commission to continue inforce until revoked by this or a future Congress.

By order of the Congress

John Hancock President[4]

———

JUNE 19
TO BURWELL BASSETT

Did George Washington feel inadequate to the command of the Continental Army? Did he fear failure, and the subsequent ruin of his reputation? Much as it contradicts the popular image of Washington as an imperturbable demigod, the answer to both questions is yes. In this letter to Martha Washington's brother-in-law, he confessed many of the worries that haunted his mind.

Philadelphia, June 19th 1775.

Dear Sir,

I am now Imbarked on a tempestuous Ocean from whence, perhaps, no friendly harbour is to be found. I have been called upon by the unanimous Voice of the Colonies to the Command of the Continental Army—It is an honour I by no means aspired to—It is an honour I wished to avoid, as well from an unwillingness to quit the peaceful enjoyment of my Family as from a thorough conviction of my own Incapacity & want of experience in the conduct of so momentous a concern—but the partiallity of the Congress added to some political motives, left me without a choice—May God grant therefore that my acceptance of it may be attended with some good to the common cause & without Injury (from want of knowledge) to my own reputation—I can answer but for three things, a firm belief of the justice of our Cause—close attention in the prosecution of it—and the strictest Integrety—If these cannot supply the places of Ability & Experience, the cause will suffer, & more than probable my character along with it, as reputation derives it[s'] principal support from success—but it will be remembered I hope that no desire, or insinuation of mine, placed me in this situation. I shall not be deprived therefore of a comfort in the worst event if I retain a consciousness of having acted to the best of my judgment.

. . .

Go: Washington

P.S. I must Intreat you & Mrs Bassett, if possible, to visit at Mt Vernon as also my Wife's other friends—I could wish you to take her down, as I have no expectations of returning till Winter & feel great uneasiness at her lonesome Situation—I have sent my Chariot & Horses back.[5]

———

JUNE 23
TO MARTHA WASHINGTON

At sunrise on June 23, Washington made his final preparations to leave Philadelphia. Well-wishers and curiosity seekers packed the streets, spilling through the doors of his boardinghouse and literally into his bedchamber. Somehow, he found the time and space to pen a final letter to his beloved wife.

Phila. June 23d 1775.

My dearest,
    As I am within a few Minutes of leaving this City, I could not think of departing from it without dropping you a line; especially as I do not

know whether it may be in my power to write again till I get to the Camp at Boston—I go fully trusting in that Providence, which has been more bountiful to me than I deserve, & in full confidence of a happy meeting with you sometime in the Fall—I have not time to add more, as I am surrounded with Company to take leave of me—I retain an unalterable affection for you, which neither time or distance can change, my best love to Jack & Nelly, & regard for the rest of the Family concludes me with the utmost truth & sincerety Yr entire

Go: Washington[6]

JULY 4
GENERAL ORDERS

On July 2, after a ten-day journey, Washington arrived at Cambridge, Massachusetts, where about 14,000 Yankee minutemen besieged about 6,000 British regular troops in Boston. The Americans assembled for inspection on the following day, wearing filthy, threadbare clothing. Their equipment was a shambles; their discipline nonexistent. Washington's job was to transform this unpromising material into the "Troops of the United Provinces of North America."

Head Quarters, Cambridge, July 4th 1775.

. . .

The Continental Congress having now taken all the Troops of the several Colonies, which have been raised, or which may be hereafter raised, for the support and defence of the Liberties of America; into their Pay and Service: They are now the Troops of the United Provinces of North America; and it is hoped that all Distinctions of Colonies will be laid aside; so that one and the same spirit may animate the whole, and the only Contest be, who shall render, on this great and trying occasion, the most essential service to the great and common cause in which we are all engaged.

It is required and expected that exact discipline be observed, and due Subordination prevail thro' the whole Army, as a Failure in these most essential points must necessarily produce extreme Hazard, Disorder and Confusion; and end in shameful disappointment and disgrace.

The General most earnestly requires, and expects, a due observance of those articles of war, established for the Government of the army, which forbid profane cursing, swearing & drunkeness; And in like manner requires & expects, of all Officers, and Soldiers, not engaged on actual duty, a punctual attendance on divine service, to implore the blessings of heaven upon the means used for our safety and defence.

All Officers are required and expected to pay diligent Attention, to keep their Men neat and clean—to visit them often at their quarters, and inculcate upon them the necessity of cleanliness, as essential to their health and service. They are particularly to see, that they have Straw to lay on, if to be had, and to make it known if they are destitute of this article. They are also to take care that Necessarys be provided in the Camps and frequently filled up to prevent their being offensive and unhealthy. Proper Notice will be taken of such Officers and Men, as distinguish themselves by their attention to these necessary duties.[7]

———

JULY 14
GENERAL ORDERS

Washington could take nothing for granted where his army was concerned. Basic principles of sanitation and military etiquette had to be spelled out in the simplest terms. The absence of proper uniforms forced the adoption of some unusual methods of distinguishing rank.

Head Quarters, Cambridge, July 14th 1775
As the Health of an Army principally depends upon Cleanliness; it is recommended in the strongest manner, to the Commanding Officer of Corps, Posts and Detachments, to be strictly diligent, in ordering the Necessarys to be filled up once a Week, and new ones dug; the Streets of the encampments and Lines to be swept daily, and all Offal and Carrion, near the camp, to be immediately buried: The Officers commanding in Barracks, or Quarters, to be answerable that they are swept every morning, and all Filth & Dirt removed from about the houses: Next to Cleanliness, nothing is more conducive to a Soldiers health, than dressing his provisions in a decent and proper manner. The Officers commanding Companies, should

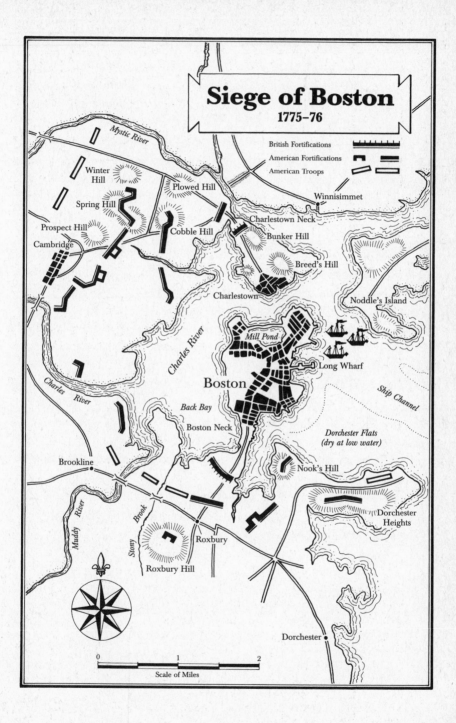

Siege of Boston
1775–76

British Fortifications
American Fortifications
American Troops

Mystic River

Winter Hill

Plowed Hill

Winnisimmet

Spring Hill

Charlestown Neck

Prospect Hill

Cobble Hill

Bunker Hill

Cambridge

Breed's Hill

Charlestown

Noddle's Island

Charles River

Mill Pond

Long Wharf

Boston

Charles River

Ship Channel

Back Bay

Boston Neck

Dorchester Flats
(dry at low water)

Brookline

Nook's Hill

Muddy River

Stony Brook

Dorchester
Heights

Roxbury

Roxbury Hill

Dorchester

0   1   2
Scale of Miles

therefore daily inspect the Camp Kitchens, and see the Men dress their Food in a wholesome way.

The Commanding Officers in those parts of the Lines and Redoubts, where the Pikes are placed, will order the Quarter Masters of Corps, to see the pikes greas'd twice a week; they are to be answerable also that the pikes are kept clean, and always ready and fit for service.

The General observing great remissness, and neglect in the several Guards in and about the Camp, orders the Officers commanding any Guard to turn out his Guard immediately upon the near Approach of The Commander in Chief or any of the General Officers, and upon passing the Guard; The Commander in Chief is to be received with *rested Arms;* the Officer to salute, and the Drums to beat a march: The Majors General with *rested Arms,* the Officer to salute and the Drums to beat two Ruffles; The Brigadiers General with *rested Arms,* the Officer to salute and the Drums to beat one Ruffle. There being something awkward, as well as improper, in the General Officers being stopp'd at the out-posts; ask'd for passes by the Sentries, and obliged often to send for the Officer of the Guard (who it sometimes happens is as much unacquainted with the Persons of the Generals, as the private Men) before they can pass in or out: It is recommended to both Officers and Men, to make themselves acquainted with the persons of all the Officers in General Command, and in the mean time to prevent mistakes: The General Officers and their Aids-de-Camp, will be distinguished in the following manner.

The Commander in Chief by a light blue Ribband, wore across his breast, between his Coat and Waistcoat.

The Majors and Brigadiers General, by a Pink Ribband wore in the like manner.

The Aids-de-Camp by a green ribband.[8]

. . .

———

JULY 23
TO BRIGADIER GENERAL JOHN THOMAS

In this letter to Brigadier General John Thomas of Massachusetts, who had threat-ened to resign rather than accept a rank lower than what he thought he deserved,

George Washington displayed his belief in the importance of self-sacrifice. Thomas heeded Washington's arguments—and got the rank he wanted—but died of small-pox in Canada less than a year later.

Cambridge July 23d 1775.

Sir

    The Retirement of a general Officer, possessing the Confidence of his Country & the Army; at so critical a Period, appears to me to be big with fatal Consequences both to the Publick Cause, & his own Reputation. While it is unexecuted, I think it my Duty to make this last Effort to prevent it; & after suggesting those Reasons which occur to me against your Resignation, your own Virtue, & good Sense must decide upon it. In the usual Contests of Empire, & Ambition, the Conscience of a Soldier has so little Share, that he may very properly insist upon his Claims of Rank, & extend his Pretensions even to Punctilio: but in such a Cause as this, where the Object is neither Glory nor Extent of Territory, but a Defence of all that is dear & valuable in Life, surely every Post ought to be deem'd honourable in which a Man can serve his Country. What Matter of Triumph will it afford our Enemies, that in less than one Month, a Spirit of Discord should shew itself in the highest Ranks of the Army, not to be extinguished by any Thing less than a total Desertion of Duty? How little Reason shall we have to boast of American Union, & Patriotism if at such a Time, & in such a Cause, smaller & partial Considerations cannot give Way to the great & general Interest. These Remarks can only affect you as a Member of the great American Body; but as an Inhabitant of Massachusetts Bay, your own Province, & the other Colonies have a peculiar & unquestionable Claim to your Services and in my Opinion you cannot refuse them, without relinquishing in some Degree, that Character for publick Virtue & Honour, which you have hitherto supported. If our Cause is just, it ought to be supported, but where shall it find Support, if Gentlemen of Merit & Experience unable to conquer the Prejudices of a Competition, withdraw themselves in an Hour of Danger: I admit, Sir, that your Claim & Services have not had due Respect—it is by no means a singular Case; worthy Men of all Nations & Countries have had Reason to make the same Complaint, but they did not for this abandon the publick Cause, they nobly stiffled the Dictates of Resentment, & made their Enemies ashamed of their Injustice. And can America shew no such Instances of Magnanimity? For the Sake of your bleeding Country, your devoted Province, your Charter Rights, & by the Memory of those brave Men who have already fell in this great Cause, I conjure you to banish from your Mind every Suggestion of Anger & Disappointment: your Country will do ample Justice to your Merits—they already do it, by the Sorrow & Regret expressed on the Occasion and the Sacrifice you are called to make, will in the Judgment of every good Man, & Lover of his Country, do you more real Honour than the most distinguished Victory.

You possess the Confidence & Affection of the Troops of this Province particularly; many of them are not capable of judging the Propriety & Reasons of your Conduct: should they esteem themselves authorized by your Example to leave the Service, the Consequences may be fatal & irretrievable—there is Reason to fear it, from the personal Attachments of the Men to their Officers, & the Obligations that are supposed to arise from those Attachments. But, Sir, the other Colonies have also their Claims upon you, not only as a Native of America, but an Inhabitant of this Province. They have made common Cause with it, they have sacrificed their Trade, loaded themselves with Taxes & are ready to spill their Blood in Vindication of the Rights of Massachusetts Bay, while all the Security, & Profit of a Neutrality has been offered them: But no Arts or Temptations could seduce them from your Side, & leave you a Prey to a cruel & perfidious Ministry. Sure these Reflections must have some Weight, with a Mind as generous & considerate as yours.

How will you be able to answer it to your Country & your own Conscience, if the Step you are about to take should lead to a Division of the Army or the Loss & Ruin of America be ascribed to Measures which your Councils & Conduct could have prevented? Before it is too late I intreat Sir, you would weigh well the greatness of the Stake, & upon how much smaller Circumstances the Fate of Empires has depended. Of your own Honour & Reputation you are the best & only Judge, but allow me to say, that a People contending for Life & Liberty are seldom disposed to look with a favourable Eye upon either Men or Measures whose Passions, Interests or Consequences will clash with those inestimable Objects. As to myself Sir, be assured, that I shall with Pleasure do all in my Power to make your Situation both easy, & honourable, & that the Sentiments here expressed, flow from a clear Opinion that your Duty to your Country, your Posterity, & yourself most explicitly require your Continuance in the

Service—The Order & Rank of the Commissions is under the Consideration of the Continental Congress, whose Determination will be received
in a few Days. It may argue a Want of Respect to that August Body not to
wait the Decision; But at all Events I shall flatter myself that these Reasons
with others which your own good Judgment will suggest, will strengthen
your Mind against those Impressions which are incident to Humanity &
laudable to a certain Degree; and that the Result will be, your Resolution
to assist your Country in this Day of Distress—That you may reap the full
Reward of Honour, & publick Esteem which such a Conduct deserves is
the sincere Wish of Sir, Your very Obed: & most Hbble Servt

Go: Washington[9]

AUGUST 11
TO GENERAL THOMAS GAGE

*The treatment of prisoners of war was an issue with repercussions extending well
beyond the fates of the captives themselves. Americans viewed their soldiers as legiti-
mate combatants in a war between two independent nations, but the British considered them traitors. One of Washington's greatest accomplishments was to convince
the British to agree—in principle, if not always in fact—that prisoners on both sides
should be treated humanely, and exchanged on equitable terms according to rank.
Some arm-twisting was necessary.*

Cambridge August 11th 1775

Sir

I understand that the Officers engaged in the Cause of Liberty, and
their Country, who by the Fortune of War, have fallen into your Hands
have been thrown indiscriminately, into a common Gaol appropriated for
Felons—That no Consideration has been had for those of the most respectable Rank, when languishing with Wounds and Sickness. That some
have been even amputated, in this unworthy Situation.

Let your Opinion, Sir, of the Principle which actuates them be what
it may, they suppose they act from the noblest of all Principles, a Love of
Freedom, and their Country. But political Opinions I conceive are foreign
to this Point, the Obligations arising from the Rights of Humanity, &

Claims of Rank, are universally binding and extensive, except in Case of Retaliation. These, I should have hoped, would have dictated a more tender Treatment of those Individuals, whom Chance or War had put in your Power—Nor can I forbear suggesting, its fatal Tendency to widen that unhappy Breach, which you, and those Ministers under whom you act, have repeatedly declared you wish'd to see forever closed.

My Duty now makes it necessary to apprize you, that for the future I shall regulate my Conduct towards those Gentlemen who are or may be in our Possession, exactly by the Rule which you shall observe, towards those of ours, who may be in your Custody. If Severity, & Hardship mark the Line of your Conduct, (painful as it may be to me) your Prisoners will feel its Effects: But if Kindness & Humanity are shewn to ours, I shall with Pleasure consider those in our Hands, only as unfortunate, and they shall receive the Treatment to which the unfortunate are ever intitled. . . .

Go: Washington[10]

AUGUST 20

TO MAJOR GENERAL PHILIP SCHUYLER

Seized from the French only a dozen years before, Canada was Great Britain's last major military and commercial base in continental North America. Militarily speaking, an American invasion of that vast region might force the British to evacuate New England, and encourage the powerful Native American tribes of the Northwest to join the patriot cause. The conquest of Canada would establish a continental American empire, and end the war in one devastating blow. In June, Congress had instructed Major General Philip Schuyler to assemble a force for the invasion of Canada, proceeding from Fort Ticonderoga to Montreal. Washington, hoping to strengthen Schuyler's invasion force under the command of Brigadier General Richard Montgomery, sought and received permission from Congress to launch a second attack against Quebec through the wilds of what is now Maine. His choice to lead the thousand-man force, which began leaving Cambridge on September 11, was a brilliant, vain, and erratic young Connecticut merchant, Colonel Benedict Arnold.

Camp at Cambridge August 20th 1775

Dr Sir

. . .

The Design of this Express is to communicate to you a Plan of an Expedition, which has engrossed my Thoughts for several Days: It is to penetrate into Canada, by Way of Kennebeck River, and so to Quebec, by a Rout 90 Miles below Montreal—I can very well spare a Detachment of 1000 or 1200 Men, and the Land Carriage by the Rout proposed is too inconsiderable to make an Objection. If you are resolved to proceed, (which I gather from your last Letter is your Intention) it would make a Diversion, that would distract [General Guy] Carlton and facilitate your Views. He must either break up and follow this party to Quebec, by which he will leave you a free passage or suffer that important Place to fall into our Hands: an Event which would have a decisive Effect and Influence on the public Interests.

There may be some Danger that such a sudden Incursion might alarm the Canadians and detach them from that Neutrality they have hitherto observed but I should hope that with suitable Precautions and a strict Discipline observed, any Jealousies and apprehensions might be quickly removed—The few whom I have consulted upon it, approve it much: but the final Determination is deferr'd until I hear from you. You will therefore by the Messenger inform me of your ultimate Resolution. If you mean to proceed acquaint me as particularly as you can with the Time and Force— What late Accounts you have had from Canada—Your Opinion of the Temper of the Inhabitants as well as Indians upon a penetration into their Country? What Number of Troops are at Quebec, and whether any Men of War and all other Circumstances which may be material in the Consideration of a Measure of such Importance.

Not a Moment's Time is to be lost in the Preparation for this Enterprize, if the advices from you favor it. . . .

. . .

Go. Washington[11]

AUGUST 20
TO LUND WASHINGTON

*In this letter to his Mount Vernon farm manager, Lund Washington, GW remarks
on a rumored plot to kidnap Martha Washington, and also offers candid observations on New England's officers and government officials.*

Camp at Cambridge Augt 20th 1775.

Dear Lund,

. . .

I can hardly think that Lord Dunmore can act so low, & unmanly a
part, as to think of siezing Mrs Washington by way of revenge upon me;
however as I suppose she is, before this time gone over to Mr Calverts, &
will soon after returning, go down to New Kent, she will be out of his
reach for 2 or 3 Months to come, in which time matters may, & probably
will, take such a turn as to render her removal either absolutely necessary,
or quite useless—I am nevertheless exceedingly thankful to the Gentlemen
of Alexandria for their friendly attention to this point & desire you will if
there is any sort of reason to suspect a thing of this kind provide a Kitchen
for her in Alexandria, or some other place of safety elsewhere for her and
my Papers.

The People of this Government have obtained a Character which they
by no means deserved—their Officers generally speaking are the most
indifferent kind of People I ever saw. I have already broke one Colo. and
five Captain's for Cowardice, & for drawing more Pay & Provision's than
they had Men in their Companies. there is two more Colonels now under
arrest, & to be tried for the same Offences—in short they are by no means
such Troops, in any respect, as you are led to believe of them from the Accounts which are published, but I need not make myself Enemies among
them, by this declaration, although it is consistent with truth. I daresay
the Men would fight very well (if properly Officered) although they are
an exceeding dirty & nasty people. had they been properly conducted at
Bunkers Hill (on the 17th of June) or those that were there properly supported, the Regulars would have met with a shameful defeat; & a much
more considerable loss than they did, which is now known to be exactly
1057 Killed & Wounded—it was for their behaviour on that occasion that

the above Officers were broke, for I never spared one that was accused of Cowardice but brot 'em to immediate Tryal.

Our Lines of Defence are now compleated, as near so at least as can be—we now wish them to come out, as soon as they please, but they (that is the Enemy) discover no Inclination to quit their own Works of Defence; & as it is almost impossible for us to get to them, we do nothing but watch each other's motion's all day at the distance of about a Mile; every now and then picking of a stragler when we can catch them without their Intrenchments; in return, they often Attempt to Cannonade our Lines to no other purpose than the waste of a considerable quantity of Powder to themselves which we should be very glad to get.

. . .

Remember me kindly to all the Neighbours who enquire after Yr Affecte friend & Servt

Go: Washington[12]

AUGUST 29

TO RICHARD HENRY LEE

More complaints about the New Englanders—in particular, their democratic system of "discipline," anathema to Washington—appear in this letter to the prominent Viriginia patriot Richard Henry Lee, who had served with Washington in the House of Burgesess and in both Continental Congresses.

Camp at Cambridge Augt 29th 1775

Dear Sir,

. . .

As we have now nearly compleated our Lines of Defence, we have nothing more, in my opinion, to fear from the Enemy provided we can keep our men to their duty and make them watchful & vigilant; but it is among the most difficult tasks I ever undertook in my life to induce these people to believe that there is, or can be, danger till the Bayonet is pushed at their Breasts; not that it proceeds from any uncommon prowess, but rather from an unaccountable kind of stupidity in the lower class of these people, which believe me prevails but too generally among the Officers of the Massachusets part of the Army, who are nearly of the same Kidney with the Privates; and adds not a little to my difficulties; as there is no such thing as getting Officers of this stamp to exert themselves in carrying orders into execution—to curry favour with the men (by whom they were chosen, & on whose Smiles possibly they may think they may again rely) seems to be one of the principal objects of their attention.

. . .

I have made a pretty good Slam among such kind of officers as the Massachusets Government abound in since I came to this Camp, having Broke one Colo. and two Captains for Cowardly behaviour in the action on Bunker's Hill—Two captains for drawing more provisions and pay than they had men in their Company—and one for being absent from his Post when the Enemy appeared there, and burnt a House just by it. Besides these, I have at this time one Colo., one Major, one Captn, & two Subalterns under arrest for tryal—In short I spare none & yet fear it will not all do, as these Peeple seem to be too inattentive to every thing but their Interest.

. . .

There has been so many great, and capital errors, & abuses to rectify—so many examples to make—& so little Inclination in the Officers of inferior Rank to contribute their aid to accomplish this work, that my life has been nothing else (since I came here) but one continued round of annoyance & fatigue; in short no pecuniary recompense could induce me to undergo what I have especially as I expect, by shewing so little Countenance to irregularities & publick abuses to render myself very obnoxious to a greater part of these People. But as I have already greatly exceeded the bounds of a Letter I will not trouble you with matters relative to my own feelings.

As I expect this Letter will meet you in Philadelphia I must request the favour of you to present my Affectionate & respectful Compliments to Doctor Shippen, his lady, and Family, my Brothers of the Deligation, and any other enquiring friends—& at the same time do me the justice to believe that I am with a sincere regard Yr Affecte friend & Obedt Servt

Go: Washington[13]

SEPTEMBER 14

TO COLONEL BENEDICT ARNOLD

Washington placed high hopes in Colonel Benedict Arnold and his Canadian expedition, which departed Cambridge on September 11. Little did he realize that Arnold was about to embark upon one of the most dramatic and disastrous military epics in American history.

Cambridge Head Quarters Septr 14. 1775

Sir,

You are intrusted with a Command of the utmost Consequence to the Interest & Liberties of America: Upon your Conduct & Courage & that of the Officers and Soldiers detached on this Expedition, not only the Success of the present Enterprize & your own Honour, but the Safety and Welfare of the whole Continent may depend. I charge you therefore and the Officers & Soldiers under your Command as you value your own Safety and Honour, & the Favour and Esteem of your Country that you consider yourselves as marching not through an Enemies Country, but that of our Friends and Brethren, for such the Inhabitants of Canada & the Indian Nations have approved themselves in this unhappy Contest between Great Brittain & America.

That you check by every Motive of Duty, and Fear of Punishment every Attempt to Plunder or insult any of the Inhabitants of Canada. Should any American Soldier be so base and infamous as to injure any Canadian or Indian in his Person or Property, I do most earnestly enjoin you to bring him to such severe & exemplary Punishment as the Enormity of the Crime may require. Should it extend to Death itself, it will not be disproportionate to its Guilt at such a Time and in such a Cause. But I hope and trust that the brave Men who have voluntarily engaged in this Expedition will be govern'd by different Views that Order, Discipline, & Regularity of Behaviour will be as conspicuous as their Courage & Valour. I also give it in Charge to you to avoid all Disrespect or Contempt of the Religion of the Country and its Ceremonies—Prudence, Policy and a true Christian Spirit will lead us to look with Compassion upon their Errors without insulting them—While we are Contending for our own Liberty, we should be very cautious of violating the Rights of Conscience in others; ever considering that God alone is the Judge of the Hearts of Men and to him only in this Case they are answerable.

Upon the whole, Sir, I beg you to inculcate upon the Officers, the Necessity of preserving the Strictest Order during their March thro' Canada to represent to them the Shame & Disgrace and Ruin to themselves & Country if they should by their Conduct turn the Hearts of our Brethren in Canada against us. And on the other Hand the Honour and Rewards which await them, if by their Prudence, and good Behaviour they conciliate the Affections of the Canadians & Indians to the great Interests of America, & convert those favourable Dispositions they have shewn into a lasting Union and Affection.

Thus wishing you and the Officers and Soldiers under your Command all Honour, Safety and Success I remain Sir Your most Obedt Humble Servt

Go: Washington[14]

CIRCA SEPTEMBER 14
ADDRESS TO THE PEOPLE OF CANADA

Washington gave Arnold copies of this address, some translated into French, for distribution to the people of Canada. His reassuring words had little effect on the Canadians; most of them sided with the British.

Friends and Brethren,

The unnatural Contest between the English Colonies and Great-Britain, has now risen to such a Heighth, that Arms alone must decide it. The Colonies, confiding in the Justice of their Cause, and the Purity of their Intentions, have reluctantly appealed to that Being, in whose Hands are all human Events. He has hitherto smiled upon their virtuous Efforts—The Hand of Tyranny has been arrested in its Ravages, and the British Arms which have shone with so much Splendor in every Part of the Globe, are now tarnished with Disgrace and Disappointment. Generals of approved Experience, who boasted of subduing this great Continent, find themselves circumscribed within the Limits of a single City and its Suburbs, suffering all the Shame and Distress of a Siege. While the trueborn Sons of America, animated by the genuine Principles of Liberty and Love of their Country, with increasing Union, Firmness and Discipline repel every Attack, and despise every Danger.

Above all, we rejoice, that our Enemies have been deceived with Regard to you—They have perswaded themselves, they have even dared to say, that the Canadians were not capable of distinguishing between the Blessings of Liberty, and the Wretchedness of Slavery; that gratifying the Vanity of a little Circle of Nobility—would blind the Eyes of the People of Canada. By such Artifices they hoped to bend you to their Views, but they have been deceived, instead of finding in you that Poverty of Soul, and Baseness of Spirit, they see with a Chagrin equal to our Joy, that you are enlightned, generous, and virtuous—that you will not renounce your own Rights, or serve as Instruments to deprive your Fellow Subjects of theirs. Come then, my Brethren, unite with us in an indissoluble Union, let us run together to the same Goal. We have taken up Arms in Defence of our Liberty, our Property, our Wives, and our Children, we are determined to preserve them, or die. We look forward with Pleasure to that Day not far remote (we hope) when the Inhabitants of America shall have one Sentiment, and the full Enjoyment of the Blessings of a free Government.

Incited by these Motives, and encouraged by the Advice of many Friends of Liberty among you, the Grand American Congress have sent an Army into your Province, under the Command of General Schuyler; not to plunder, but to protect you; to animate, and bring forth into Action those Sentiments of Freedom you have disclosed, and which the Tools of Despotism would extinguish through the whole Creation. To co-operate with this Design, and to frustrate those cruel and perfidious Schemes, which would deluge our Frontiers with the Blood of Women and Children; I have detached Colonel Arnold into your Country, with a Part of the Army under my Command—I have enjoined upon him, and I am certain that he will consider himself, and act as in the Country of his Patrons, and best Friends. Necessaries and Accommodations of every Kind which you may furnish, he will thankfully receive, and render the full Value. I invite you therefore as Friends and Brethren, to provide him with such Supplies as your Country affords; and I pledge myself not only for your Safety and Security, but for ample Compensation. Let no Man desert his Habitation—Let no one flee as before an Enemy. The Cause of America, and of Liberty, is the Cause of every virtuous American Citizen; whatever may be his Religion or his Descent, the United Colonies know no Distinction but such as Slavery, Corruption and arbitrary Domination may create. Come then, ye generous Citizens, range yourselves under the Standard of general Liberty—against which all the Force and Artifice of Tyranny will never be able to prevail.

G. Washington.[15]

———

NOVEMBER 10

TO COLONEL WILLIAM WOODFORD

What makes a good officer? Washington emphasized solid education and strict discipline, as appears in this letter to an inexperienced fellow Virginian, Colonel William Woodford.

Cambridge, 10 November, 1775.

Dear Sir,

Your favor of the 18th of September came to my hands on Wednesday last, through Boston, and open, as you may suppose. It might be well to recollect by whom you sent it, in order to discover if there has not been some treachery practised.

I do not mean to flatter, when I assure you, that I highly approve of your appointment. The inexperience you complain of is a common case, and only to be remedied by practice and close attention. The best general advice I can give, and which I am sure you stand in no need of, is to be strict in your discipline; that is, to require nothing unreasonable of your officers and men, but see that whatever is required be punctually complied with. Reward and punish every man according to his merit, without partiality or prejudice; hear his complaints; if well founded, redress them; if otherwise, discourage them, in order to prevent frivolous ones. Discourage vice in every shape, and impress upon the mind of every man, from the first to the lowest, the importance of the cause, and what it is they are contending for. For ever keep in view the necessity of guarding against surprises. In all your marches, at times, at least, even when there is no possible danger, move with front, rear, and flank guards, that they may be familiarized to the use; and be regular in your encampments, appointing necessary guards for the security of your camp. In short, whether you expect an enemy or not, this should be practised; otherwise your attempts will be confused and awkward, when necessary. Be plain and precise in your orders, and keep copies of them to refer to, that no mistakes may happen. Be easy and condescending in your deportment to your officers, but not too familiar, lest you subject yourself to a want of that respect, which is necessary to support a proper command. These, Sir, not because I think you need the advice, but because you have been condescending enough to ask it, I have presumed to give as the great outlines of your conduct.

As to the manual exercise, the evolutions and manoeuvres of a regiment, with other knowledge necessary to the soldier, you will acquire them from those authors, who have treated upon these subjects, among whom Bland (the newest edition) stands foremost; also an Essay on the Art of War; Instructions for Officers, lately published at Philadelphia; the Partisan; Young; and others.

My compliments to Mrs. Woodford; and that every success may attend you, in this glorious struggle, is the sincere and ardent wish of, dear Sir, your affectionate humble servant.[16]

NOVEMBER 28
TO LIEUTENANT COLONEL JOSEPH REED

New Jersey lawyer Joseph Reed served with Washington in the First Continental Congress, and subsequently became his first military secretary and close confidant. Washington's growing frustrations at the perceived corruption and cynicism of his fellow Americans appear in this letter. Washington risked all of his most prized possessions—including his family, estate, and reputation—in the American cause, and decried the unwillingness of other men to do the same.

Cambridge 28th Novr 1775.

Dear Sir,

. . .

I could wish, my good friend, that these things may give a spur to your Inclination to return, and that I may see you here as soon as convenient, as I feel the want of your ready pen, &ca, greatly.

. . .

Such a dearth of Publick Spirit, & want of Virtue; such stock jobbing, and fertility in all the low Arts to obtain advantages, of one kind or another, in this great change of Military arrangement I never saw before, and pray God I may never be Witness to again. what will be the ultimate end of these Manouvres is beyond my Scan—I tremble at the prospect—We have been till this time Enlisting about 3500 Men—To engage these I have been obliged to allow Furloughs as far as 50 Men a Regiment; & the Officers, I am perswaded, endulge as many more—The Connecticut Troops will not be prevail'd upon to stay longer than their term (saving those who have enlisted for the next Campaign, & mostly on Furlough) and such a dirty, mercenary Spirit pervades the whole, that I should not be at all surprized at any disaster that may happen—In short, after the last of this Month, our lines will be so weakened that the Minute Men and Militia must be call'd in for their defence—these being under no kind of Government themselves, will destroy the little subordination I have been labouring to establish, and run me into one evil, whilst I am endeavouring to avoid another; but the lesser must be chosen. could I have foreseen what I have, & am like to experience, no consideration upon Earth should have induced me to accept this Command. A Regiment, or any subordinate department would have been accompanied with ten times the satisfaction—perhaps the honour. . . . believe me, it is beyond the powers of conception to discover the absurdities, & partiality of these People, and the trouble & vexation I have had in the New arrangement of Officers—after five, I think, different meetings of the General Officers I have, in a manner, been obliged to give into the humour & whimsies of the People, or get no Army. The Officers of one Government would not serve in the Regiments of another (although there was to be an entire new Creation)—a Captain must be in this Regiment—a Subaltern in that Company In short I can scarce tell at this moment in what manner they are fixed. Sometime hence strangers may be brought in, but it could not be done now, except in an Instance or two, without putting too much to the hazard.

I have this Instant by Express, received the agreeable News of the Capitulation of Montreal—The account of it, you also, undoubtedly have—Poor Arnold I wonder where he is—Enos left him with the Rear division of his Army and is now hear under Arrest. . . . I shall add no more than that I am Dr Sir Yr Most Obedt & Affecte Ser.

Go: Washington[17]

———

1776

On New Year's Day, 1776, most of the army that Washington had worked so hard to organize and discipline simply dissolved. Their terms of enlistment expired, thousands of soldiers left for home. Raw recruits replaced them. Once again, Washington had to build an army from scratch.

Head Quarters, Cambridge, January 1st 1776
This day giving commencement to the new-army, which, in every point of View is entirely Continental; The General flatters himself, that a laudable Spirit of emulation, will now take place, and pervade the whole of it; without such a Spirit, few Officers have ever arrived to any degree of Reputation, nor did any Army ever become formidable: His Excellency hopes that the Importance of the great Cause we are engaged in, will be deeply impressed upon every Man's mind, and wishes it to be considered, that an Army without Order, Regularity & Discipline, is no better than a Commission'd Mob; Let us therefore, when every thing dear and valuable to Freemen is at stake; when our unnatural Parent is threat'ning of us with destruction from every quarter, endeavour by all the Skill and Discipline in our power, to acquire that knowledge, and conduct, which is necessary in War—Our men are brave and good; Men who with pleasure it is observed, are addicted to fewer Vices than are commonly found in Armies;

but it is Subordination & Discipline (the Life and Soul of an Army) which next under providence, is to make us formidable to our enemies, honorable in ourselves, and respected in the world; and herein is to be shewn the Goodness of the Officer.

In vain is it for a General to issue Orders, if Orders are not attended to, equally vain is it for a few Officers to exert themselves, if the same spirit does not animate the whole; it is therefore expected, (it is not insisted upon) that each Brigadier, will be attentive to the discipline of his Brigade, to the exercise of, and the Conduct observed in it, calling the Colonels, and Field Officers of every regiment, to severe Account for Neglect, or Disobedience of orders—The same attention is to be paid by the Field Officers to the respective Companies of their regiments—by the Captains to their Subalterns, and so on: And that the plea of Ignorance, which is no excuse for the Neglect of Orders (but rather an Aggravation) may not be offer'd, It is order'd, and directed, that not only every regiment, but every Company, do keep an Orderly-book, to which frequent recourse is to be had, it being expected that all standing orders be rigidly obeyed, until alter'd or countermanded—It is also expected, that all Orders which are necessary to be communicated to the Men, be regularly read, and carefully explained to them. As it is the first wish of the General to have the business of the Army conducted without punishment, to accomplish which, he assures every Officer, & Soldier, that as far as it is in his power, he will reward such as particularly distinguish themselves; at the same time, he declares that he will punish every kind of neglect, or misbehaviour, in an exemplary mannor.

As the great Variety of occurrences, and the multiplicity of business, in which the General is necessarily engaged, may withdraw his attention from many objects & things, which might be improved to Advantage; He takes this Opportunity of declaring, that he will thank any Officer, of whatsoever Rank, for any useful hints, or profitable Informations, but to avoid trivial matters; as his time is very much engrossed, he requires that it may be introduced through the channel of a General Officer, who is to weigh the importance before he communicates it.

All standing Orders heretofore issued for the Government of the late Army, of which every Regiment has, or ought to have Copies; are to be strictly complied with, until changed, or countermanded.

. . .

This being the day of the Commencement of the new-establishment,

The General pardons all the Offences of the old, and commands all Prisoners (except Prisoners of war) to be immediately released.[1]

––––––––

JANUARY 4

TO LIEUTENANT COLONEL JOSEPH REED

Washington's contempt for the British was matched only by his contempt for American soldiers who had chosen to leave the army, "retiring into a Chimney Corner" at their country's hour of crisis.

Cambridge 4th Jany 1776

Dear Sir,

. . .

It is easier to conceive, than to describe the Situation of My Mind for sometime past, & my feelings under our present Circumstances; search the vast volumes of history through, & I much question whether a case similar to ours is to be found. to wit, to maintain a Post against the flower of the British Troops for Six Months together without—and at the end of them to have one Army disbanded and another to raise within the same distance of a Reinforced Enemy—it is too much to attempt—what may be the final Issue of the last Manouvre time only can tell—I wish this Month was well over our heads—The same desire of retiring into a Chimney Corner siez'd the Troops of New Hampshire, Rhode Island, & Massachusets (so soon as their time expired) as had Work'd upon those of Connecticut, notwithstanding many of them made a tender of their Services to continue till the Lines could be sufficiently strengthned—We are now left with a good deal less than half rais'd Regiments, and about 5000 Militia who only stand Ingaged to the middle of this Month; when, according to custom, they will depart, let the necessity of their stay be never so urgent. thus it is that for more than two Months past I have scarcely immerged from one difficulty before I have plunged into another—how it will end God in his great goodness will direct, I am thankful for his protection to this time. We are told that we shall soon get the Army compleated, but I have been told so many things which have never come to pass, that I distrust every thing. . . .[2]

JANUARY 18
TO MAJOR GENERAL PHILIP SCHUYLER

As Washington organized the army at Cambridge, news arrived of the disastrous failure of the Canadian expedition. "My Amiable Friend the Gallant Montgomery is no more," Major General Schuyler wrote to him on January 13. "The Brave Arnold is wounded & we have met with a severe Check, in an unsuccessful Attempt on Quebec; May Heaven be graciously pleased that the Misfortune may terminate here; I tremble for our People in Canada, And Nothing my Dear Sir seems left, to prevent the most fatal Consequences, but an immediate Reinforcement, that is no where to be had but from You."³ Unfortunately, Washington could do little to help.

Cambridge Jany 18th 1776.

Dear Sir.

I received your Favour of the 13th Instant with its Inclosures and am heartily sorry & most sincerely condole with you upon the unhappy Fall of the brave and worthy Montgomery & those gallant officers & Men, who have experienced a like Fate. In the Death of this Gentleman, America has sustained a heavy Loss, as he had approved himself a steady Friend to her Rights and of Ability to render her the most essential Services. I am much concerned for the intrepid and enterprizing Arnold and greatly fear that Consequences of the most alarming Nature will result from this well intended but unfortunate Attempt.

It would give me the greatest Happiness, if I could be the happy Means of relieving our Fellow Citizens now in Canada and preventing the Ministerial Troops from exulting long and availing themselves of the Advantages arising from this Repulse—But it is not in my power—Since the Dissolution of the old Army, the progress in raising Recruits for the new has been so very slow & inconsiderable that five thousand Militia have been called in to the Defence of our Lines. . . . In short I have not a Man to spare.

. . .

Go: Washington⁴

34

JANUARY 23

TO LIEUTENANT COLONEL JOSEPH REED

Washington's headquarters could never have functioned without the men of his "military family," or aides-de-camp, who penned most of his correspondence. In this letter, Washington begs Reed, who had left headquarters, to return, and discusses the qualifications of a good aide.

Cambridge 23d Jan: 1776.

Dear Sir,

Real necessity, compells me to ask you whether I may entertain any hopes of your returning to my Family? if you can make it convenient, and will hint the matter to Colo. [Robert Henson] Harrison, I dare venture to say that Congress will make it agreeable to you in every shape they can— My business Increases very fast, and my distresses for want of you, along with it—Mr Harrison is the only Gentleman of my Family that can afford me the least assistance in writing—He and Mr [Stephen] Moylan, whose time must now be solely Imployed in his department of Commissary, have heretofore afforded me their aid. & I have hinted to them in consequence of what you signified in some former Letter that each (as they have really had a great deal of trouble) should receive one third of your pay, reserving the other third, contrary to your desire, for yourself; My distress, and Imbarrassment, is in a way of being very considerably Increased by an Occurrance in Virginia which will I fear compell Mr Harrison to leave me, or suffer considerably by his stay. He has wrote however by the last post to see if his return cannot be dispensed with—If he should go, I shall really be distressed beyond Measure as I know no Persons able to supply your places (in this part of the World) with whom I would chuse to live in unbounded confidence. In short, for want of an acquaintance with the People hitherwards, I know of none which appear to me qualified for the Office of Secretary.

The business, as I hinted to you before, is considerably Increased, by being more comprehensive; and, at this time (from the great changes which have, and are happening every day) perplexed; so that you would want a good Writer, and a Methodical Man, as an Assistant, or Copying Clerk—such an one I have no doubt will be allowed, and the choice I leave to yourself, as he should be a person in whose Integrety you can confide, and on whose capacity—care—& method you can rely. At present, my time is so much taken up at my Desk, that I am obliged to neglect many other essential parts of my Duty; it is absolutely necessary therefore for me to have person's that can think for me, as well as execute Orders—This it is that pains me, when I think of Mr White's expectation of coming into my Family, if an opening happens. I can derive no earthly assistance from such a Man—and my friend [George] Baylor is much such another Although as good, and as obliging a person as any in the World.

. . .

I am with the greatest truth & Sincerety Dr Sr Yr Affect.

Go: Washington[5]

JANUARY 31
TO LIEUTENANT COLONEL JOSEPH REED

Most Americans and Europeans had no idea of Washington's appearance. A London publisher answered the public's curiosity by preparing two mezzotint portraits of Washington, one of which depicted him riding on horseback with drawn sword, looking stern and bold. The publisher claimed to have based the mezzotints on originals drawn from life by one Alexander Campbell of Williamsburg, who did not in fact exist. Washington regarded the fraudulent portraits, which became popular on both continents, with wry amusement.

. . .

Mrs Washington desires I will thank you for the Picture sent her. Mr Campbell whom I never saw (to my knowledge) has made a very formidable figure of the Commander in Chief giving him a sufficient portion of Terror in his Countenance.[6]

FEBRUARY 1

TO LIEUTENANT COLONEL JOSEPH REED

The Canadian expedition's failure confirmed Washington's distrust of the militia, which most Americans still regarded as the cornerstone of a citizen army.

Cambridge Feby 1st 1776.

My dear Sir,

. . . The Acct given of the behaviour of the Men under Genl Montgomerie is exactly consonant to the opinion I have form'd of these People, and such as they will exhibit abundant proofs of in similar cases whenever called upon—Place them behind a Parapet—a Breast Work—Stone Wall—or anything that will afford them Shelter, and from their knowledge of a Firelock, they will give a good Account of their Enemy, but I am as well convinced as if I had seen it, that they will not March boldly up to a Work—or stand exposed in a plain—and yet, if we are furnished with the Means, and the Weather will afford us a Passage, and we can get in Men (for these three things are necessary) something must be attempted. The Men must be brought to face danger—they cannot allways have an Intrenchment, or a Stone Wall as a safe guard or Shield—and it is of essential Importance that the Troops In Boston should be destroyed if possible before they can be re-inforced, or remove—this is clearly my opinion—whether Circumstances will admit of the tryal—& if tryed what will be the Event, the allwise disposer of them alone can tell.

The Evils arising from short, or even any limited Inlistment of the Troops are greater, and more extensively hurtful than any person (not an eyewitness to them) can form any Idea of—It takes you two or three Months to bring New men in any tolerable degree acquainted with their duty—it takes a longer time to bring a People of the temper, and genius of these into such a subordinate way of thinking as is necessary for a Soldier—Before this is accomplished, the time approaches for their dismission, and your beginning to make Interest with them for their continuance for another limited period; in the doing of which you are oblig'd to relax in your discipline, in order as it were to curry favour with them, by which means the latter part of your time is employed in undoing what the first was accomplishing and instead of having Men always ready to take advantage of Circumstances you must govern your Movements by the Circumstances of your Inlistment—this is not all—by the time you have got Men arm'd & equip'd—the difficulty of doing which is beyond description—and with every new sett you have the same trouble to encounter without the means of doing it. In short the disadvantages are so great, & apparent to me, that I am convinc'd, uncertain as the continuance of the War is, that the Congress had better determine to give a Bounty of 20, 30, or even 40 Dollars to every Man who will Inlist for the whole time, be it long or short.

. . .

Go: Washington[7]

FEBRUARY 10

TO LIEUTENANT COLONEL JOSEPH REED

Washington's concern for his reputation and appearance in the public eye at times bordered on the obsessive; yet he remained willing to risk everything in the struggle for freedom against King George III and his "diabolical Ministry."

Cambridge Feby 10th 1776.

My dear Sir

. . .

If my dear Sir, you conceive that I took any thing wrong, or amiss, that was conveyed in any of your former Letters you are really mistaken—I only meant to convince you, that nothing would give me more real satisfaction than to know the Sentiments which are entertained of me by the Publick, whether they be favourable, or otherwise—and, urged as a reason that the Man who wished to steer clear of Shelves & Rocks must know where they lay—I know—but to declare it unless to a friend, may be an argument of vanity—the Integrety of my own Heart—I know the unhappy predicament I stand in. I know, that much is expected of me—I know that without Men, without Arms, without Ammunition, without any thing fit for the accomodation of a Soldier that little is to be done—and, which is mortifying; I know, that I cannot stand justified to the World without exposing my own Weakness & injuring the cause by declaring my wants, which I am determined not to do further than unavoidable necessity brings every Man acquainted with them—If under these disadvantages I am able to keep above Water (as it were) in the esteem of Mankind I shall feel myself happy; but, if from the unknown, peculiarity of my Circumstances, I suffer in the opinion of the World I shall not think you take the freedom of a friend if you conceal the reflections that may be cast upon my conduct. My own Situation feels so irksome to me at times, that, if I did not consult the publick good more than my own tranquility I should long e're this have put every thing to the cast of a Dye—So far from my having an Army of 20,000 Men well Armed &ca I have been here with less than one half of it, including Sick, furloughed, & on Command, and those neither Arm'd or Cloathed, as they should be. In short my Situation has been such that I have been obliged to use art to conceal it from my own Officers.

. . .

With respect to myself, I have never entertained an Idea of an Accomodation since I heard of the Measures which were adopted in consequence of the Bunkers Hill fight. The Kings Speech has confirmed the Sentiments I entertained upon the News of that Affair—and, if every Man was of my Mind the Ministers of G[reat] B[ritain] should know, in a few Words, upon what Issue the cause should be put. I would not be deceived by artful declarations, or specious pretences—nor would I be amused by unmeaning propositions. but in open, undisguised, and Manly terms proclaim our Wrongs & our Resolutions to be redressed. I would tell them, that we had born much—that we had long, & ardently sought for reconciliation upon honourable terms—that it had been denied us—that all our attempts after Peace had proved abortive and had been grossly misrepresented—that we had done every thing that could be expected from the best of Subjects— that the Spirit of Freedom beat too high in us, to Submit to Slavery; & that, if nothing else would satisfie a Tyrant & his diabolical Ministry, we were determined to shake of all Connexions with a State So unjust, & unnatural. This I would tell them, not under Covert, but in Words as clear as the Sun in its Meridian brightness.

. . .

G.W.[8]

FEBRUARY 18–21
TO JOHN HANCOCK

On February 11, Lieutenant Colonel Rufus Putnam wrote to Washington with a plan for occupying and fortifying Dorchester Heights, which overlooked Boston Harbor from the south. Washington's preference was for a direct assault on the city; but his officers, assembled in a council of war, endorsed Lieutenant Colonel Putnam's plan, followed by a protracted bombardment of the British positions by heavy artillery pieces that Colonel Henry Knox had brought from Ticonderoga. Such, they hoped, would force the British either to fight or to withdraw.

Frustrated with delays in gathering powder for Knox's heavy artillery and feeling "the Eyes of the whole Continent" fixed upon him "with anxious expectation of hearing of some great event," Washington nevertheless continued to mull a plan for sending his infantry across the iced-over Boston Harbor for a direct assault on the British fortifications. Fortunately, his officers remained opposed to the plan, which could only have ended in disaster.

Cambridge 18th[–21] Feby 1776

Sir

The late freezing Weather having formed some pretty strong Ice from Dorchester point to Boston Neck and from Roxbury to the Common, thereby affording a more expanded and consequently a less dangerous Approach to the Town, I could not help thinking, notwithstanding the Militia were not all come In, and we had little or no Powder to begin our Operation by a regular Cannonade & Bombardment, that a bold & resolute Assault upon the Troops in Boston with such Men as we had (for it could not take Many Men to guard our own Lines at a time when the Enemy were attacked in all Quarters) might be crown'd with success; and therefore, seeing no certain prospect of a Supply of Powder on the one hand and a certain dissolution of the Ice on the other, I called the General Officers together for their opinion . . . The Result will appear in the In-closed Council of War, and being almost unanimous, I must suppose to be right; although, from a thorough conviction of the necessity of attempting something against the Ministerial Troops before a Re-inforcement should arrive, and while we were favour'd with the Ice, I was not only ready, but willing and desirous of making the Assault; under a firm hope, if the

Men would have stood by me, of a favourable Issue; notwithstanding the Enemy's advantage of Ground—Artillery—&ca.

Perhaps the Irksomeness of my Situation, may have given different Ideas to me, than those which Influenced the Gentlemen I consulted, and might have inclin'd me to put more to the hazard than was consistent with prudence—If it had, I am not sensible of it, as I endeavoured to give it all the consideration that a matter of such Importance required—True it is, & I cannot help acknowledging, that I have many disagreeable Sensation's on account of my Situation; for to have the Eyes of the whole Continent fixed with anxious expectation of hearing of some great event, & to be restrain'd in every Military Operation for want of the necessary means of carrying it on, is not very pleasing; especially, as the means used to conceal my Weakness from the Enemy conceals it also from our friends, and adds to their Wonder.

I do not utter this by way of Complaint—I am sensible that all that the Congress could do, they have done, and I should feel, most powerfully, the weight of conscious Ingratitude were I not to acknowledge this; but as we have Accounts of the arrival of Powder in Captain Mason I would beg to have it sent on in the most expeditious manner, otherwise we not only lose all chance of the Benefits resulting from the Season, but of the Militia which are brought in at a most Inormous expence, upon a presumption that we should long e're this have been amply Supplied with Powder under the contracts enter'd into with the Committee of Congress.

. . .

Go: Washington[9]

FEBRUARY 20
TO JOSEPH JOHNSON

While lamenting the weaknesses of his army at Cambridge, Washington remained congnizant of the importance of maintaining a pretense of confidence and strength toward the Indians of the Iroquois Confederacy, or the Six Nations. This letter to Mohican-turned-missionary Joseph Johnson demonstrates Washington's awareness of the important role that Native Americans would play in the Revolutionary War.

[Cambridge]

Sir,

I am very much pleased to find by the Strong recommendations you produce, that we have amongst our Brothers of the Six Nations a person who can explain to them, the Sense of their Brothers, on the dispute between us and the Ministers of Great Britain; you have seen a part of our Strength, and can inform our Brothers, that we can withstand all the force, which those who want to rob us of our Lands and our Houses, can send against us.

You can tell our friends, that they may always look upon me, whom the Whole United Colonies have chosen to be their Chief Warrior, as their brother, whilst they Continue in Friendship with us, they may depend upon mine and the protection of those under my Command.

Tell them that we don't want them to take up the hatchett for us, except they chuse it, we only desire that they will not fight against us, we want that the Chain of friendship should always remain bright between our friends of the Six Nations and us—Their attention to you, will be a proof to us that they wish the same, we recommend you to them, and hope by your Spreading the truths of the Holy Gospel amongst them, it will Contribute to keep the Chain so bright, that, the malicious insinuations, or practices of our Enemies will never be able to break this Union, so much for the benefit of our Brothers of the Six Nations and of us—And to prove to them that this is my desire, and of the Warriors under me, I hereto Subscribe my name at Cambridge this 20th day of February 1776.

Go: Washington[10]

FEBRUARY 28

TO PHILLIS WHEATLEY

The African-American poet Phillis Wheatley (ca. 1753–1784) had been kidnapped from Africa as a child and shipped as a slave to Boston, where she began writing poetry while acting as a servant to a tailor's wife. She sent a poetic tribute to Washington in October 1775, and apparently visited him at headquarters in March 1776.

Cambridge February 28th 1776.

Mrs Phillis,

Your favour of the 26th of October did not reach my hands 'till the middle of December. Time enough, you will say, to have given an answer ere this. Granted. But a variety of important occurrences, continually interposing to distract the mind and withdraw the attention, I hope will apologize for the delay, and plead my excuse for the seeming, but not real, neglect.

I thank you most sincerely for your polite notice of me, in the elegant Lines you enclosed; and however undeserving I may be of such encomium and panegyrick, the style and manner exhibit a striking proof of your great poetical Talents. In honour of which, and as a tribute justly due to you, I would have published the Poem, had I not been apprehensive, that, while I only meant to give the World this new instance of your genius, I might have incurred the imputation of Vanity. This, and nothing else, determined me not to give it place in the public Prints.

If you should ever come to Cambridge, or near Head Quarters, I shall be happy to see a person so favoured by the Muses, and to whom nature has been so liberal and beneficent in her dispensations. I am, with great Respect, Your obedt humble servant,

G. Washington[11]

––––––––

MARCH 7–9
TO JOHN HANCOCK

On the evening of March 2, with adequate supplies of powder finally in place, American artillery began to bombard the British positions around Boston. Two days later, Washington sent his troops to occupy Dorchester Heights. The operation was conducted with an efficiency that stunned the British, and by the morning of March 5 the heights bristled with American infantry and artillery. An elated Washington hoped that the British would attack; but General William Howe, the British commander, more prudently decided to hasten his plans for the evacuation of the city.

Cambridge March 7[–9] 1776

Sir

On the 26 Ultimo I had the honour of addressing you and then mentioned that we were making preparations for taking possession of Dorchester Heights. I now beg leave to Inform you, that a Council of General Officers having determined a previous Bombardment & Cannonade expedient and proper, in order to harrass the Enemy and divert their attention from that Quarter, on Saturday, Sunday and Monday nights last, we carried them on from our Posts at Cobble Hill, Letchmores Point & Lams Dam— Whether they did the Enemy any considerable & what Injury, I have not yet heard, but have the pleasure to acquaint you, that they greatly facilitated our Schemes, and wou'd have been attended with success equal to our most sanguine expectations, had It not been for the unlucky bursting of Two Thirteen & three Ten Inch Mortars . . . To what cause to attribute this misfortune I know not, whether to any defect in them, or to the Inexperience of the Bombardiers. But to return, on Monday Evening as soon as our firing commenced, a considerable detachment of our men under the command of Brigadier General Thomas crossed the Neck and took possession of the Two Hills without the least interruption or annoyance from the Enemy, and by their great activity and Industry before the morning advanced the Works so far, as to be secure against their Shot—They are now going on with such expedition that in a little time I hope they will be compleat, and enable our Troops stationed there, to make a vigorous and Obstinate stand—during the whole Cannonade, which was Incessant the last two nights, we were fortunate enough to lose but two men, One a Lieutenant by a Cannon Ball's taking off his thigh, the other a private by the explosion of a shell which also slightly wounded four or five more.

Our taking possession of Dorchester Heights is only preparatory to taking Post on Nuke Hill and the points opposite the South end of Boston—It was absolutely necessary that they should be previously fortified in order to cover and command them—As soon as the Works on the former are finished and compleat, measures will be immediately adopted for Securing the latter and making them as strong and defensible as we can—their contiguity to the Enemy will make them of much Importance and of great service to us. . . . I flatter myself from the Posts we have just taken & are about to take, that It will be in our Power to force the Ministerial Troops to an attack, or to dispose of 'em in some way that will be of advantage to us—I think from these Posts they will be so galled and annoyed, that they must either give us Battle or quit their present possessions. I am resolved that nothing on my part shall be wanting to effect the one or the other.

. . .

When the Enemy first discovered our Works in the morning, they seemed to be in great confusion, and from their movements to have Intended an Attack. It is much to be wished, that it had been made—The event I think must have been fortunate, and nothing less than success and victory on our side, as our Officers and men appeared Impatient for the appeal, and to have possessed the most animated sentiments and determined resolution.

. . .

March 9. Yesterday evening a Captain Irvine who escaped from Boston the night before with Six of his Crew, came to Head Quarters and gave the following Intelligence—"That our Bombardment and Cannonade caused a good deal of Surprize and alarm in Town, as many of the Soldiery said they never heard or thought we had Mortars or Shells: That several of the Officers acknowledged they were well and properly directed—That they made much distress and confusion—That the Cannon Shot for the greatest part went thro the Houses, and he was told, that one took of the Legs and Arms of Six men lying in the Barracks on the Neck—That a Soldier who came from the Lines there on Tuesday morning Informed him that 20 men had been wounded the night before—It was reported that others were also hurt, and one of the light Horse torn to peices by the explosion of a Shell—This was afterwards contradicted: That early on Tuesday morning Admiral Shuldham discovering the works our people were throwing up on Dorchester Heights, immediately sent an Express to General Howe to inform him, and that It was necessary they shou'd be attacked and dislodged from thence, or he wou'd be under the necessity of withdrawing the Ships from the Harbour, which were under his command: That preparations were directly made for that purpose as It was said, and from Twelve to Two OClock about 3,000 men embarked on board the Transports which fell down to the Castle with a design of Landing on that part of Dorchester next to It, and Attacking the works on the Heights at 5 OClock next morning: That Lord Piercy was appointed to command—That It was generally beleived the attempt would have been made, had It not been for the violent

Storm which happened that night as I have mentioned before—That he heard several of the Privates and one or two Serjeants say as they were embarking, that It wou'd be another Bunker Hill affair—He further Informs that the Army is preparing to leave Boston and that they will do It in a day or two—That the Transports necessary for their embarkation were getting ready with the utmost expedition—That there had been great movements & confusion among the Troops the night & day preceding his coming out, in hurrying down their Cannon, Artillery & other Stores to the wharffs with the utmost precipitation, and were putting em on board the Ships in such haste that no Account or Memorandum was taken of them—That most of the Cannon were removed from their works and embarked & embarking. That he heard a woman say which he took to be an Officers wife, that she had seen men go under the ground at the lines on the neck without returning—That the Ship he commanded was taken up, places fitted & fitting for Officers to lodge, and Several Shot, Shells & Cannon already on board—That the Tories were to have the liberty of going where they please, If they can get Seamen to man the Vessells, of which there was a great scarcity—That on that account many Vessells cou'd not be carried away and wou'd be burnt—That many of the Inhabitants apprehended the Town would be destroy'd, And that It was generally thought their destination is Hallifax."

. . .

Go: Washington[12]

———————

MARCH 11
GENERAL ORDERS

While Washington awaited the British evacuation of Boston, he issued orders for the establishment of his personal guard.

Head Quarters, Cambridge, March 11th 1776

. . .

The General being desirous of selecting a particular number of men, as a Guard for himself, and baggage, The Colonel, or commanding Officer, of each of the established Regiments, (the Artillery and Riffle-men excepted) will furnish him with four, that the number wanted may be chosen out of them. His Excellency depends upon the Colonels for good Men, such as they can recommend for their sobriety, honesty, and good behaviour; he wishes them to be from five feet, eight Inches high, to five feet, ten Inches; handsomely and well made, and as there is nothing in his eyes more desireable, than Cleanliness in a Soldier, he desires that particular attention may be made, in the choice of such men, as are neat, and spruce. They are all to be at Head Quarters to morrow precisely at twelve, at noon, when the Number wanted will be fixed upon. The General neither wants men with uniforms, or arms, nor does he desire any man to be sent to him, that is not perfectly willing, and desirous, of being of this guard. They should be drill'd men. . . .[13]

MARCH 19
TO JOHN HANCOCK

The British evacuation took place on March 17. It was the first important American victory of the war.

Head Quarters Cambridge 19 March 1776

Sir

It is with the greatest pleasure I inform you that on Sunday last, the 17th Instant, about 9 O'Clock in the forenoon, The Ministerial Army evacuated the Town of Boston, and that the Forces of the United Colonies are now in actual possession thereof. I beg leave to congratulate you Sir, & the honorable Congress—on this happy Event, and particularly as it was effected without endangering the lives & property of the remaining unhappy Inhabitants.

. . .

The Situation in which I found their Works evidently discovered that their retreat was made with the greatest precipitation—They have left their Barracks & other Works of Wood at Bunkers Hill &c. all standing, & have destroy'd but a small part of their Lines. They have also left a number of fine pieces of Cannon, which they first spik'd up, also a very large Iron Mortar, and (as I am inform'd) they have thrown another over the end of your Wharf—I have employ'd proper Persons to drill the Cannon & doubt not shall save the most of them. I am not yet able to procure an exact list of all the Stores they have left, as soon as it can be done I shall take care to transmit it to you. From an Estimate of what the Quarter Master Gen'ral has already discover'd the Amount will be 25 or 30,000£.

. . . I have the honor to be, with sincere respect Sir Your most obedt Servt.[14]

MARCH 22

TO JOHN MORGAN

Washington's proclamation aside, the property of known Tories was considered fair play, and plundered at will. He refused to join in, however, declining the offer of a horse that had been siezed from a loyalist doctor. Morgan was the director general and chief physician of the Continental Army's hospitals.

Friday-Morning. 22d Mar. 1776.
The General presents his best respects to Doctor Morgan—Upon enquiry of Colonel [Thomas] Mifflin, concerning the Horse (the Doctor very kindly made a tender of to him) he is given to understand, that this Horse did not belong to the King, or any of his Officers; but was the property of a Doctor Loyd, an avow'd Enemy to the American Cause—As the General does not know under what predicament the property of these kind of People may fall; In short, if there was no kind of doubt in the case, as the Horse is of too much value for the General to think of robbing the Doctor of, he begs leave to return him; accompanied with sincere thanks for the politeness with which he was presented; and this request, that the Doctor will not think the General meant to slight his favours.[15]

MARCH 31

TO JOHN AUGUSTINE WASHINGTON

Washington's reflections on the campaign just concluded were bittersweet.

Cambridge 31st March 1776

Dear Brother,

. . .

I believe I may, with great truth affirm, that no Man perhaps since the first Institution of Armys ever commanded one under more difficult Circumstances than I have done—to enumerate the particulars would fill a volume—many of my difficulties and distresses were of so peculiar a cast that in order to conceal them from the Enemy, I was obliged to conceal them from my friends, indeed from my own Army thereby subjecting my Conduct to interpretations unfavourable to my Character—especially by those at a distance, who could not, in the smallest degree, be acquainted with the Springs that govern'd it—I am happy however to find, and to hear from different Quarters, that my reputation stands fair—that my Conduct hitherto has given universal Satisfaction—the Addresses which I have received, and which I suppose will be published, from the general Court of this Colony (the same as our General Assembly) and from the Selectmen of Boston upon the evacuation of the Town & my approaching departure from the Colony, exhibits a pleasing testimony of their approbation of my conduct, and of their personal regard, which I have found in various other Instances; and which, in retirement, will afford many comfortable reflections.

The share you have taken in these Publick disputes is commendable and praiseworthy—it is a duty we owe our Country—a Claim posterity has on us—It is not sufficient for a Man to be a passive friend & well wisher to the Cause. This, and every other Cause, of such a Nature, must inevitably perish under such an opposition. every person should be active in some department or other, without paying too much attention to private Interest, It is a great stake we are playing for, and sure we are of winning if the Cards are well managed—Inactivity in some—disaffection in others—and timidity in many, may hurt the Cause; nothing else can, for Unanimity will carry us through triumphantly in spite of every exertion of Great Britain, if link'd together in one indissoluble Band—this they now know, & are practising every strategem which Human Invention can devise, to divide us, & unite their own People—upon this principle it is, the restraining Bill is past, and Commissioners are coming over. The device to be sure is shallow—the covering thin—But they will hold out to their own People that the Acts (complained of) are repealed, and Commissioners sent to each Colony to treat with us, neither of which will we attend to &ca—this upon weak Minds among us will have its effect—they wish for reconciliation—or in other Words they wish for Peace without attending to the Conditions.

. . .

I shall only add therefore my Affectionate regards to my Sister and the Children, & Compliments to any enquiring friends and that I am with every Sentiment of true Affection yr Loving Brother & faithful friend.

Go: Washington[16]

———

JULY 3

TO JOHN HANCOCK

With the British army and fleet departed to Halifax, Nova Scotia—where nobody expected them to stay for long—Washington left Cambridge. He arrived in New York City on April 13, where new challenges awaited him. Although he had begun preparations for the city's defense many months earlier, Manhattan and Long Island would be almost impossible to hold against a determined enemy with command of the sea. On June 28, Washington received news that the British fleet had left Halifax, and enemy ships were sighted off Sandy Hook, New Jersey, a few days later.

New York July the 3d 1776

Sir

Since I had the honor of addressing you and on the same day, several Ships more arrived within the Hook, making the number that came in then a hundred & Ten, and there remains no doubt of the whole of the Fleet from Hallifax being now here.

Yesterday evening fifty of them came up the Bay, and Anchored on the Staten Island side. their views I cannot precisely determine, but am extremely apprehensive as part of 'em only came, that they mean to surround the Island and secure the Stock upon It. I had consulted with a Committee of the Provincial Congress upon the Subject before the arrival of the Fleet and they appointed a person to superintend the business and to drive the Stock off. I also wrote Brigadier Genl Herd and directed him to the measure, lest It might be neglected, but am fearfull It has not been affected.

Our reinforcement of Militia is but yet small. I cannot ascertain the amount not having got a return. However I trust if the Enemy make an Attack they will meet with a repulse, as I have the pleasure to inform you, that an agreable spirit and willingness for Action seem to animate and pervade the whole of our Troops.

. . .

Go: Washington[17]

JULY 9
GENERAL ORDERS

While the British fleet grew offshore and his troops awaited the enemy landing, Washington announced that Congress had approved a Declaration of Independence from Great Britain.

. . .

The Honorable the Continental Congress, impelled by the dictates of duty, policy and necessity, having been pleased to dissolve the Connection which subsisted between this Country, and Great Britain, and to declare the United Colonies of North America, free and independent STATES: The several brigades are to be drawn up this evening on their respective Parades, at six OClock, when the declaration of Congress, shewing the grounds & reasons of this measure, is to be read with an audible voice.

The General hopes this important Event will serve as a fresh incentive to every officer, and soldier, to act with Fidelity and Courage, as knowing that now the peace and safety of his Country depends (under God) solely on the success of our arms: And that he is now in the service of a State, possessed of sufficient power to reward his merit, and advance him to the highest Honors of a free Country. . . .[18]

JULY 10
TO JOHN HANCOCK

At almost the same moment, redcoats began landing on Staten Island, to the evident joy of its mostly loyalist inhabitants. On Manhattan and Long Island, Washington fielded an army of about 20,000 Continentals and militia, against a concentrated enemy force of 25,000 men, including British redcoats and German mercenaries— the largest army that Great Britain had ever fielded outside of Europe.

New York July 10th 1776

Sir

. . .

I perceive that Congress have been employed in deliberating on measures of the most Interesting nature. It is certain that It is not with us to determine in many Instances what consequences will flow from our Counsels, but yet It behoves us to adopt such, as under the smiles of a Gracious & All kind Providence will be most likely to promote our happiness; I trust the late decisive part they have taken is calculated for that end, and will secure us that freedom and those privileges which have been and are refused us, contrary to the voice of nature and the British Constitution. Agreable to the request of Congress I caused the Declaration [of Independence] to be proclaimed before all the Army under my Immediate command and have the pleasure to inform them that the measure seemed to have their most hearty assent, The expressions and behavior both of Officers and men testifying their warmest approbation of It.

. . .

The Intelligence we have from a few deserters that have come over to us, and from Others, is, that General Howe has between Nine & Ten thousand men who are chiefly landed on the Island, posted in different parts and securing the several communications from the Jerseys with small Works and Intrenchments to prevent our people from paying 'em a visit— That the Islanders have all Joined them, seem well disposed to favor their cause & have agreed to take up Arms in their behalf—they look for Admiral Howe's arrival every day with his fleet and a large reinforcement; and in high spirits, and talk confidently of success and carrying All before 'em when he comes. I trust through divine favor and our own exertions they will be disappointed in their views, and at all events any Advantages they may gain will cost them very dear. If our Troops will behave well, which I hope will be the case, having every thing to contend for that Freemen hold dear, they will have to wade through much blood & Slaughter before they can carry any part of our Works, If they carry 'em at all, and at best be in possession of a melancholy and mournfull victory. May the sacredness of our cause Inspire our Soldiery with sentiments of Heroism, and lead 'em to the performance of the noblest exploits. . . .

Go: Washington[19]

———

JULY 14
TO JOHN HANCOCK

A British attempt to address Washington without using his proper military title interrupted the battle preparations with a crisis of punctilio. From the British perspective, dignifying Washington with the title of "General" would legitimize him and the American troops as honorable combatants rather than rebels and traitors; conversely, for the Americans to accept a letter addressed to "Mister Washington" would be to deny their claims to sovereignty. After another attempt to address Washington without mentioning his military title, this time as "Geo. Washington &c. &c. &c.," the British relented and called him "General Washington."

New York July the 14th 1776

Sir

. . .

About 3 OClock this afternoon I was informed that a Flag from Lord Howe was coming up and waited with two of our Whale boats untill directions should be given. I immediately convened such of the General officers as were not upon other duty who agreed in opinion that I ought not to receive any Letter directed to me as a private Gentleman, but if otherwise and the Officer desired to come up to deliver the Letter himself as was suggested, he should come under a safe conduct—Upon this I directed Colo. Reed to go down & manage the affair under the above general Instruction. On his return he Informed me, after the common Civilities the Officer acquainted him that he had a Letter from Lord Howe to Mr Washington which he shewed under a superscription to George Washington Esqr. Col.

Reed replied there was no such person in the Army and that a Letter Intended for the General could not be received under such a direction—The
Officer expressed great concern, said It was a Letter rather of a civil than
Military nature. That Lord Howe regretted he had not arrived sooner. That
he (Lord Howe) had great Powers. the anxiety to have the Letter received
was very evident, though the Officer disclaimed all Knowledge of Its contents. However Col. Reeds Instructions being positive they parted—after
they had got some distance the Officer with the Flag again put about
and asked under what direction Mr Washington chose to be addressed. to
which Colo. Reed answered his station was well known and that certainly
they could be at no loss how to direct to him. The Officer said they knew
It & lamented It and again repeated his wish that the Letter could be received—Col. Reed told him a proper direction would obviate all difficulties & that this was no new matter. this subject having been fully discussed
in the course of the last year, of which Lord Howe could not be ignorant
upon which they parted.

I would not upon any occasion sacrifice Essentials to Punctilio, but in
this Instance, the Opinion of Others concurring with my own, I deemed
It a duty to my Country and my appointment to insist upon that respect
which in any other than a public view I would willingly have waived. Nor
do I doubt but from the supposed nature of the Message and the anxiety
expressed they will either repeat their Flag or fall upon some mode to communicate the Import and consequence of It. . . .[20]

———

AUGUST 1
GENERAL ORDERS

*Even with the enemy in sight, Washington struggled to create a sense of unity in his
army.*

Head Quarters, New York, August 1st 1776.
It is with great concern, the General understands, that Jealousies &c: are
arisen among the troops from the different Provinces, of reflections frequently thrown out, which can only tend to irritate each other, and injure
the noble cause in which we are engaged, and which we ought to support

with one hand and one heart. The General most earnestly entreats the officers, and soldiers, to consider the consequences; that they can no way assist our cruel enemies more effectually, than making division among ourselves; That the Honor and Success of the army, and the safety of our bleeding Country, depends upon harmony and good agreement with each other; That the Provinces are all United to oppose the common enemy, and all distinctions sunk in the name of an American; to make this honorable, and preserve the Liberty of our Country, ought to be our only emulation, and he will be the best Soldier, and the best Patriot, who contributes most to this glorious work, whatever his Station, or from whatever part of the Continent, he may come: Let all distinctions of Nations, Countries, and Provinces, therefore be lost in the generous contest, who shall behave with the most Courage against the enemy, and the most kindness and good humour to each other—If there are any officers, or soldiers, so lost to virtue and a love of their Country as to continue in such practices after this order; The General assures them, and is directed by Congress to declare, to the whole Army, that such persons shall be severely punished and dismissed the service with disgrace.[21]

AUGUST 13
GENERAL ORDERS

. . .

The Enemy's whole reinforcement is now arrived, so that an Attack must, and will soon be made; The General therefore again repeats his earnest request, that every officer, and soldier, will have his Arms and Ammunition in good Order; keep within their quarters and encampment, as much as possible; be ready for action at a moments call; and when called to it, remember that Liberty, Property, Life and Honor, are all at stake; that upon their Courage and Conduct, rest the hopes of their bleeding and insulted Country; that their Wives, Children and Parents, expect Safety from them only, and that we have every reason to expect Heaven will crown with Success, so just a cause. The enemy will endeavour to intimidate by shew and appearance, but remember how they have been repulsed, on various occasions, by a few brave Americans; Their Cause is bad; their men are conscious of it, and if opposed with firmness, and coolness, at their first onsett, with our advantage of Works, and Knowledge of the Ground; Victory is most assuredly ours. Every good Soldier will be silent and attentive, wait for Orders and reserve his fire, 'till he is sure of doing execution: The Officers to be particularly careful of this. The Colonels, or commanding Officers of Regiments, are to see their supernumerary officers so posted, as to keep the men to their duty; and it may not be amiss for the troops to know, that if any infamous Rascal, in time of action, shall attempt to skulk, hide himself or retreat from the enemy without orders of his commanding Officer; he will instantly be shot down as an example of Cowardice: On the other hand, the General solemnly promises, that he will reward those who shall distinguish themselves, by brave and noble actions; and he desires every officer to be attentive to this particular, that such men may be afterwards suitably noticed. . . .[22]

AUGUST 13
TO JOHN HANCOCK

The bold words of today's General Orders aside, Washington understood the value of prudence when it came to one of his most valuable possessions: his papers. He sent them to safety secretly, lest any of his soldiers suspect he contemplated defeat.

New York Augt 13th 1776

Sir

As there is reason to beleive that but little Time will elapse before the Enemy make their Attack, I have thought It advisable to remove All the papers in my hands respecting the Affairs of the States from this place. I hope the Event will shew the precaution was unnecessary, but yet prudence required that It should be done, Lest by any Accident they might fall into their hands.

They are all contained in a large Box nailed up & committed to the care of Lt Colo. Reed, Brother of the Adjutant General to be delivered to Congress, In whose Custody I would beg leave to deposit them, untill our Affairs shall be so circumstanced as to admit of their return. The Enemy since my Letter of Yesterday have received a further augmentation of Thirty Six Ships to their Fleet, making the whole that have arived since Yesterday morning Ninety Six. . . . I would Observe that I have sent off the Box privately that It might raise no disagreable Ideas, & have enjoined Colo. Reed to Secrecy.

G.W.[23]

AUGUST 17

TO THE NEW YORK CONVENTION

Fearing the approaching battle would cause massive civilian casualties, Washington called for a partial evacuation of Manhattan.

Head Qrs N. York Augt 17: 1776

Gentn

When I consider that the City of New York will in all human probability very soon be the scene of a bloody conflict: I can not but view the great Numbers of Women, Children & infirm persons remaining in It with the most melancholy concern—When the Men of War passed up the River the Shrieks & Cries of these poor creatures running every way with their Children was truly distressing & I fear will have an unhappy effect on the Ears & Minds of our Young & inexperienced Soldiery. Can no method be devised for their removal? Many doubtless are of Ability to remove themselves; but there are Others in a different situation—Some provision for them afterwards would also be a necessary consideration—It would releive me from Great anxiety If your Honorable body would Immediately deliberate upon It & form & execute some plan for their Removal and releif in which I will co-operate & assist to the utmost of my power—In the mean Time I have thought It proper to recommend to persons under the above description to convey themselves without delay to some place of safety with their most valuable Effects. I have the honor &c.

G.W.[24]

AUGUST 23
TO THE NEW YORK CONVENTION

As the Americans and the British prepared for battle, rumors spread that Washington intended to burn Manhattan if his men were forced to abandon the city. Although Washington denied the rumors, he thought privately that in case of an American defeat it would be best to burn Manhattan so that it could not provide shelter to the British.

Head Quarters New York 23d Augt 1776

Gentlemen

I am favoured with yours of the 22d acquainting me with a Report now circulating "that if the American Army should be obliged to retreat from this City, any Individual may set it on fire."

I can assure you Gentlemen, this Report is not founded upon the least Authority from me. On the contrary I am so sensible of the Value of such a City and the Consequences of its Destruction to many worthy Citizens & their Families that nothing but the last Necessity and that such as should justify me to the whole World, would induce me to give Orders for that purpose.

The unwillingness shewn by many Families to remove notwithstanding your and my Recommendation may perhaps have led some persons to propagate the Report with honest and innocent Intentions. But as your Letter first informed me of it, I cannot pretend to say by whom or for what purpose it has been done.

As my Views with Regard to the Removal of the Women and Children have happily coincided with your Sentiments and a Committee appointed to carry them into Execution, I submit it to your Judgment whether it would not be proper for the Committee to meet immediately in this City and give Notice of their Attendance on this Business. There are many who anxiously wish to remove but have not the means.[25]

AUGUST 26

TO LUND WASHINGTON

On August 22, General Howe began ferrying his troops from Staten Island to Long Island. Within a few days there were 20,000 British soldiers on the island. They faced about 4,000 Americans, entrenched around Brooklyn Heights under the command of Major General John Sullivan.

New York Augt 26th 1776.

Dear Lund,

. . .

The Enemy on Wednesday night, and thursday last, landed a pretty considerable part of their Force on long Island; at a place called Graves end bay about Ten Miles from our Works on the Island; and Marched through the Flat & level Land, which is quite free of Wood, till they (or part of them) got within abt three Miles of our Lines, where they are now Incamped; A Wood & broken ground lying between Us. What there real design is I know not; whether they think our Works round this City are too strong, and have a Mind to bend their whole force that way—or whether it is intended as a feint—or is to form part of their Attack, we cannot as yet tell—however I have strengthend the Post as much as I can, to prevent a Surprize, and have lined the Wood between them and Us, from whence some Skirmishes have ensued and lives lost on both sides. A few days more I should think will bring matters to an Issue one way or other or else the Season for Action will leave them as we [are] verging close upon September.

I am not at all surprized that our Numbers should be so much magnified with you, when in the very Neighbourhood they are thought to be double what they really are—but this you may be assured of, that our numbers are a good deal short of those of the Enemy, who have this further great advantage of us that by knowing their own points of Attack, they can regulate matters accordingly, where as we are obliged, as far as we are able, to be prepared at all points. Our Officers and Men (such as are fit for duty) seem to be in good Spirits, but we are exceedingly Sickly, more so than the Army has been at any one time since I have Commanded it. I have no doubt however, at least I am flattered into a belief, that Victory, if unfortunately it should decide in favour of the Enemy will not be purchased at a very easy rate.

I, in behalf of the Noble cause we are Ingaged in, and myself, thank with a grateful Heart all those who supplicate the throne of grace for success to the one & preservation of the other. That being from whom nothing can be hid will, I doubt not, listen to our Prayers, and protect our Cause and the supporters of it, as far as we merit his favour and Assistance. If I did not think our struggle just, I am sure it would meet with no assistance from me—and sure I am that no pecuniary Satisfaction upon Earth can compensate the loss of all my domestick happiness and requite me for the load of business which constantly presses upon and deprives me of every enjoyment. . . .

Go: Washington[26]

AUGUST 31

GENERAL ORDERS

On the morning of August 27, General Howe attacked Major General John Sullivan's force on upper Long Island—reinforced to 8,000 men, but still less than half the size of the British force—and routed it, capturing Sullivan and Major General William Alexander, who styled himself Lord Stirling, along with most of their men. By early afternoon, the British had cleared the entire island except for the fortified American camp at Brooklyn Heights, just across the Hudson from lower Manhattan. Four or five thousand Continentals were there, along with Washington, who had crossed the river to investigate. Had the British stormed the fortifications, they would have taken serious casualties, but probably captured the entire American force, possibly along with Washington himself. Inexplicably, Howe halted his victorious troops, allowing the Americans time to recover and prepare to evacuate. Yet although the evacuation of Long Island on the night of August 29–30 saved a portion of Washington's army, it also constituted a defeat. Washington did what he could to shore up his army's faltering morale.

Head Quarters, New York, August 31st 1776.

. . .

Both officers and soldiers are informed that the Retreat from Long Island was made by the unanimous advice of all the General Officers, not from any doubts of the spirit of the troops, but because they found the

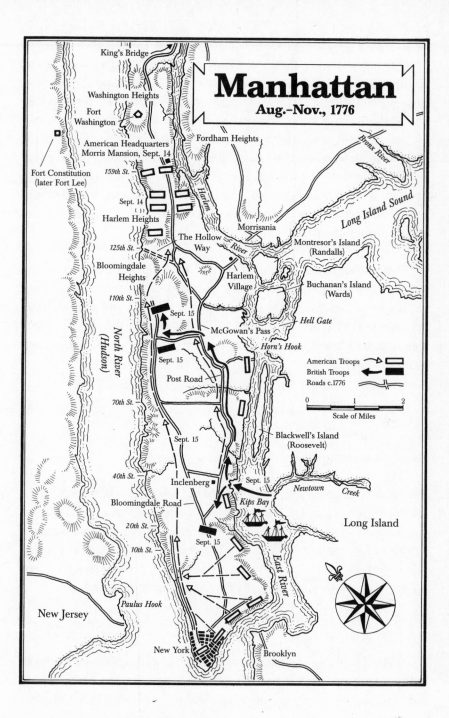

King's Bridge

Washington Heights

Fort
Washington

American Headquarters
Morris Mansion, Sept. 14

Fordham Heights

Fort Constitution
(later Fort Lee)

159th St.

Manhattan
Aug.–Nov., 1776

Bronx River

Sept. 14

Harlem Heights

Harlem River

Morrisania

Long Island Sound

125th St.

The Hollow
Way

Bloomingdale
Heights

Sept. 15

110th St.

Harlem
Village

Montresor's Island
(Randalls)

Buchanan's Island
(Wards)

McGowan's Pass

Hell Gate

Sept. 15

Post Road

Horn's Hook

American Troops
British Troops
Roads c.1776

70th St.

North River
(Hudson)

0   1   2
Scale of Miles

Blackwell's Island
(Roosevelt)

40th St.

Inclenberg

Sept. 15

Sept. 15

Bloomingdale Road

Kips Bay

Newtown   Creek

Long Island

20th St.

10th St.

Sept. 15

Paulus Hook

East River

New Jersey

New York

Brooklyn

troops very much fatigued with hard duty and divided into many detach-ments, while the enemy had their Main Body on the Island, and capable of receiving assistance from the shipping: In these circumstances it was thought unsafe to transport the whole of an Army on an Island, or to engage them with a part, and therefore unequal numbers; whereas now one whole Army is collected together, without Water intervening, while the enemy can receive little assistance from their ships; their Army is, and must be divided into many bodies, and fatigued with keeping up a commu-nication with their Ships; whereas ours is connected, and can act together: They must affect a landing under so many disadvantages, that if officers and soldiers are vigilant, and alert, to prevent surprise, and add spirit when they approach, there is no doubt of our success.

. . .

The General hopes the several officers, both superior and inferior, will now exert themselves, and gloriously determine to conquer, or die—From the justice of our cause—the situation of the harbour, and the bravery of her sons, America can only expect success—Now is the time for every man to exert himself, and make our Country glorious, or it will become contemptable.[27]

SEPTEMBER 2
TO JOHN HANCOCK

The defeat of the American army on Long Island, where many soldiers surrendered without firing a shot, and the militia's continuing refusal to lend significant support convinced Washington more than ever of the need for a standing army composed of men enlisted for the duration of the war. In this letter to the president of Congress, Washington also hinted at the efficacy of a measure he had rejected only a few weeks before—the destruction of New York City. Congress refused to sanction it.

New York Septr the 2d 1776

Sir

As my Intelligence of late has been rather unfavourable and would be received with anxiety & concern, peculiarly happy should I esteem myself, were It in my power at this time, to transmit such information to Congress, as would be more pleasing and agreable to their Wishes—But unfortunately for me—Unfortunately for them, It is not.

Our situation is truly distressing—The check our Detachment sustained on the 27th Ulto, has dispirited too great a proportion of our Troops and filled their minds with apprehension and despair—The Militia instead of calling forth their utmost efforts to a brave & manly opposition in order to repair our Losses, are dismayed, Intractable, and Impatient to return. Great numbers of them have gone off; in some Instances, almost by whole Regiments—by half Ones & by Companies at a time—This circumstance of Itself, Independent of others, when fronted by a well appointed Enemy, superior in number to our whole collected force, would be sufficiently disagreable, but when their example has Infected another part of the Army— When their want of discipline & refusal of almost every kind of restraint & Government, have produced a like conduct, but too common to the whole, and an entire disregard of that order and subordination necessary to the well doing of an Army, and which had been Inculcated before, as well as the nature of our Military establishment would admit of, our condition is still more alarming, and with the deepest concern I am obliged to confess my want of confidence in the Generality of the Troops. All these circumstances fully confirm the opinion I ever entertained, and which I more than once in my Letters took the liberty of mentioning to Congress, that no dependence could be put in a Militia or other Troops than those enlisted and embodied for a longer period than our regulations heretofore have prescribed. I am persuaded and as fully convinced, as I am of any One fact that has happened, that our Liberties must of necessity be greatly hazarded, If not entirely lost If their defence is left to any but a permanent, standing Army I mean One to exist during the War. . . . Till of late I had no doubt in my own mind of defending this place nor should I have yet If the Men would do their duty, but this I despair of—It is painfull and extremely grating to me to give such unfavourable accounts, but It would be criminal to conceal the truth at so critical a juncture—Every power I possess shall be exerted to serve the Cause, & my first wish is, that whatever may be the event, the Congress will do me the Justice to think so. If we should be obliged to abandon this Town, ought It to stand as Winter Quarters for the Enemy? They would derive great conveniences from It on the one hand—and much property would be destroyed on the other—It is an important question, but will admit of but little time for deliberation—At present I dare say the Enemy mean to preserve It if they can—If Congress therefore should resolve upon the destruction of It, the Resolution should be a profound secret as the knowledge of It will make a Capital change in their plans. . . .

Go: Washington[28]

SEPTEMBER 8

TO JOHN HANCOCK

Fight and face possible destruction, or withdraw and live to fight another day? This classic military dilemma faced Washington and his generals in early September, and forced a reappraisal of American strategy. Unfortunately, the generals could agree only on half measures—partially withdrawing from New York, while still attempting to defend the city. The consequences of such indecision were nearly disastrous for the American cause. Six days later, Washington wrote Hancock again to announce that he and his generals had decided to abandon New York—but the British had already begun operations intended to cut off the American army in lower Manhattan.

New York Head Qrs Septr 8th 1776

Sir

Since I had the honour of addressing you on the 6th Instt I have called a Council of the General Officers in order to take a full & comprehensive view of our situation & thereupon form such a plan of future defence as may be immediately pursued . . . It is now extremely obvious from all Intelligence—from their movements, & every other circumstance that having landed their whole Army on Long Island, (except about 4,000 on Staten Island) they mean to inclose us on the Island of New York by taking post in our Rear, while the Shipping effectually secure the Front; and thus either by cutting off our Communication with the Country oblige us to fight them on their own Terms or Surrender at discretion, or by a Brilliant stroke endeavour to cut this Army in peices & secure the collection of Arms & Stores which they will know we shall not be able soon to replace. Having therefore their System unfolded to us, It became an important consideration how It could be most successfully opposed—On every side there is a choice of difficulties, & every measure on our part, (however painfull the reflection is from experience) to be formed with some apprehension that all our Troops will not do their duty. In deliberating on this great Question, it was impossible to forget that History—our own experience— the advice of our ablest Friends in Europe—The fears of the Enemy, and even the Declarations of Congress demonstrate that on our side the War should be defensive, It has been even called a War of posts, that we should on all occasions avoid a general Action or put anything to the risque unless compelled by a necessity into which we ought never to be drawn. The Arguments on which such a System was founded were deemed unanswerable & experience has given her sanction—With these views & being fully persuaded that It would be presumption to draw out our young Troops into open Ground against their superiors both in number and discipline, I have never spared the Spade & Pickax: I confess I have not found that readiness to defend even strong posts at all hazards which is necessary to derive the greatest benefit from them. The honour of making a brave defence does not seem to be a sufficient stimulus when the success is very doubtfull and the falling into the Enemy's hands probable: But I doubt not this will be gradually attained. We are now in a strong post but not an Impregnable one, nay acknowledged by every man of Judgement to be untenable unless the Enemy will make the Attack upon Lines when they can avoid It and their Movements Indicate that they mean to do so—To draw the whole Army together in order to arrange the defence proportionate to the extent of Lines & works would leave the Country open for an approach and put the fate of this Army and Its stores on the Hazard of making a successfull defence in the City or the issue of an Engagement out of It—On the other hand to abandon a City which has been by some deemed defensible and on whose Works much Labor has been bestowed has a tendency to dispirit the Troops and enfeeble our Cause . . . With these and many other circumstances before them, the whole Council of Genl Officers met yesterday in order to adopt some Genl line of conduct to be pursued at this Important crisis. . . . All agreed the Town would not be tenable If the Enemy resolved to bombard & cannonade It—But the difficulty attending a removal operated so strongly, that a course was taken between abandoning It totally & concentring our whole strength for Its defence—Nor were some a little Influenced in their opinion to whom the determination of Congress was known, against an evacuation totally, as they were led to suspect Congress wished It to be maintained at every hazard. . . . There were some Genl Officers in whose Judgement and opinion much confidence is to be reposed, that were for a total and immediate removal from the City, urging the great danger of One part of the Army being cut off before the other can support It, the Extremities being at least Sixteen miles apart—that our Army when collected is inferior to the Enemy's—that they can move with their whole force to any point of attack & consequently must succeed by weight of Numbers if they have only a part to oppose them—That by removing from hence we deprive the Enemy of the Advantage of their Ships which will make at least one half of the force to attack the Town—That we should keep the Enemy at Bay—put nothing to the hazard but at all events keep the Army together which may be recruited another Year, that the unspent Stores will also be preserved & in this case the heavy Artillery can also be secured—But they were overruled by a Majority who thought for the present a part of our force might be kept here and attempt to maintain the City a while longer.

I am sensible a retreating Army is encircled with difficulties, that the declining an Engagement subjects a General to reproach and that the Common cause may be affected by the discouragement It may throw over the minds of many. Nor am I insensible of the contrary Effects if a brilliant stroke could be made with any probability of Success, especially after our Loss upon Long Island—But when the Fate of America may be at Stake on the Issue, when the wisdom of Cooler moments & experienced men have decided that we should protract the War, if possible, I cannot think it safe or wise to adopt a different System when the Season for Action draws so near a Close—That the Enemy mean to winter in New York there can be no doubt—that with such an Armament they can drive us out is equally clear. The Congress having resolved that It should not be destroyed nothing seems to remain but to determine the time of their taking possession—It is our Interest & wish to prolong It as much as possible provided the delay does not affect our future measures.

. . .

Go: Washington[29]

- *1776* -

SEPTEMBER 16

TO JOHN HANCOCK

British troops landed on the early morning of September 15 at Kip's Bay, at the east end of what is now 34th Street. The American troops defending the bay fled almost as soon as the landing began, despite Washington's attempts to rally them, sometimes with the flat of his sword. The British moved inland too slowly to cut off the thousands of Americans still withdrawing from lower Manhattan, and the army withdrew successfully to Harlem Heights; but Washington's humiliation at his inability to rally the troops would plunge him almost into despair.

Head Qrs at Col. Roger Morris's House Septr 16th 1776

Sir

On Saturday about Sunset Six more of the Enemy's Ships, One or Two of which were men of War; passed between Governors Island & Red Hook and went up the East River to the Station taken by those mentioned in my Last . . . in the morning they began their Operations—Three Ships of War came up the North River as high [as] Bloomingdale which put a total stop to the removal by Water of any more of our provision &c. and about Eleven OClock those in the East River began a most severe and Heavy Cannonade to scour the Grounds and cover the landing of their Troops between Turtle-Bay and the City, where Breast Works had been thrown up to oppose them. As soon as I heard the Firing, I road with all possible dispatch towards the place of landing when to my great surprize and Mortification I found the Troops that had been posted in the Lines retreating with the utmost precipitation and those ordered to support them, parson's & Fellows's Brigades, flying in every direction and in the greatest confusion, notwithstanding the exertions of their Generals to form them. I used every means in my power to rally and get them into some order but my attempts were fruitless and ineffectual, and on the appearance of a small party of the Enemy, not more than Sixty or Seventy, their disorder increased and they ran away in the greatest confusion without firing a Single Shot—Finding that no confidence was to be placed in these Brigades and apprehending that another part of the Enemy might pass over to Harlem plains and cut off the retreat to this place, I sent orders to secure the Heights in the best manner with the Troops that were stationed on and near them, which being done, the retreat was effected with but little or no loss of Men, tho of a considerable part of our Baggage occasioned by this disgracefull and dastardly conduct—Most of our Heavy Cannon and a part of our Stores and provisions which we were about removing was unavoidably left in the City, tho every means after It had been determined in Council to evacuate the post, had been used to prevent It. We are now encamped with the Main body of the Army on the Heights of Harlem where I should hope the Enemy would meet with a defeat in case of an Attack, If the Generality of our Troops would behave with tolerable bravery, but experience to my extreme affliction has convinced me that this is rather to be wished for than expected; However I trust, that there are many who will act like men, and shew themselves worthy of the blessings of Freedom. I have sent out some reconoitring parties to gain Intelligence If possible of the disposition of the Enemy and shall inform Congress of every material event by the earliest Opportunity . . .[30]

SEPTEMBER 22
TO JOHN HANCOCK

A fire that began in New York on September 21 destroyed a quarter of the city, or about a thousand buildings. Who started the fire has never been determined, but Washington was far from regretting it. "Providence," he wrote to Lund Washington on October 6, "or some good honest Fellow, has done more for us than we were disposed to do for ourselves."[31]

Head Qrs Heights of Harlem Septr 22d 1776

Sir

. . .

On Friday night, about Eleven or Twelve OClock, a Fire broke out in the City of New York, near the New or St Pauls Church, as It is said, which continued to burn pretty rapidly till after Sun rise the next morning. I have not been Informed how the Accident happened, nor received any certain account of the damage. Report says many of the Houses between the Broadway and the River were consumed. . . .

Go: Washington[32]

SEPTEMBER 25
TO JOHN HANCOCK

On New Year's Day, 1776, Washington had watched most of his soldiers leave for home as their one-year enlistments expired, oblivious to his appeals for patriotism and self-sacrifice. And in August and September, he watched his men throw down their weapons and flee the enemy, sometimes without firing a shot. The lesson—that men are guided by self-interest before idealism—was painful, but necessary; Washington draws on it in this remarkable letter, in which he sets out a definite standard by which the country should build and maintain an army capable of winning the war.

Colo. Morris's on the Heights of Harlem Septr 25th 1776.
Sir,

From the hours allotted to Sleep, I will borrow a few moments to convey my thoughts on sundry important matters to Congress. I shall offer them with that sincerety which ought to characterize a Man of candour; and with the freedom which may be used in giving useful information, without incurring the imputation of presumption.

We are now as it were, upon the eve of another dissolution of our Army—the remembrance of the difficulties which happened upon that occasion last year—the consequences which might have followed the change, if proper advantages had been taken by the Enemy—added to a knowledge of the present temper and Situation of the Troops, reflect but a very gloomy prospect upon the appearance of things now and satisfie me, beyond the possibility of doubt, that unless some speedy, and effectual measures are adopted by Congress; our cause will be lost.

It is in vain to expect that any (or more than a trifling) part of this Army will again engage in the Service on the encouragement offered by Congress—When Men find that their Townsmen & Companions are receiving 20, 30, and more Dollars for a few Months Service (which is truely the case) it cannot be expected; without using compulsion; & to force them into the Service would answer no valuable purpose. When Men are irritated, & the Passions inflamed, they fly hastily, and chearfully to Arms, but after the first emotions are over to expect, among such People as compose the bulk of an Army, that they are influenced by any other principles than those of Interest, is to look for what never did, & I fear never will happen; the Congress will deceive themselves therefore if they expect it.

A Soldier reasoned with upon the goodness of the cause he is engaged in and the inestimable rights he is contending for, hears you with patience, & acknowledges the truth of your observations; but adds, that it is of no more Importance to him than others—The Officer makes you the same reply, with this further remark, that his pay will not support him, and he cannot ruin himself and Family to serve his Country, when every member of the community is equally Interested and benefitted by his Labours—The few therefore, who act upon Principles of disinterestedness, are, comparitively speaking—no more than a drop in the Ocean. It becomes evidently clear then, that as this contest is not likely to be the Work of a day—as the War must be carried on systematically—and to do it, you must have good Officers, there are, in my judgment, no other possible means to obtain them but by establishing your Army upon a permanent footing; and giving your Officers good pay. this will induce Gentlemen, and Men of Character to engage; and till the bulk of your Officers are composed of Such persons as are actuated by Principles of honour, and a spirit of enterprize, you have little to expect from them. They ought to have such allowances as will enable them to live like, and support the Characters of Gentlemen; and not be driven by a scanty pittance to the low, & dirty arts which many of them practice to filch the Public of more than the difference of pay would amount to upon an ample allowe—besides, something is due to the Man who puts his life in his hand—hazards his health—& forsakes the Sweets of domestic enjoyments—Why a Captain in the Continental Service should receive no more than 5/. Currency per day for performing the same duties that an Officer of the same Rank in the British Service receives 10/. Sterling for, I never could conceive; especially when the latter is provided with every necessary he requires upon the best terms, and the former can scarce procure them at any Rate. There is nothing that gives a Man consequence, & renders him fit for Command, like a support that renders him Independant of every body but the State he Serves.

With respect to the Men, nothing but a good bounty can obtain them upon a permanent establishment; and for no shorter time than the continuance of the War, ought they to be engaged. . . . I shall therefore take the freedom of givg it as my opinion, that a good Bounty be immediately offered, aided by the proffer of at least 100 or 150 Acres of Land and a

Suit of Cloaths & Blanket to each Non Commissioned Officer & Soldier, as I have good Authority for saying, that however high the Mens pay may appear, it is barely sufficient in the present scarcity & dearness of all kinds of goods, to keep them in Cloaths, much less afford support to their Families—If this encouragement then is given to the Men, and such Pay allowed the Officers as will induce Gentlemen of Character & liberal Sentiments to engage, and proper care & precaution used in the nomination (having more regard to the Characters of Persons, than the number of Men they can Inlist) we should in a little time have an Army able to cope with any that can be opposed to it; as there are excellent Materials to form one out of: but while the only merit an Officer possesses is his ability to raise Men—while those Men consider, and treat him as an equal; & (in the Character of an Officer) regard him no more than a broomstick, being mixed together as one common herd, no order, nor no discipline can prevail—nor will the Officer ever meet with that respect which is essensially necessary to due subordination.

To place any dependance upon Militia, is, assuredly, resting upon a broken staff. Men just dragged from the tender Scenes of domestick life—unaccustomed to the din of Arms—totally unacquainted with every kind of Military skill, which being followed by a want of Confidence in themselves when opposed to Troops regularly trained—disciplined, and appointed—superior in knowledge, & superior in Arms, makes them timid, and ready to fly from their own Shadows. Besides, the sudden change in their manner of living (particularly in the lodging) brings on sickness in many; impatience in all; & such an unconquerable desire of returning to their respective homes that it not only produces shameful, & scandalous Desertions among themselves, but infuses the like spirit in others—Again, Men accustomed to unbounded freedom, and no controul, cannot brooke the Restraint which is indispensably necessary to the good Order and Government of an Army; without which Licentiousness, & every kind of disorder triumphantly reign. To bring men to a proper degree of Subordination is not the work of a day—a Month— or even a year—and unhappily for us, and the cause we are Ingaged in, the little discipline I have been labouring to establish in the Army under my immediate Command, is in a manner done away by having such a mixture of Troops as have been called together within these few Months.

. . .

The Jealousies of a standing Army, and the Evils to be apprehended from one, are remote; and in my judgment, situated & circumstanced as we are, not at all to be dreaded; but the consequence of wanting one, according to my Ideas; formed from the present view of things, is certain, and inevitable Ruin; for if I was called upon to declare upon Oath, whether the Militia have been most Serviceable or hurtful upon the whole I should subscribe to the latter.

. . .

Another matter highly worthy of attention, is, that other Rules and Regulation's may be adopted for the Government of the Army than those now in existence, otherwise the Army, but for the name, might as well be disbanded—For the most atrocious offences (one or two Instances only excepted) a Man receives no more than 39 Lashes, and these perhaps (thro the collusion of the Officer who is to see it inflicted) are given in such a manner as to become rather a matter of sport than punishment; but when inflicted as they ought, many hardend fellows who have been the Subjects, have declared that for a bottle of Rum they would undergo a Second operation—it is evident therefore that this punishment is inadequate to many Crimes it is assigned to—as a proof of it, thirty and 40 Soldiers will desert at a time; and of late, a practice prevails (as you will see by my Letter of the 22d) of the most alarming nature; and which will, if it cannot be checked, prove fatal both to the Country and Army—I mean the infamous practice of Plundering, for under the Idea of Tory property—or property which may fall into the hands of the Enemy, no Man is secure in his effects, & scarcely in his Person; for in order to get at them, we have several Instances of People being frieghtned out of their Houses under pretence of those Houses being ordered to be burnt, & this is done with a view of siezing the Goods; nay, in order that the Villainy may be more effectually concealed, some Houses have actually been burnt to cover the theft.

I have with some others used my utmost endeavours to stop this horrid practice, but under the present lust after plunder, and want of Laws to punish Offenders, I might almost as well attempt to remove Mount Atlas— I have ordered instant corporal Punishment upon every Man who passes our Lines, or is seen with Plunder that the Offender might be punished for disobedience of Orders; and Inclose you the proceedings of a Court Martial held upon an Officer, who with a Party of Men had robbed a House a little beyond our Lines of a number of valuable Goods; among which (to shew that nothing escapes) were four large Peer looking Glasses— Womens Cloaths, and other Articles which one would think, could be of no Earthly use to him—He was met by a Major of Brigade who ordered him to return the Goods as taken contrary to General Orders, which he not only peremptorily refused to do, but drew up his Party and swore he would defend them at the hazard of his Life; on which I ordered him to be Arrested, and tryed for Plundering, Disobedience of Orders, and Mutiny; for the Result, I refer to the Proceedings of the Court; whose judgment appeared so exceedingly extraordinary, that I ordered a Reconsideration of the matter, upon which, and with the assistance of a fresh evidence, they made Shift to Cashier him.

I adduce this Instance to give some Idea to Congress of the Current Sentiments & general run of the Officers which compose the present Army; & to shew how exceedingly necessary it is to be careful in the choice of the New sett even if it should take double the time to compleat the Levies—An Army formed of good Officers moves like Clock work; but there is no Situation upon Earth less enviable, nor more distressing, than that Person's who is at the head of Troops, who are regardless of Order and discipline; and who are unprovided with almost every necessary—In a word, the difficulties which have forever surrounded me since I have been in the Service, and kept my Mind constantly upon the stretch—The Wounds which my Feelings as an Officer have received by a thousand things which have happened, contrary to my expectation and Wishes—the effect of my own conduct, and present appearance of things, so little pleasing to myself, as to render it a matter of no Surprize (to me) if I should stand capitally censured by Congress—added to a consciousness of my inability to govern an Army composed of such discordant parts, and under such a variety of intricate and perplexing circumstances, induces not only a belief, but a thorough conviction in my Mind, that it will be impossible unless there is a thorough change in our Military System for me to conduct matters in such a manner as to give Satisfaction to the Publick, which is all the recompense I aim at, or ever wished for.

Before I conclude I must appologize for the liberties taken in this Letter and for the blots and scratchings therein—not having time to give it more correctly. With truth I can add, that with every Sentiment of respect & esteem I am Yrs & the Congresses Most Obedt & Most H. Servt

Go: Washington[33]

SEPTEMBER 30
TO LUND WASHINGTON

Washington expounded more candidly on his worries in this letter to Lund. So despondent was he that he even considered resignation.

Col. Morris's, on the Heights of Harlem, 30 September, 1776.
Dear Lund,

. . .

In short, such is my situation that if I were to wish the bitterest curse to an enemy on this side of the grave, I should put him in my stead with my feelings; and yet I do not know what plan of conduct to pursue. I see the impossibility of serving with reputation, or doing any essential service to the cause by continuing in command, and yet I am told that if I quit the command inevitable ruin will follow from the distraction that will ensue. In confidence I tell you that I never was in such an unhappy, divided state since I was born. To lose all comfort and happiness on the one hand, whilst I am fully persuaded that under such a system of management as has been adopted, I cannot have the least chance for reputation, nor those allowances made which the nature of the case requires; and to be told, on the other, that if I leave the service all will be lost, is, at the same time that I am bereft of every peaceful moment, distressing to a degree. But I will be done with the subject, with the precaution to you that it is not a fit one to be publicly known or discussed. If I fall, it may not be amiss that these circumstances be known, and declaration made in credit to the justice of my character. And if the men will stand by me (which by the by I despair of), I am resolved not to be forced from this ground while I have life; and a few days will determine the point, if the enemy should not change their plan of operations; for they certainly will not—I am sure they ought not—to waste the season that is now fast advancing, and must be precious to them. I thought to have given you a more explicit account of my situation, expectation, and feelings, but I have not time. I am wearied to death all day with a variety of perplexing circumstances—disturbed at the conduct of the militia, whose behavior and want of discipline has done great injury to the other troops, who never had officers, except in a few instances, worth the bread they eat. My time, in short, is so much engrossed that I have not leisure for corresponding, unless it is on mere matters of public business.

. . .

I am with truth and sincerity, Dr Lund yr affect'e friend.[34]

———

NOVEMBER 16
TO JOHN HANCOCK

Washington evacuated Harlem Heights on October 17 and withdrew to the village of White Plains. Howe appeared there on the twenty-eighth, attacked, and once again defeated the Americans, forcing Washington to commence a slow, painful retreat west across New Jersey. Another entry in the year's catalog of disasters was added on November 16 when the British captured Fort Washington on the Hudson River with almost 3,000 American troops. A chagrined Washington watched the surrender from across the river at Fort Lee. Within a few days he was forced to abandon that, too.

General Greens Quarters [Fort Lee, N.J.]
16th Novr 1776

Sir

Since I had the Honor of addressing you last, an important Event has taken place; of which I wish to give you the earliest Intelligence.

The preservation of the Passage of the North River was an Object of so much Consequence that I thought no pains or Expence too great for that purpose, and therefore after sending off all the valuable Stores except such as were necessary for its Defence, I determined agreeable to the Advice of most of the General Officers, to risque something to defend the Post on the East Side call'd Mount Washington.

When the Army moved up in Consequence of Genl Howe's landing at Frog Point, Colo. [Robert] Magaw was left on that Command with about 1200 Men, and Orders given to defend it to the last. Afterwards reflecting upon the smallness of the Garrison, and the Difficulty of their holding it if Genl Howe should fall down upon it with his whole Force, I wrote to Genl [Nathanael] Greene who had the Command on the Jersey Shore, directing him to govern himself by Circumstances, and to retain or evacuate the post as he should think best, and revoking the absolute Order to Colo. Magaw to defend the post to the last Extremity.

Genl Greene struck with the Importance of the Post, and the Discouragement which our Evacuation of Posts must necessarily have given, reinforced Colo. Magaw with Detachments from several Regiments of the Flying Camp, but cheifly of Pennsylvania, so as to make up the Number about 2000. In this Situation things were Yesterday, when Genl Howe demanded the Surrendry of the Garrison, to which Colo. Magaw returned a spirited Refusal. Immediately upon receiving an Account of this Transaction, I came from Hackinsack to this place, and had partly cross'd the North River when I met Genl [Israel] Putnam and Genl Greene who were just returning from thence, and informed me that the Troops were in high Spirits and would make a good Defence, and it being late at Night I returned.

Early this Morning Colo. Magaw posted his Troops partly in the Lines thrown up by our Army on our first coming thither from New York, and partly on a commanding Hill laying North of Mount Washington (the Lines being all to the Southward). In this Position the Attack began about Ten O'Clock, which our Troops stood, and returned the Fire in such a Manner as gave me great Hopes the Enemy was intirely repulsed. But at this time a Body of Troops cross'd Harlem River in Boats and landed inside of the second Lines, our Troops being then engaged in the first.

Colo. [Lambert] Cadwalader who commanded in the Lines sent off a Detatchment to oppose them, but they being overpowered by Numbers gave way; upon which Colo. Cadwalader ordered his Troops to retreat in Order to gain the Fort. It was done with much Confusion, and the Enemy crossing over, came in upon them in such a Manner that a Number of them surrendered.

At this Time the Hessians advanced on the North Side of the Fort in very large Bodies, they were received by the Troops posted there with proper Spirit and kept back a considerable time. But at Length they were also obliged to submit to a superiority of Numbers and retire under the Cannon of the Fort.

The Enemy having advanced thus far halted, and immediately a Flag went in with a Repetition of the demand of the Fortress as I suppose. At this Time I sent a Billet to Colo. Magaw, directing him to hold out, and

I would endeavour this Evening to bring off the Garrison, if the Fortress could not be maintained, as I did not expect it could, the Enemy being possessed of the adjacent Ground. But before this reached him he had entered too far into a Treaty to retract. After which, Colo. Cadwalader told another Messenger who went over, that they had been able to obtain no other Terms than to surrender as prisoners of War. In this Situation Matters now stand. I have stopped Genl [Rezin] Beall's and Genl [Nathaniel] Heards Brigades to preserve the Post and Stores here, which with the other Troops I hope we shall be able to effect.

I dont yet know the Numbers killed or wounded on either Side, but from the heaviness and Continuance of Fire in some places, I imagine there must have been considerable Execution.

The Loss of such a Number of Officers and Men, many of whom have been trained with more than common Attention, will I fear be severely felt. But when that of the Arms and Accoutrements is added much more so, and must be a farther Incentive to procure as considerable a Supply as possible for the New Troops as soon as it can be done. . . .

Go: Washington[35]

DECEMBER 8
TO JOHN HANCOCK

Washington arrived at Trenton, New Jersey, on December 4 with an army of a little over 4,000 men, almost all of them due to depart when their enlistments expired at the end of the month. Several thousand more soldiers lay scattered in detachments across New York and New Jersey, the largest under the command of Major General Charles Lee, who persistently ignored Washington's orders to rejoin the main army. Unable to unite his troops or resist the British, who seemed bent on capturing Philadelphia before Christmas, Washington withdrew his troops across the Delaware River to Pennsylvania on the night of December 7–8.

Mr Berkley's Sommerseat Decr 8th 1776

Sir

Colo. Reed would inform you of the Intelligence which I first met with on the Road from Trenton to Princeton Yesterday. Before I got to the latter, I received a Second express informing me, that as the Enemy were advancing by different Routs and attempting by One to get in the rear of our Troops which were there & whose numbers were small and the place by no means defensible, they had judged it prudent to retreat to Trenton—The retreat was accordingly made, and since to this side of the River.

This information I thought it my duty to communicate as soon as possible, as there is not a moments time to be lost in assembling such force as can be collected and as the object of the Enemy cannot now be doubted in the smallest degree. Indeed I shall be out in my conjecture (for it is only conjecture), if the late imbarkation at New York, is not for Delaware river, to cooperate with the Army under the immediate command of Genl Howe, who I am informed from good authority is with the British Troops and his whole force upon this Route.

I have no certain intelligence of Genl Lee, although I have sent frequent Expresses to him and lately a Colo. Humpton to bring me some accurate Accounts of his situation. I last night dispatched another Gentleman to him—Major Hoops, desiring he would hasten his march to the Delaware in which I would provide Boats near a place called Alexandria for the transportation of his Troops. I can not account for the slowness of his March.

In the disordered & moving state of the Army I cannot get returns, but from the best accounts we had between Three thousand & 3500 Men before the Philadelphia Militia and German Batallion arrived, they amount to about Two thousand. . . .[36]

———

DECEMBER 10–17
TO LUND WASHINGTON

By mid-December, affairs looked so bad—General Lee was captured while dawdling near Basking Ridge, New Jersey, on December 13, the Middle Atlantic states seemed prepared to capitulate to the British, and the army was less than three weeks from dissolution—that Washington sent Lund Washington secret instructions for the evacuation of Mount Vernon.

Falls of Delaware So. Side, 10[–17]th Decr 1776.

Dear Lund,

. . .

I wish to Heaven it was in my power to give you a more favourable Acct of our situation than it is—our numbers, quite inadequate to the task of opposing that part of the Army under the Command of Genl Howe, being reduced by Sickness, Desertion, & Political Deaths (on & before the first Instant, & having no assistance from the Militia) were obliged to retire before the Enemy, who were perfectly well informed of our Situation till we came to this place, where I have no Idea of being able to make a stand, as My numbers, till joined by the Philadelphia Militia did not exceed 3000 Men fit for duty—now we may be about 5000 to oppose Howes whole Army, that part of it excepted which sailed under the Command of General Clinton. I tremble for Philadelphia, nothing in my opinion but General Lee's speedy arrival, who has been long expected, thô still at a distance (with about 3000 Men) can save it. We have brought over, and destroyed, all the Boats we could lay our hands on, upon the Jersey Shore for many Miles above and below this place; but it is next to impossible to guard a Shore for 60 Miles with less than half the Enemys numbers; when by force, or Stratagem they may suddenly attempt a passage in many differ-ent places. at present they are Incamp'd or quartered along the other shore above & below us (rather this place for we are obliged to keep a face to-wards them) for fifteen Miles.

. . .

. . . hitherto by our destruction of the Boats, and vigilance in watch-ing the Fords of the River above the Falls (which are now rather high) we have prevented them from crossing; but how long we shall be able to do it, God only knows, as they are still hovering about the River, and if every thing else fails will wait till the first of January when their will be no other Men to oppose them but Militia. . . . Our Cause has also received a severe blow in the Captivity of General Lee—Unhappy Man! taken by his own Imprudence! going three or four Miles from his own Camp to lodge, & within 20 of the Enemy; notice of which by a rascally Tory being given, a party of light Horse siez'd him in the Morning after travelling all Night & carried him off in high triumph, and with every Mark of Indignity—not even suffering him to get his Hat, or Sartout Coat. the Troops that were under his Command are not yet come up with us, though I think they may be expected to morrow. A large part of the Jerseys have given every proof of disaffection that a people can do, & this part of Pensylvania are equally inemical; in short your immagination can scarce extend to a situation more distressing than mine—Our only dependance now, is upon the Speedy Inlistment of a New Army; if this fails us, I think the game will be pretty well up, as from disaffection, and want of spirit & fortitude, the Inhabitants instead of resistance, are offering Submission, & taking protections from Genl Howe in Jersey.

. . .

Matters to my view, but this I say in confidence to you, as a friend, wears so unfavourable an aspect (not that I apprehend half so much danger from Howes Army, as from the disaffection of the three States of New York, Jersey & Pensylvania) that I would look forward to unfavorable Events, & prepare Accordingly in such a manner however as to give no alarm or suspicion to any one; as one step towards it, have my Papers in such a Situation as to remove at a short notice in case an Enemy's Fleet should come up the River—When they are removed let them go immediately to my Brothers in Berkeley.

. . .

Go: Washington[37]

DECEMBER 20

TO JOHN HANCOCK

Washington took extreme care throughout the war to avoid even the appearance of impinging on civilian authority. By mid-December 1776, however, he could no longer refer important civil and military matters to Congress before making decisions. Worried by the evident British threat to Philadelphia, the delegates had fled to Baltimore; and as Washington explained in this letter, so much time must elapse in any applications to Congress that it would "defeat the end in view." The critical situation of his army would not admit of delay. Washington therefore asked Congress for extensive civil and military powers within his army's sphere of operations, including—as laid out in this letter—the right to recruit troops and form regiments on his own authority. The delegates complied—one day after the Battle of Trenton—lead-

ing some men to question whether Washington was on the verge of establishing a military dictatorship.

Camp above Trenton Falls Decr 20th 1776.

Sir

   . . .

In short, the present exigency of our Affairs will not admit of delay either in Council or the Feild, for well convinced I am, that if the Enemy go into Quarters at all, it will be for a short season; but I rather think, the design of Genl Howe, is to possess himself of Philadelphia this Winter, if possible, and in truth, I do not see what is to prevent him, as ten days more will put an end to the existence of our Army; that One great point, is to keep us as much harrassed as possible with a view to injure the recruiting service, and hinder a collection of Stores; and other necessaries for the next campaign, I am as clear in, as I am of my existence; If therefore we have to provide in this short interval and make these great & arduous preparations, every matter that in its nature is self evident, is to be referred to Congress, at the distance of 130 or 40 miles, so much time must necessarily elapse as to defeat the end in view.

It may be said, that this is an application for powers, that are too dangerous to be intrusted. I can only add, that desperate diseases, require desperate remedies, and with truth declare, that I have no lust after power but wish with as much fervency as any man upon this wide extended Continent for an Opportunity of turning the Sword into a ploughshare; But my feelings as an Officer and a man, have been such, as to force me to say, that no person ever had a greater choice of difficulties to contend with than I have. It is needless to add, that short inlistments, and a mistaken dependance upon Militia, have been the Origin of all our misfortunes, and the great accumulation of our Debt.

   . . .

It may be thought, that, I am going a good deal out of the line of my duty, to adopt these measures, or to advise thus freely. A character to loose—an Estate to forfeit—the inestimable blessing of liberty at Stake, and a life devoted, must be my excuse. . . . I have the Honor to be with great respect Sir Your Most Obedt Servt

Go: Washington[38]

DECEMBER 23
TO COLONEL JOSEPH REED

*By December 20, a series of small reinforcements had brought Washington's army to
6,000 men, most of them due to leave as their enlistments expired at the end of the
month. That gave him eleven days to accomplish something. On the evening of the
twenty-second, Washington convened a secret council of war. Howe, he pointed out,
had established several winter cantonments in New Jersey, and evidently intended to
wait until the Delaware River froze before resuming his advance on Philadelphia.
These cantonments were isolated and vulnerable to attack, especially at Trenton,
where Colonel Johann Rall commanded approximately 1,500 Hessian troops. Washington proposed to lead what remained of his army across the Delaware at night,
surround and destroy Rall's post, and withdraw across the river before the British
could react. The American generals, perhaps sensing that they had nothing to lose,
agreed. Their troops would cross the Delaware on Christmas night.*

Camp above Trenton Falls 23d December 1776.
Dr Sir,
    The bearer is sent down to know whether your plan was attempted
last Night—and if not, to inform you that Christmas day at Night, one
hour before day is the time fixed upon for our Attempt on Trenton. For
heaven's sake keep this to yourself, as the discovery of it may prove fatal
to us, our numbers, sorry I am to say, being less than I had any conception of—but necessity, dire necessity will—nay must justify any Attempt.
Prepare, & in concert with Griffin attack as many of their Posts as you
possibly can with a prospect of success. the more we can attack, at the
same Instant, the more confusion we shall spread and greater good will
result from it.
    If I had not been fully convinced before of the Enemys designs I have
now ample testimony of their Intentions to attack Philadelphia so soon as
the Ice will afford the means of conveyance.
    . . .
    I shall not be particular—we could not ripen matters for our attack,
before the time mentioned in the first part of this Letter—so much out
of sorts, & so much in want of every thing, are the Troops under Sullivan
&ca—Let me know by a careful express the Plan you are to pursue. The
Letter herewith sent forward on to Philadelphia—I could wish it to be in,

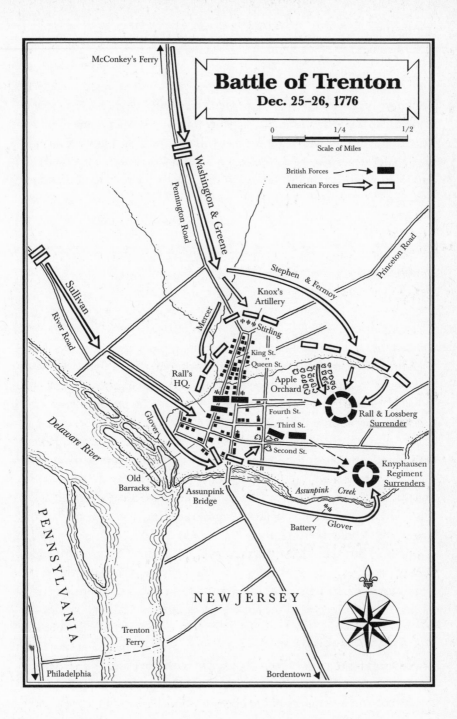

McConkey's Ferry

Battle of Trenton
Dec. 25–26, 1776

0   1/4   1/2
Scale of Miles

British Forces
American Forces

Washington & Greene

Pennington Road

Sullivan

River Road

Stephen & Fermoy

Princeton Road

Knox's Artillery

Mercer

Stirling

King St.
Queen St.

Rall's HQ.

Apple Orchard

Fourth St.

Third St.

Second St.

Rall & Lossberg
Surrender

Glover

Delaware River

Old Barracks

Assunpink Bridge

Assunpink Creek

Knyphausen Regiment Surrenders

Battery   Glover

PENNSYLVANIA

NEW JERSEY

Trenton Ferry

Philadelphia

Bordentown

in time for the Southern Post's departure which will be, I believe by 11 Oclock to morrow. I am Dr Sir Yr Most Obt St

Go: Washington

P.S. I have orderd our Men to be provided with three days Provisions ready Cook'd; with which, and their Blankets they are to March, for if we are successful which heaven grant & other Circumstances favour we may push on. I shall direct every Ferry & Ford to be well Guarded & not a Soul sufferd to pass without an officers going down with the permit. do the same with you.[39]

DECEMBER 25

GENERAL ORDERS

Each Brigade to be furnish'd with two good Guides.

General [Adam] Stevenss Brigade to form the advanced party & to have with them a detachment of the Artillery without Cannon provided with Spikes and Hamners to Spike up the enemies Cannon in case of necesity or to bring them off if it can be effected. the party to be provided with drag ropes for the purpose of dragging off the Cannon. General Stevens is to attack and force the enemies Guards and seize such posts as may prevent them from forming in the streets and in case they are annoy'd from the houses to set them on fire. The Brigades of [Hugh] Mercer & Lord Stirling under the Command of Major General Greene to support General Stevens, this is the second division or left wing of the Army and to march by the way of the Pennington Road.

[Arthur] St Clairs [John] Glovers & [Paul Dudley] Sargents Brigades under Major General [John] Sullivan to march by the river road, this is the first division of the Army and to form the right wing. Lord Stirlings Brigade to form the reserve of the left wing and General St Clairs Brigade the reserve of the right wing. These reserves to form a second line in Conjunction or a second Line to each division as circumstances may require—Each Brigadier to make the Colonels acquainted with the posts of their respective Regiments in the Brigade and the Major Generals will inform them of the posts of their Brigades in the Line.

Four peices of artillery to march at the head of each Column, three peices at the head of the second Brigade of each Division and two peices with each of the Reserves. The troops to be assembled one Miles back of McKonkeys ferry and as soon as it begins to grow dark the troops to be March'd to McKonkeys ferry and embark onboard the boats in following order under the direction of Colonel Knox.

General Stevens Brigade with the detachment of Artillery men to embark first General Mercers next; Lord Stirlings next, Genl Fermoys next who will march in the rear of the Second Division and file off from the Penington to the Princeton Road in such direction that he can with the greatest ease & safety secure the passes between Princeton & Trenton. the Guides will be the best judges of this. he is to take two peices of artillery with him.

St Clair Glover & Sargents Brigades to embark in order. Immediately upon their debarkation the whole to form & march in Subdivisions from the Right.

The Commanding Officers of Regiments to observe that the Divisions be equal & that proper officers be appointed to each—a profound silence to be enjoyn'd & no man to quit his Ranks on the pain of Death—each Brigadier to appoint flanking parties—the reserve Brigades to appoint the rear Guards of the Columns—The heads of the Columns to be appointed to arrive at Trenton at five oClock.

Capt. [William] Washington & Capt. Flahaven with a party of 40 men each to march before the Divisions & post themselves on the road about three miles from Trenton & make prisoners of all going in or coming out of Town.

General Stevens will appoint a Guard to form a chain of centries round the landing place at a sufficient distance from the river to permit the troops to form This Guard not to suffer any person to go in or come out—but to detain all persons who attempts either this Guard to join their Brigade when the troops are all over.[40]

———

DECEMBER 27

GENERAL ORDERS

The crossing of the Delaware at McConkey's Ferry on Christmas night and subse-
quent attack on Trenton on December 26 is the best-known military operation of the
Revolutionary War. Only one of the four columns that Washington dispatched—
the one he commanded, with 2,400 men—actually arrived in time to participate in
the attack, but no matter; Rall's Hessians were completely surprised, and surrendered
after a short fight. In military terms, Washington's victory was insignificant; but its
effect on American morale was profound.

Head Quarters: Newton [Pa.], Dec. 27, 1776.
The General, with the utmost sincerity and affection, thanks the Officers
and soldiers for their spirited and gallant behavior at Trenton yesterday.
It is with inexpressible pleasure that he can declare, that he did not see a
single instance of bad behavior in either officers or privates; and that if
any fault could be found, it proceeded from a too great eagerness to push
forward upon the Enemy. Much! very much, indeed, is it to be lamented
that when Men are brought to play the part of Soldiers thus well, that any
of them, for the sake of a little temporary ease, should think of abandoning the cause of Liberty and their Country at so important a crisis.—As
a reward to the officers and soldiers for their spirited behavior in such
inclement weather, the General will (in behalf of the Continent) have all
the Field pieces, the Arms, Accoutrements, Horses and everything else
which was taken yesterday, valued and a proportionate distribution of the
Amount made among the Officers (if they choose to partake) and the Men
who crossed the River.

The Commissary is strictly ordered to provide Rum for the Troops that
it may be served out as Occasion shall require.

Col. Bradley's Regiment or such part of them as have overstayed the
time for which they were engaged, and are still in Camp, have the General's thanks for so doing, and may be dismissed if they choose it; But
as we have begun the glorious work of driving the Enemy, he hopes
they will not now turn their backs upon them, and leave the business
half finished at this important Crisis, a Crisis, which may, more than
probably determine the fate of America. The General therefore not only
invites them to a longer continuance, but earnestly exhorts the Officers

86

and Soldiers of all those Regiments whose term of service expires in a few days, to remain.

The Colonels and Commanding Officers of each Regiment are, without delay, to have the Plunder of every kind (taken by his Regiment) collected and given in to the Quarter Master Gen'l that the men may receive the value of it.[41]

———

DECEMBER 27
TO JOHN HANCOCK

Head Quarters Newtown 27th Decemr 1776.
Sir

I have the pleasure of congratulating you upon the Success of an Enterprize, which I had formed against a Detatchment of the Enemy lying in Trenton, and which was executed yesterday Morning.

The Evening of the 25th I ordered the Troops intended for this Service to parade back of McKonkey's Ferry, that they might begin to pass as soon as it grew dark, imagining we should be able to throw them all over, with the necessary Artillery, by 12 OClock, and that we might easily arrive at Trenton by five in the Morning, the distance being about nine Miles. But the quantity of Ice, made that Night, impeded the passage of Boats so much, that it was three OClock before the Artillery could all be got over, and near four, before the Troops took up their line of march.

This made me despair of surprizing the Town, as I well knew we could not reach it before the day was fairly broke, but as I was certain there was no making a Retreat without being discovered, and harassed on repassing the River, I determined to push on at all Events. I formed my Detatchment into two divisions one to march by the lower or River road, the other, by the upper or Pennington Road. As the Divisions had nearly the same distance to march, I ordered each of them, immediately upon forcing the out Guards, to push directly into the Town, that they might charge the Enemy before they had time to form. The upper division arrived at the Enemys advanced post, exactly at eight OClock, and in three Minutes after, I found from the fire on the lower Road that, that Division had also got up. The Out Guards made but small Opposition, tho', for their

Numbers, they behaved very well, keeping up a constant retreating fire from behind Houses.

We presently saw their main Body formed, but from their Motions, they seem'd undetermined how to act.

Being hard pressed by our Troops, who had already got possession of part of their Artillery, they attempted to file off by a road on their right leading to Princetown, but perceiving their Intention, I threw a Body of Troops in their Way which immediately checked them. Finding from our disposition, that they were surrounded, and that they must inevitably be cut to peices if they made any further Resistance, they agreed to lay down their Arms. The Number, that submitted in this manner, was 23 Officers and 886 Men. Colo. Rall the commanding Officer and seven others were found wounded in the Town. I dont exactly know how many they had killed, but I fancy not above twenty or thirty, as they never made any regular Stand. Our Loss is very trifling indeed, only two Officers and one or two privates wounded.

I find, that the Detatchment of the Enemy consisted of the three Hessian Regiments of Lanspatch, Kniphausen and Rohl amounting to about 1500 Men, and a Troop of British Light Horse; but immediately, upon the beginning of the Attack, all those, who were not killed or taken, pushed directly down the Road towards Bordentown. These would likewise have fallen into our hands, could my plan have been compleatly carried into Execution. Genl [James] Ewing was to have crossed before day at Trenton Ferry, and taken possession of the Bridge leading out of Town, but the Quantity of Ice was so great, that tho' he did every thing in his power to effect it, he could not get over. This difficulty also hindered Genl Cadwallader from crossing, with the Pennsylvania Militia, from Bristol, he got part of his Foot over, but finding it impossible to embark his Artillery, he was obliged to desist. I am fully confident, that could the Troops, under Generals Ewing and Cadwallader, have passed the River, I should have been able, with their Assistance, to have driven the Enemy from all their posts below Trenton. But the Numbers I had with me, being inferior to theirs below me, and a strong Battalion of Light Infantry being at Princetown above me, I thought it most prudent to return the same Evening, with the prisoners and the Artillery we had taken. We found no Stores of any Consequence in the Town.

In justice to the Officers and Men, I must add, that their Behaviour upon this Occasion, reflects the highest honor upon them. The difficulty of passing the River in a very severe Night, and their March thro' a violent Storm of Snow and Hail, did not in the least abate their Ardour. But when they came to the Charge, each seemed to vie with the other in pressing forward, and were I to give a preferance to any particular Corps, I should do great injustice to the others. . . .

Go: Washington[42]

DECEMBER 31
TO ROBERT MORRIS

The enemy seemed vulnerable, and Washington was in position to take advantage of it—if only he could convince his soldiers to stay in service a little longer. Exhortations to patriotism and duty, Washington knew, would accomplish little without additional material incentives to back them up. Assembling his troops on New Year's Eve, with the help of Robert Morris and Colonel Henry Knox, the commander in chief asked his troops to stay in service for another month in return for $10 bounty money per man. Hundreds of soldiers ignored him and left, but 3,335 agreed to his terms and remained. Reinforced to 6,500 by militia and some newly raised Pennsylvania regiments, Washington would venture again into New Jersey.

Trenton Decem. 31. 1776

Sir

Our Affairs are at present in a most delicate—tho' I hope a fortunate Situation: But the great & radical Evil which pervades our whole System & like an Ax at the Tree of our Safety Interest & Liberty here again shews its baleful Influence—Tomorrow the Continental Troops are all at Liberty—I wish to push our Success to keep up the Pannick & in order to get their Assistance have promised them a Bounty of 10 Dollars if they will continue for one Month—But here again a new Difficulty presents itself we have not Money to pay the Bounty, & we have exhausted our Credit by such frequent Promises that it has not the Weight we could wish. If it be possible, Sir, to give us Assistance do it—borrow Money where it can be done we are doing it upon our private Credit—every Man of Interest & every Lover of his Country must strain his Credit upon such an Occasion.

No Time my dear Sir is to be lost. I am most Obedt & sincerely D. Sir Your very Hbble Servt

Go: Washington

The Bearer will escort the Money.[43]

———

1777

JANUARY 1
TO JOHN HANCOCK

Just as he resumed his advance into New Jersey, Washington received word that Congress had agreed to grant him the extraordinary civil and military powers that he had requested before the Battle of Trenton.

Trenton January the 1st 1777

Sir

    Your Resolves of the 27th Ulto were transmitted me last night by Messrs Clymer, Morris & Walton. The confidence which Congress have honoured me with by these proceedings, has a claim to my warmest acknowledgments. At the same time, I beg leave to assure them, that all my faculties shall be employed to direct properly the powers they have been pleased to vest me with, and to advance those Objects and only those, which gave rise to this honourable mark of distinction. If my exertions should not be attended with the desired success, I trust the failure will be imputed to the true cause, the peculiarly distressed situation of our Affairs, and the difficulties I have to combat, rather than to a want of zeal for my Country and the closest attention to her interests, to promote which has ever been my study.

    On Monday morning I passed the Delaware myself; the whole of our Troops & Artillery not till yesterday owing to the ice which rendered their passage extremely difficult and fatiguing. Since their arrival we have been parading the Regiments whose time of service is now expired, in order to know what force we should have to depend on, & how to regulate our views accordingly. After much persuasion and the exertions of their Officers, half or a greater proportion of those from the Eastward, have consented to stay Six Weeks, on a bounty of Ten Dollars. I feel the inconvenience of this advance, and I know the consequences which will result from it; But what could be done? Pensylvania had allowed the same to her Militia, The Troops felt their importance, and would have their price. Indeed as their aid is so essential and not to be dispensed with, it is to be wondered, they had not estimated it at a higher rate. I perceive that Congress, apprehensive of this event, had made unlimited provision for it. Genl Mifflin is at Borden Town with about Eighteen hundred Men & Genl Cadwalader at Croswix with about the same number. We are now making our Arrangements and concerting a Plan of Operations, which I shall attempt to execute as soon as possible & which I hope will be attended with some success. As to the number and situation of the Enemy, I cannot obtain certain intelligence, but from the accounts most to be relied on, they have collected the Principal part of their force from Brunswic & the neighbouring Posts at Princeton, where they are throwing up some Works. The number there, is reported to be from Five to Six Thousand, and it is confidently said they have sent the cheif part of their Baggage to Brunswick. It is added, that Genl Howe landed at Amboy a day or two ago with a thousand light Troops, and is on his march from thence.

I have sent into different parts of Jersey, men of influence, to spirit up the Militia, and flatter myself that the many injuries they have received will induce some to give their aid. If what they have suffered does not rouse their resentment, they must not possess the common feelings of humanity. to oppression, ravage and a deprivation of property, they have had the more mortifying circumstance of insult added. After being stripped of All they had, without the least compensation, protections have been granted them for the free enjoyment of their effects. I have the Honor to be with sentiments of great esteem & regard Sir yr Most Obedt Servt

Go: Washington

P.S: I have not been able to procure returns of our force owing to our situation; I suppose that about Two or three and Twenty hundred passed with me, which number is now reduced to Fifteen or Sixteen hundred. No

Estimate of our force can be formed from the number of Regiments; many of 'em by reason of Sickness cannot turn out more than a hundred men.[1]

———

JANUARY 5

TO JOHN HANCOCK

Washington won another victory at Princeton on January 3, but it was a close-run affair.

Pluckamin [N.J.] January 5th 1777

Sir

I have the honor to inform you, that since the date of my last from Trenton, I have removed with the Army under my command to this place. The difficulty of crossing the Delaware on account of the ice made our passage over it tedious, and gave the Enemy an opportunity of drawing in their several cantonments and assembling their whole Force at Princeton. Their large Picquets advanced towards Trenton, their great preparations & some intelligence I had received, added to their knowledge, that the first of January brought on a dissolution of the best part of our Army, gave me the strongest reasons to conclude, that an attack upon us was meditating.

Our situation was most critical and our force small. to remove immediately was again destroying every dawn of hope which had begun to revive in the breasts of the Jersey Militia, and to bring those Troops which had first crossed the Delaware, and were laying at Croswix's under Genl Cadwalader & those under Genl Mifflin at Bordenton (amounting in the whole to about 3600) to Trenton, was to bring them to an exposed place; One or the other however was unavoidable, the latter was preferred & they were ordered to join us at Trenton, which they did by a Night march on the 1st Instant.

On the 2d according to my expectation the Enemy began to advance upon us, and after some skirmishing the Head of their Column reached Trenton about 4 OClock, whilst their rear was as far back as Maidenhead. They attempted to pass Sanpink Creek, which runs through Trenton at different places, but finding the Fords guarded, halted & kindled their Fires—We were drawn up on the other side of the Creek. In this situation we remained till dark, cannonading the Enemy & receiving the fire of their Field peices which did us but little damage.

Having by this time discovered that the Enemy were greatly superior in number and that their design was to surround us, I ordered all our Baggage to be removed silently to Burlington soon after dark, and at twelve OClock after renewing our fires & leaving Guards at the Bridge in Trenton and other passes on the same stream above, marched by a roundabout Road to Princeton, where I knew they could not have much force left and might have Stores. One thing I was certain of, that it would avoid the appearance of a retreat, (which was of course or to run the hazard of the whole Army being cut off) whilst we might by a fortunate stroke withdraw Genl Howe from Trenton and give some reputation to our Arms. happily we succeeded. We found Princeton about Sunrise with only three Regiments and three Troops of light Horse in it, two of which were on their march to Trenton— These three Regiments, especially the Two first, made a gallant resistance and in killed wounded and Prisoners must have lost 500 Men, upwards of One hundred of them were left dead in the Feild, and with what I have with me & what were taken in the pursuit & carried across the Delaware, there are near 300 prisoners 14 of which are Officers—all British.

This peice of good fortune is counterballanced by the loss of the brave and worthy Genl Mercer, Cols. Hazlet and Potter, Captn Neal of the Artillery, Captn Fleming who commanded the first Virginia Regiment and four or five other valuable Officers who with about twenty five or thirty privates were slain in the feild—Our whole loss cannot be ascertained, as many who were in pursuit of the Enemy, who were chaced three or four Miles, are not yet come in.

The rear of the Enemy's Army laying at Maidenhead (not more than five or Six miles from Princeton) was up with us before our pursuit was over, but as I had the precaution to destroy the Bridge over Stoney Brooke (about half a mile from the Feild of action) they were so long retarded there as to give us time to move off in good order for this place. We took Two Brass Feild peices but for want of Horses could not bring them away. We also took some Blankets—Shoes—and a few other trifling Articles— burnt the Hay & destroyed such other things as the shortness of the time would admit of.

My Original plan when I set out from Trenton was to have pushed on to Brunswic, but the harrassed State of our own Troops (many of them having had no rest for two nights & a day) and the danger of loosing the advantage we had gained by aiming at too much induced me by the advice of my Officers to relinquish the attempt, but in my Judgement Six or Eight hundred fresh Troops upon a forced march would have destroyed all their Stores and Magazines—taken as we have since learnt their Military Chest containing 70,000£ and put an end to the War. The Enemy from the best intelligence I have been able to get were so much alarmed at the apprehension of this, that they marched immediately to Brunswick without halting except at the Bridges, (for I also took up those on Millstone on the different routs to Brunswick) and got there before day.

From the best information I have received, Genl Howe has left no men either at Trenton or Princeton. The truth of this I am endeavouring to ascertain that I may regulate my movements accordingly—The Militia are taking spirit and I am told, are coming in fast from this State, but I fear those from Philadelphia will scarcely submit to the hardships of a winter Campaign much longer, especially as they very unluckily sent their Blankets with their Baggage to Burlington—I must do them justice however to add, that they have undergone more fatigue and hardship than I expected Militia (especially Citizens) would have done at this inclement Season. I am just moving to Morris town where I shall endeavour to put them under the best cover I can. hitherto we have been without any and many of our poor Soldiers quite bear foot & ill clad in other respects. I have the Honor to be with great respect Sir Yr Most Obedt

Go: Washington[2]

FEBRUARY 10
TO THE NEW YORK CONVENTION

Washington's victory at Princeton and subsequent narrow escape from British pursuit to the security of Morristown did not put an end to his worries. Smallpox—the plague of armies, especially in winter encampments, from time immemorial—threatened to wreck the Continental Army without prompt countermeasures. Fortunately Washington was alert to the potential crisis.

Head Quarters Morris Town 10th Feby 1777.

Gentlemen,

After every attempt to stop the progress of the small Pox, I found, that it gained such head among the Southern Troops, that there was no possible way of saving the lives of most of those who had not had it, but by introducing innoculation generally. The physicians are now making the proper preparations to innoculate all at the several posts in this quarter and Doctor Shippen will innoculate all the Recruits that have not had the disorder, as fast as they come into Philada. They will lose no time by this operation, as they will go thro', while their Cloathing Arms and Accoutrements are preparing.

That the Army may be kept as clean as possible of this terrible disorder, I have recommended it to every State, which is to send Troops to the Army in this department, immediately to begin upon the innoculation of their Recruits, and to continue till they have gone thro' the whole. By these Means, very few will be down at a Time, & of those many will be fit for duty (should the occasion be pressing) the whole time.

I think your Hospital, for this purpose, should be at or in the Neighbourhood of Peeks Kill, because if the Enemy should hear that many of our men were down, and should make an Attempt to fall upon us at that Time, many of the patients would, as I said Before, be as able to give opposition, as if they were intirely well.

We intend for the present to keep the Matter as much a Secret as possible, and I would Advise you to do the same. After the first and Second division of Patients, (who should be innoculated at an interval of five or six days) have gone thro' the thing will become extremely light, and of little Consequence, whether it is known or not. . . .

Go: Washington[3]

APRIL 27

TO ELIZABETH MALLAM NEIL

At this point in the war, Congress had made no provision to support widows or orphans of soldiers killed in the line of duty, leaving Washington to do what he could in a private capacity, as in the case of this widow of a captain killed at the Battle of Princeton.

Morris Town April 27th 1777.

Madam,

    I hoped to have given you a more favourable Account of my application to Congress, in your behalf, than the Inclosed resolution will convey. but that Honorable body have, I presume, thought it rather too early to adopt a measure of this kind yet—what they may do hereafter, I cannot undertake to say. In the meantime, as I sincerely feel for your distress, I beg your acceptance of the Inclosd as a small testimony of my Inclination to serve you upon any future occasion. I am Madam, Yr Most Obedt Servt

Go: Washington

P.S. I have receivd, & am much obliged to you for the Piece of Buff Cloth.

G: W——n

Fifty Dollars sent.[4]

MAY 1

TO CAPTAIN CALEB GIBBS

This letter to one of Washington's aides provides a rare glimpse into daily life at the commander in chief's headquarters, which Martha was visiting at this time.

Morris Town May 1 1777.

Dear Gibbs,

    A Letter from Mr Fitzgerald, written to you a few days ago, would inform you that we have no longer any expectation of the Person recommended by Doctor [John] Cochran as a Steward; and, that it was necessary for you to exert yourself in obtaining one. If you could get a Man who had been employed in that capacity, or as a Butler in a Gentlemans Family & who could be well recommended & by such as may be depended upon for his honesty—Sobriety—& care, he would answer the purpose much better than a mere greenhorn; who in the first place would be ignorant of his duty, & in the next (which would be a consequence of the other) be diffident, & suffer himself to be imposed upon by our Servents; who stand so much in need of being checked for their extravagance, and roguery, in making away with Liquors, & other Articles laid in for the use of the Family.

I dare say you are better acquainted with our Wants than I am, but I shall mention two, which seem to be pretty severely felt at present—namely, Loaf Sugar and Tea. If I was to add Wine, I believe I should not much err, and whilst you are in the humour of getting, I wish you would procure for me two pair of Brown thread Stockings for Boots.

What did you pay Mrs Thompson a Month, and where is she? Mrs Washington wishes I had mention'd my Intentions of parting with the old Woman, before her, as she is much in want of a Housekeeper— How do you think she would suit? as her conduct from the beginning has been more under your immediate Inspection, & notice, than any [*mutilated text*] of the Family, you can answer [*mutilated text*] question with more precission and certainty than any of them & Mrs Washington would be glad of your opinion of the matter.

I had like to have forgot one thing wanted, and that is, cloth to make my Servant Will, as also the Hostler, Cloaths—get Russia Drill enough, if you can, to make each of them two Waistcoats, and two pair of Breeches—the Coats may be made of a light coloured cloth of any kind, lined with red Shalloon—a bit of red Cloth for capes, or Collars to them. Buttons & every kind of trimming must be sent, as nothing of the kind is to be had here. . . .

If your health admits of it, I could wish you to return as soon as you can execute the several matters and things required of you, as I am now calling in Men to form a Guard of, and your presence I believe pretty much wanted in other respects. . . .

Go: Washington[5]

MAY 8

GENERAL ORDERS

With a new army recruited, this time on three-year enlistments, Washington turned his attention to preparing it for the summer campaign. As always, Washington laid special emphasis on enforcing morality among his soldiers.

Head-Quarters, Morristown May 8th 1777. As few vices are attended with more pernicious consequences, in civil life; so there are none more fatal in a military one, than that of GAMING; which often brings disgrace and ruin upon officers, and injury and punishment upon the Soldiery: And reports prevailing, which, it is to be feared are too well founded, that this destructive vice has spread its baneful influence in the army, and, in a peculiar manner, to the prejudice of the recruiting Service, The Commander in chief, in the most pointed and explicit terms, forbids ALL officers and soldiers, playing at cards, dice—or at any games, except those of EXERCISE, for diversion; it being impossible, if the practice be allowed, at all, to discriminate between innocent play, for amusement, and criminal gaming, for pecuniary and sordid purposes.

Officers, attentive to their duty, will find abundant employment, in training and disciplining their men—providing for them—and seeing that they appear neat, clean and soldierlike—Nor will any thing redound more to their honor—afford them more solid amusement—or better answer the end of their appointment, than to devote the vacant moments, they may have, to the study of Military authors.

The Commanding Officer of every corps is strictly enjoined to have this order frequently read, and strongly impressed upon the minds of those under his command. Any officer, or soldier, or other person belonging to, or following, the army, either in camp, in quarters, on the recruiting service, or elsewhere, presuming, under any pretence, to disobey this order, shall be tried by a General Court Martial. . . .[6]

JULY 9

TO THE PENNSYLVANIA SUPREME EXECUTIVE COUNCIL

In June 1777, General Howe's army emerged from winter quarters and attempted to draw Washington away from Morristown and into open country. When Washington declined to offer battle, the British turned and marched toward the coast at Sandy Hook, New Jersey, where they began boarding transports in early July. What they intended to do next was unclear, but Washington, suspecting they would attack Philadelphia via the Delaware River, prepared for a summer campaign in the surrounding region. Procuring maps was a priority.

Head Quarters Morris Town July 9th 1777

Gentlemen

I find accurate Draughts or Maps of the Country which is or may be the Seat of War so essentially necessary, that I must beg Leave to recommend such a Measure with all possible Expedition, so far as regards the Shores of the Delaware where the Enemy may probably land & march. When the Enemy have once possessed themselves of any Part of the Country every Attempt to delineate it becomes difficult if not wholly impracticable; the Propriety therefore of doing it with all possible Advantage, I trust will be too obvious to your Honourable Board to make it necessary to press it farther.

In the Execution of this Work I would wish the Eminences, Distances of Places Woods, Streams of Water, Marshy Places & Passes may be particularly noted. And that it be done on as large a Scale as is tolerably convenient. I am Gentlemen with due Respect & Regard Your most Obedt & very Hbble Servt

Go: Washington

P.S. I scarcely think it necessary to suggest Secrecy & Caution in the Execution of this Work, as its Value & Importance must very much depend not only on the Ability but Fidelity of those to whom it is intrusted.[7]

AUGUST 5–9

TO JOHN AUGUSTINE WASHINGTON

The departure of the British fleet off Sandy Hook left Washington almost paralyzed
with indecision—would they sail south to Philadelphia, as he originally believed,
attempt to link up with General John Burgoyne's army advancing from Canada
toward Albany, New York, or head for Charleston, South Carolina?

German Town near Philada, Augt 5[–9]th 1777.

Dear Brother

. . . Since Genl Howes remove from the Jerseys, the Troops under my
Command have been More harrassed by Marching, & Counter Marching,
than by any thing that has happen'd to them in the course of the Campaign.

After Genl Howe had Imbarked his Troops, the presumption that he
would operate upon the North River, to form a junction with General Burgoyne, was so strong, that I removed from Middle Brook to Morristown,
& from Morristown to the Clove (a narrow pass leading through the Highlands) about 18 Miles from the River—Indeed, upon some pretty strong
presumptive evidence, I threw two divisions over the North River. In this
Situation we lay till about the 24th Ulto; when Receiving certain Information that the Fleet had actually Sailed from Sandy hook (the outer point
of New York harbour) and the concurring Sentiment of every one, (tho I
acknowledge my doubts of it were strong) that Philadelphia was the object
we counter Marched—and got to Coryells Ferry on the Delaware (about
33 Miles above the City) on the 27th where I lay till I receiv'd Information
from Congress that the Enemy were actually at the Capes of Delaware—
This brought us in great haste to this place for defence of the City, but in
less than 24 hours after our arrival we got Accounts of the disappearance
of the Fleet on the 31st; since which nothing having been heard of them,
we remain here in a very irksome state of Suspence. Some imagining that
they are gone to the Southward, whilst a Majority (in whose opinion upon
this occasion I concur) are satisfied they are gone to the Eastward [to New
England]. The fatigue however, & Injury, which Men must Sustain by long
Marches in such extreme heat as we have felt for the last five days, must
keep us quiet till we hear something of the destination of the Enemy.

I congratulate you very sincerely on the happy passage of my Sister and the rest of your Family, through the Small pox—Surely the daily Instances which present themselves, of the amazeing benefits of Inoculation must make converts of the most rigid opposers, and bring on a repeal of that most impolitic Law which restrains it.

. . .

I have from the first, been among those few who never built much upon a French War—I ever did, and still do think they never meant more than to give us a kind of underhand assistance, that is, to supply us with Arms &ca for our Money, & Trade—this may indeed, if G.B. has spirit & strength to resent it, bring on a War; but the declaration, if on either side, must, I am convinced, come from the last mentioned power. . . . My love and best Wishes are presented to my Sister, & the rest of your Family, & with sincerest Affection believe & be assured, I am Dr Sir Yr

Go: Washington

P.S. Augt 9th being disappointed in sending of this Letter, I have to add that we have no further Acct of the Enemys Fleet, & therefore concluding that they are gone to the Eastward we have again turned our Faces that way & shall move slow till we get some acct of it.[8]

AUGUST 19
TO BENJAMIN HARRISON

When a young officer named the Marquis de Lafayette appeared in camp on July 31, he was just one of many French volunteers seeking a commission. Washington had little use for such officers unless they demonstrated substantial technical expertise in areas such as artillery and engineering. Most of them knew little more about war than the Americans did, being just naive young aristocrats eager for glory and adventure.

Neshamony Bridge [Pa.] August 19. 1777

Dear sir

If I did not misunderstand what you, or some other Member of Congress said to me respecting the appointment of the Marquis de le Fiatte, he has misceived the design of his appointment, or Congress did not understand the extent of his views, for certain it is, If I understand him, that he does not conceive his Commission is merely honorary; but given with a view to command a division of this Army. True, he has said that he is young, & inexperienced, but at the same time has always accompanied it with a hint, that so soon as I shall think him fit for the Command of a division, he shall be ready to enter upon the duties of it; & in the meantime, has offer'd his service for a smaller Command; to which I may add, that he has actually applied to me (by direction he says from Mr Hancock) for Commissions for his Two Aid de Camps.

What the designs of Congress respecting this Gentleman were—& what line of Conduct I am to pursue, to comply with their design, & his expectations, I know no more than the Child unborn, & beg to be instructed. If Congress meant that this rank should be unaccompanied by Command I wish it had been sufficiently explain'd to him—If on the other hand it was intended to vest him with all the powers of a Major Genl why have I been led into a contrary belief, & left in the dark with respect to my own conduct towards him?—this difficulty with the numberless applications for Imployment by Foreigners, under their respective appointments, adds no small embarrassment to a command which, without it, is abundantly perplexed by the different tempers I have to do with, & different modes which the respective States have pursued to nominate & arrange their officers; the combination of all which, is but a too just representation of a great Chaos from whence we are endeavouring (how successfully time can only tell) to draw some regularity & order.

I was going to address Congress for Instructions in the case of the Marquis de Le Fyatte, but upon second thought concluded to ask some direction of My conduct in this matter through a Member, and therefore have imposed this task upon you. Let me beseech you then my good Sir to give me the sentiments of Congress on this matter, that I may endeavour, as far as it is in my power, to comply with them, with respect to Commissions for his Aid de Camps, I told him that I should write to Mr Hancock about them and wish to be instructed. The Marquis is now in Philadelphia but expected up this day or to morrow. With sincere regard I am Dr Sir Your most Affecte

G. Washington[9]

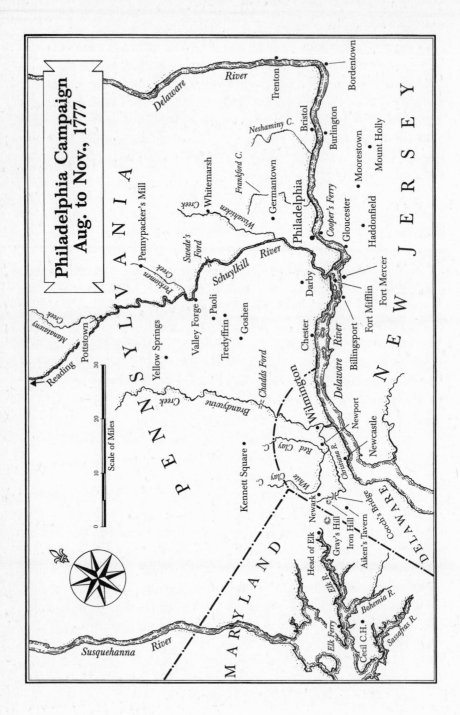

Philadelphia Campaign
Aug. to Nov., 1777

AUGUST 22
TO ISRAEL PUTNAM

The appearance of the British fleet in the Chesapeake Bay ended Washington's uncertainty; they obviously intended to come ashore at the north end of the bay and march on Philadelphia. That left the New Englanders to deal with Burgoyne on their own.

Head Quarters Bucks County [Pa.] 22d Augt 1777
Dear Sir

By the inclosed which is this Moment come to hand you will perceive that the Enemy's Fleet have at length fairly entered Chesapeak Bay, Swan point being at least 200 Miles up. I desire you will immediately forward this account to Govr [Jonathan] Trumbull, to be by him sent on the Eastward. As there is not now the least danger of General Howes going to New England, I hope the whole Force of that Country will turn out, and by following the great stroke struck by Genl [John] Stark near Bennington intirely crush Genl Burgoine, who by his letter to Colo. Bern seems to be in want of almost every thing. I hope you will draw in such a Force of Militia as will effectually secure your post against any attempt from New York. I shall be obliged to draw Genl Sullivan with his division down to me, for by Genl Howe's coming so far up Chesapeak he must mean to reach Philadelphia by that Rout, tho' to be sure it is a very strange one. I am &ca.[10]

SEPTEMBER 5
GENERAL ORDERS

Howe's army came ashore at Head of Elk, Maryland, on August 22 and spent several days recuperating from a difficult voyage before beginning its advance on Philadelphia. Washington, who had turned south and marched his army through Philadelphia to Wilmington, Delaware, made preparations to oppose the British, and to ready his soldiers—mentally and materially—for combat.

Head Quarters, Wilmington Septemr 5th 1777.

. . .

From every information of the enemy's designs, and from their movements, it is manifest their aim is, if possible, to possess themselves of Philadelphia. This is their capital object—'Tis what they last year strove to effect;
but were happily disappointed: They made a second attempt at the opening
of this campaign; but after vast preparations, and expence for the purpose,
they abandoned their design, and totally evacuated the Jersies—They are
now making their last effort; To come up the Delaware it seems, was their
first intention; but, from the measures taken to annoy them in the river,
they judged the enterprise, that way, too hazardous. At length they have
landed on the eastern shore of Maryland, and advanced some little way
into the country: But the General trusts, they will be again disappointed
in their views—Should they push their design against Philadelphia, on
this route, their all is at stake—they will put the contest on the event of a
single battle: If they are overthrown, they are utterly undone—the war is
at an end—Now then is the time for our most strenuous exertions—One
bold stroke will free the land from rapine, devastations & burnings, and
female innocence from brutal lust and violence—In every other quarter the
American Arms have, of late, been rapidly successful & still greater numbers have been made prisoners—The militia at the northward, have fought
with a resolution, that would have done honor to old soldiers; they bravely
fought and conquered, and glory attends them. Who can forbear to emulate their noble spirit? Who is there without ambition, to share with them,
the applauses of their countrymen, and of all posterity, as the defenders of
Liberty, and the procurers of peace and happiness to millions in the present
and future generations? Two years we have maintained the war and struggled with difficulties innumerable. But the prospect has since brightened,
and our affairs put on a better face—Now is the time to reap the fruits of
all our toils and dangers! If we behave like men, this third Campaign will
be our last—Ours is the main army; to us our Country looks for protection—The eyes of all America, and of Europe are turned upon us, as on
those by whom the event of the war is to be determined. And the General
assures his countrymen and fellow soldiers, that he believes the critical, the
important moment is at hand, which demands their most spirited exertions
in the field. There glory waits to crown the brave—and peace—freedom
and happiness will be the rewards of victory. Animated by motives like

these, soldiers fighting in the cause of innocence, humanity and justice, will never give way, but, with undaunted resolution, press on to conquest. And this, the General assures himself, is the part the American Forces now in arms will act; and thus acting, he will insure them success.[11]

SEPTEMBER 11
TO JOHN HANCOCK

On September 10, Washington's army took post at Chadds Ford, Pennsylvania, along the Brandywine Creek, blocking the enemy's road to Philadelphia. Believing that his flanks were secure—scouts had told him that the British could not cross the creek anywhere without taking a long detour, except in front of the American guns— Washington awaited the British attack with confidence. But the scouts were wrong. Upstream, just beyond the American right flank, the British crossed Brandywine Creek over a ford about which the Americans knew nothing. The consequences were nearly disastrous.

Chester [Pa.] Septr 11. 1777. 12 o'Clock at Night.
Sir,

I am sorry to inform you that in this days engagement we have been obliged to leave the enemy masters of the field. Unfortunately the intelligence received of the enemy's advancing up the Brandywine, & crossing at a ford about six miles above us, was uncertain & contradictory, notwithstanding all my pains to get the best. This prevented my making a disposition adequate to the force with which the enemy attacked us on our right; in consequence of which the troops first engaged were obliged to retire before they could be reinforced. In the midst of the attack on the right, that body of the enemy which remained on the other side of Chad's ford, crossed it, & attacked the division there under the command of General [Anthony] Wayne & the light troops under General [William] Maxwell; who after a severe conflict also retired. The militia under the command of General [John] Armstrong, being posted at a ford about two miles below Chad's, had no opportunity of engaging. But though we fought under many disadvantages, and were from the causes above mentioned, obliged to retire; yet our loss of men is not, I am persuaded, very considerable; I believe much less than the enemys. We have also lost seven or eight pieces of cannon, according to the best information I can at present obtain. The baggage having been previously moved off is all secure; saving the mens' blankets, which being at their backs, many of them doubtless are lost.

I have directed all the troops to assemble behind Chester, where they are now arranging for this night. Notwithstanding the misfortune of the day, I am happy to find the troops in good spirits; and I hope another time we shall compensate for the losses now sustained.

The Marquis La Fayette was wounded in the leg, & General Woodford in the hand. Divers other officers were wounded, & some slain; but the numbers of either cannot now be ascertained. I have the honor to be, Sir, your obedient h'ble servant

Go: Washington

P.S. It has not been in my power to send you earlier intelligence; the present being the first leisure moment I have had since the action.[12]

SEPTEMBER 23
TO JOHN HANCOCK

The defeat at Brandywine did not inevitably lead to the fall of Philadelphia. Instead, Howe outmaneuvered Washington, as the commander in chief explained in this letter. Caught on the wrong side of the Schuylkill River, Washington could only watch as the British and their German allies victoriously entered the city on September 26. But he was not ready to give up yet.

Camp near Potts Grove [Pa.] 23d Sept. 1777

Sir

I have not had the honor of addressing you since your adjournment to Lancaster, and I sincerely wish that my first letter was upon a more agreeable subject. The Enemy, by a variety of perplexing Maneuvres thro' a Country from which I could not derive the least intelligence being to a man disaffected, contrived to pass the Schuylkill last Night at the Flat land and other Fords in the Neighbourhood of it. They marched immediately towards Philada and I imagine their advanced parties will be near

110

that City to Night. They had so far got the Start before I received certain intelligence that any considerable Number had crossed, that I found it in vain to think of overtaking their Rear with Troops harrassed as ours had been with constant marching since the Battle of Brandywine and therefore concluded by the advice of all the General Officers to march from this place tomorrow Morning towards Philadelphia, and on the way endeavour to form a junction with the Continental Troops under Genl [Alexander] Mcdougal from Peekskill and the Jersey Militia under General [Philemon] Dickenson, both of whom are I hope on this Side the Delaware. I am also obliged to wait for Genl Wayne and Genl Smallwood who were left upon the other Side of Schuylkill in hopes of falling upon the Enemy's Rear, but they have eluded them as well as us.

When I last recrossed the Schuylkill it was with a firm intent of giving the Enemy Battle wherever I should meet them, and accordingly advanced as far as the Warren Tavern upon the Lancaster Road near which place the two Armies were upon the point of coming to a general Engagement but were prevented by a most violent Flood of Rain which continued all the day and following Night. When it held up, we had the mortification to find that our Ammunition which had been compleated to Forty Rounds a Man was intirely ruined, and in that Situation we had nothing left for it but to find out a strong piece of Ground which we could easily maintain till we could get the Arms put into order and a Recruit of Ammunition. Before this could be fully effected, the Enemy marched from their position near the White Horse Tavern down the Road leading to the Swedes Ford, I immediately crossed the Schuylkill above them and threw myself full in their front hoping to meet them in their passage or soon after they had passed the River. The day before yesterday they were again in motion and marched rapidly up the Road leading towards Reading. This induced me to beleive that they had two objects in view, one to get round the right of the Army, the other perhaps to detach parties to Reading where we had considerable quantities of military Stores. To frustrate those intentions I moved the Army up on this side the River to this place, determined to keep pace with them, but early this morning I received intelligence that they had crossed at the Fords below. Why I did not follow immediately, I have mentioned in the former part of my letter. But the strongest Reason against being able to make a forced march is the want of Shoes; Mess[r]s Carroll, Chase and Penn who were some days with the Army can inform

Congress in how deplorable a Situation the Troops are for want of that necessary Article, at least one thousand Men are bare footed and have performed the marches in that condition. . . . I have planned a method of throwing a Garrison into Fort Mifflin, if it succeeds and they with the Assistance of the Ships and Gallies should keep the obstructions in the River, General Howe's Situation in Philada will not be the most agreeable, for if his supplies can be stopped by Water it may be easily done by land. To do both shall be my utmost endeavour, and I am not yet without hope that the acquisition of Philada may, instead of his good fortune, prove his Ruin. . .

Go: Washington[13]

OCTOBER 5

TO JOHN HANCOCK

Washington refused to submit quietly to the British occupation of Philadelphia. But although his attack on the British positions at Germantown, Pennsylvania, on October 4 was conducted in the spirit of Trenton, it nevertheless ended in failure.

Camp near Pennibeckers Mill [Pa.] Octr 5: 1777.

Sir

Having received intelligence through Two intercepted Letters, that Genl Howe had detached a part of his force for the purpose of reducing Billingsport and the Forts on Delaware, I communicated the Accounts to my Genl Officers, who were unanimously of Opinion, that a favourable Opportunity offered to make an Attack upon the Troops, which were at & near German Town. It was accordingly agreed, that it should take place Yesterday morning and the following dispositions were made. The Divisions of Sullivan & Wayne, flanked by [Thomas] Conways Brigade were to enter the Town by the way of Chesnut Hill, while Genl Armstrong with the Pensylvania Militia should fall down the Manatawny Road by Vandeerings Mill and get upon the Enemy's left and Rear. The Divisions of Greene & Stephen flanked by McDougals Brigade were to enter by taking a circuit by way of the Lime Kiln Road at the Market House & to attack their Right wing, & the Militia of Maryland & Jersey under Genls Smalwood & Foreman were to march by the Old York road and fall upon the rear of their Right. Lord Stirling with Nash & Maxwell's Brigades was to form a Corps de Reserve. We marched about Seven OClock the preceding Evening, and Genl Sullivans advanced party drawn from Conways Brigade attacked their picket at Mount Airy or Mr Allens House about Sun rise the next Morning, which presently gave way, and his Main body, consisting of the right Wing, following soon engaged the Light Infantry and Other Troops encamped near the picket which they forced from their Ground, leaving their Baggage. They retreated a considerable distance, having previously thrown a party into Mr Chews House, who were in a situation not to be easily forced, and had it in their power from the Windows to give us no small annoyance, and in a great measure to obstruct our advance.

The Attack from our left Column under Genl Greene began about three Quarters of an Hour after that from the Right, and was for some time equally successfull. But I cannot enter upon the particulars of what happened in that Quarter, as I am not yet informed of them, with sufficient certainty and precision.

The Morning was extremely foggy, which prevented our improving the advantages we gained so well, as we should otherwise have done. This circumstance, by concealing from us the true situation of the Enemy, obliged us to act with more caution and less expedition than we could have wished, and gave the Enemy time to recover from the effects of our first impression; and what was still more unfortunate, it served to keep our different parties in ignorance of each Others movements, and hindered their acting in concert. It also occasioned them to mistake One another for the Enemy, which, I believe, more than any thing else contributed to the misfortune which ensued. In the midst of the most promising appearances—when every thing gave the most flattering hopes of victory, the Troops began suddenly to retreat; and intirely left the Feild in spite of every effort that could be made to rally them.

Upon the whole, it may be said the day was rather unfortunate, than injurious. We sustained no material loss of Men and brought off all our Artillery, except One peice which was dismounted; The Enemy are nothing the better by the event, and our Troops, who are not in the least dispirited by it, have gained what All young Troops gain by being in Actions. We have had however several valuable Officers killed and wounded—particularly the latter. Genl Nash is among the Wounded and his life is despaired of. As soon as it is possible to obtain a return of our loss, I will transmit it.

In justice to Genl Sullivan and the whole right wing of the Army, whose conduct I had an Opportunity of observing, as they acted immediately under my eye, I have the pleasure to inform you, that both Officers & Men behaved with a degree of Gallantry that did them the highest honor. I have the Honor to be with great respect Sir Your Most Obed. Servt

Go: Washington

P.S. As I have observed, I have not received a Return of our loss, but from what I have just now learnt from Genl Greene, I fear it is more considerable than I at first apprehended in Men. The Cannon mentioned above is said to have been brought off in a Waggon.[14]

OCTOBER 6
TO GENERAL WILLIAM HOWE

Whether Howe ever thanked Washington for the return of his stray dog is unknown.

[Perkiomen, Pa.] Octr 6. 1777

General Washington's compliments to General Howe. He does himself the pleasure to return him a dog, which accidentally fell into his hands, and by the inscription on the Collar appears to belong to General Howe.[15]

OCTOBER 15
GENERAL ORDERS

News of the victory at Saratoga, New York, in which an army under Major General Horatio Gates defeated and then captured General Burgoyne's Anglo-German army, brightened the outlook of America's otherwise bleak military prospects in the autumn of 1777. Washington hoped that it would create a spirit of emulation in his own army.

Head Quarters, Towamensing [Pa.] October 15th 1777. The General has the repeated pleasure of informing the army of the success of the troops under the command of General Gates, over General Burgoyne's army—On the 7th instant the action commenced, about 3 o'clock in the afternoon, between the picquets of the two armies, which were reinforced on both sides—The contest was warm, and continued with obstinacy 'till evening, when our troops gained the advanced line of the enemy, and encamped on that ground all night—The enemy fled, and left behind them 330 tents, with kettles boiling with corn, 8 Brass Cannon, two twelve and six six-pounders, upwards of two hundred of their dead, and the baggage of their flying camp—General Frazier is among their slain—Our troops took 550 non-commissioned officers and soldiers prisoners; besides Sir Francis Carr Clark, Aid-de-Camp to General Burgoyne—A Quarter Master General—the commanding officers of artillery, of a foreign brigade and of the British Grenadiers, and a number of inferior rank—Two of our Generals, [Benjamin] Lincoln and Arnold, were wounded in the leg: besides these, our troops suffered very little—They behaved with great bravery and intrepidity; and have thus a second time triumphed over the valor of veteran troops—When the last accounts came away, General Burgoyne's army was retreating, and ours pursuing.

The General congratulates the troops upon this signal victory, the third capital advantage, which under divine providence, we have gained in that quarter; and hopes it will prove a powerful stimulus to the army under his immediate command; at least to equal their northern brethren in brave and intrepid exertions when called thereto—The General wishes them to consider that this is the Grand American Army; and that of course great things are expected from it—'Tis the army of whose superior prowess some have boasted—What shame then and dishonour will attend us, if we suffer ourselves in every instance to be outdone? We have a force sufficient, by the favor of Heaven, to crush our foes; and nothing is wanting but a spirited, persevering exertion of it, to which, besides the motives before mentioned, duty and the love of our Country irresistably impel us. The effect of such powerful motives, no man, who possesses the spirit of a soldier can withstand, and spurred on by them, the General assures himself, that on the next occasion his troops will be completely successful.

In honor of the northern Army, and to celebrate their victory, Thirteen pieces of cannon are to be discharged, at the artillery park, at five o'clock this afternoon: previous to which, the brigades and corps are to be drawn out on their respective parades, and these orders distinctly read to them by their officers. . . .[16]

OCTOBER 18
GENERAL ORDERS

Head Quarters, at Wentz's, Worcester Township [Pa.]. October 18th 1777. The General has his happiness completed relative to the successes of our northern Army. On the 14th instant, General Burgoyne, and his whole Army, surrendered themselves prisoners of war—Let every face brighten, and every heart expand with grateful Joy and praise to the supreme disposer of all events, who has granted us this signal success—The Chaplains of the army are to prepare short discourses, suited to the joyful occasion to deliver to their several corps and brigades at 5 O'clock this afternoon—immediately after which, Thirteen pieces of cannon are to be discharged at the park of artillery, to be followed by a feu-de-joy with blank cartridges, or powder, by every brigade and corps of the army, beginning on the right of the front line, and running on to the left of it, and then instantly beginning on the left of the 2nd line, and running to the right of it where it is to end—The Major General of the day will superintend and regulate the feu-de-joy.[17]

––––––––––

OCTOBER 27
TO LANDON CARTER

In this letter to his friend Landon Carter, Washington brushes aside worries about his personal safety; summarizes the year's military events and the enemy's current attempts to reduce the American forts on the Delaware River; and—already sensitive of the contrast between General Gates's successes in the north and his own multiple defeats—attempts to explain why he could not do to Howe what the New Englanders had done to Burgoyne.

Philadelphia County [Pa.] Octr 27th 1777.

Dear Sir

Accept my sincere thanks for your sollicitude on my Acct—and for the good advice contained in your little paper of the 27th Ulto—at the sametime that I assure you, that It is not my wish to avoid any danger which duty requires me to encounter I can as confidently add, that it is not my intention to run unnecessary risques. In the Instance given by you, I was acting precisely in the line of my duty, but not in the dangerous situation you have been led to believe. I was reconnoitring, but I had a strong party of Horse with me. I was, as (I afterwards found) in a disaffected House at the head of Elk, but I was equally guarded agt friend and Foe. the information of danger then, came not from me.

So many accounts have been published of the battle of brandy wine that nothing more can be said of it—the subsequent Ingagement on the 4th Instant had every appearance (after a hot contest of two hours and forty minutes) of a glorious decission; but after driving the Enemy from their Incampment—possessing their ground—and being, as we thought, upon the point of grasping victory, it was snatched from us by means altogether unaccountable; excepting that a very heavy atmosphere, aided by the smoke of our Field pieces and Small arms, rendered impossible, at times, to distinguish friend from Foe at the distance of 30 yards which caused our Men I believe to take fright at each other; since that, the Enemy have retired to Philadelphia where they have been strengthening themselves as much as possible, whilst we hover round to cut off their Supplies.

The Enemy are exerting their utmost skill, to reduce the Forts constructed for the defence of the Chevaux de frieze in Delaware, and to drive off our little Fleet, employed in aid of them. On the 22d Instant Count Donop a Hessian Officer of Rank, & great Military Abilities, with 1200 of his Countrymen undertook to storm one of these Works (called Fort Mercer at Redbank on the Jersey shore) when himself and about 400 others were killed and wounded. between two and three hundred were left slain; and badly wounded, on the spot. the rest got off with their retreating brethren, who made the best of their way to Phila.—the Count is among the wounded—supposed Mortally.

The next day, several of the Enemys Ships, having passed the lower Chevaux de frieze, aided by their Land Batteries, began a most tremendous Canonade upon Fort Mifflin (on an Island near the Pensylvania Shore) and on our Armed vessels adjoining, which continued Six hours without Intermission; and ended in the destruction of two of the Enemys Ships of War—one, a Sixty four gun Ship, the other 18—Our damage on both these occasions was inconsiderable—in the Attack on Fort Mercer we had about 30 Men killed and wounded, at Fort Mifflin, and the Ships, less. The possession of these defenses is of such essential Importance to the Enemy that they are leaving no stone unturnd to succeed—we are doing what we can (under many disadvantages) to disappoint them.

The great and important event to the Northward—of which no doubt you have heard—must be attended with the most fortunate consequences. It has caused Sir Henry Clintons expedition from New York in aid of Burgoyne to end in (something more than Smoke indeed) burning of Mills, Gentlemens Seats, and the Villages near the Water! an evident proof of their despair of carrying their diabolical designs in to execution. My Inclination leads me to give you a more minute detail of the Situation of our Army, but prudence forbids, as Letters are Subject to too many miscarriages. My best respects attends the good family at Sabine Hall—Neighbours at Mount Airy—&ca & with Affecte regard I remain Dr Sir Yr Most Obt Servt

Go: Washington

P.S. I am perswaded you will excuse this scratch'd Scrawl, when I assure you it is with difficulty I write at all.

I have this Instant receivd an Account of the Prisoners taken by the Northern Army (Including Tories in arms agt us) in the course of the Campaign—this singular Instance of Providence, and our good fortune under it exhibits a striking proof of the advantages which result from unanimity, & a spirited conduct in the Militia—the Northern army before the Surrender of Genl Gates was reinforced by upwards of 12,000 Militia who shut the only door by which Burgoyne could Retreat, and cut off all his supplies. How different our case! the disaffection of great part of the Inhabitants of this State—the langour of others, & internal distraction of the whole, have been among the great and insuperable difficulties I have met with, and have contributed not a little to my embarrassments this Campaign. but enough! I do not mean to complain, I flatter myself that a superintending Providence is ordering every thing for the best—and that, in due time, all will end well. that it may do so, and soon, is the most fervent wish of Yr

Go. Washington[18]

OCTOBER 30
TO MAJOR GENERAL HORATIO GATES

General Horatio Gates wrote letters to Congress and many others announcing his victory at Saratoga—but not to the commander in chief, George Washington. This slight forced Washington into the humiliating necessity of sending one of his aides, Colonel Alexander Hamilton, to Gates seeking information and requesting reinforcements for the army in Pennsylvania. Washington's own reinforcements to Gates earlier in the year—most notably Colonel Daniel Morgan's riflemen—had played a crucial role in Burgoyne's defeat; but Gates, who some were already speaking of as a possible replacement for Washington, felt no obligation to return the favor.

Camp near White Marsh 15 Miles from Philadelphia
Octobr 30: 1777

Sir

By this Opportunity, I do myself the pleasure to congratulate you on the signal success of the Army under your command, in compelling Genl Burgoyne and his whole force, to surrender themselves, prisoners of War. An Event that does the highest honor to the American Arms, and which, I hope will be attended with the most extensive and happy consequences. At the same time, I cannot but regret, that a matter of such magnitude and so interesting to our General Operations, should have reached me by report only, or through the channel of Letters not bearing that authenticity, which the importance of it required, and which it would have received by a line under your signature, stating the simple fact.

Our affairs having happily terminated at the Northward, I have, by the advice of my Genl Officers, sent Colo. Hamilton, One of my aids, to lay before you a full state of our situation, and that of the Enemy in this Quarter. He is well informed upon the subject, and will deliver my Sentiments upon the plan of Operations, that is now necessary to be pursued. I think it improper to enter into a particular detail, not knowing how matters are circumstanced on the North River, and fearing that by some accident, my Letter might miscarry. From Colo. Hamilton you will have a clear and comprehensive view of things, and I persuade myself, you will do every thing in your power to facilate the Objects, I have in contemplation. I am Sir Your Most Obed. Servt

Go: Washington[19]

TO JACOB DUCHÉ

The Reverend Jacob Duché (1738–1798) was the most popular preacher in Philadelphia at the beginning of the Revolutionary War. He gave the opening prayers for the first and second Continental Congresses and was appointed chaplain to Congress in July 1776. Duché had a change of heart, however, after the British occupied Philadelphia and imprisoned him in September 1777, and the following month he wrote a long, public letter to Washington decrying the Declaration of Independence, and arguing that the war was hopeless. It had always been assumed that Washington never replied to Duché's letter. Recently, however, a long, hitherto unknown letter from Washington to Duché was discovered in a Massachusetts newspaper. Full of unusual and revealing statements about religion, Washington's relations with Congress, and the origins of the war, it is an exciting discovery—although there is a possibility, in the absence of an original manuscript letter to analyze, that it is a very clever forgery that somebody managed to plant in a staunchly patriotic newspaper. This is the first time that it has appeared in print since 1779.

[October 1778]

SIR,

YOUR letter to me having been publickly shewn by you to many of your acquaintance, I have reason to suppose my answer will meet with the same treatment. This expectation alone might be sufficient to excuse a person in my particular situation from writing you any answer at all; but I am so entirely convinced of the honesty of your heart, that I am unwilling you should suspect me of slighting you in any respect. At the same time, I am so fully persuaded of the justice of the cause in which I am engaged, that I will freely profess myself to all the world ready to encounter much greater difficulties than any I have yet experienced in support of it.

I am persuaded your letter (for it is without a date) was written when the prospects of the United Colonies were less flattering than they are at present; and though it was written with the most simple integrity, yet it certainly was not dictated by a spirit of prophecy. In a word, Sir, I think you may be a well meaning divine, but your politics seem to have sophisticated your faith. Would any serious pastor, unclouded by political prejudice, and whose zeal was wholly confined to the furtherance of the true religion; would any such man hesitate a moment to assist a congregation in prayer, because they had scruples about praying for some particular potentate, or his royal family? Would any such man proclaim to all his flock, that the Christian religion was a mere state engine—that rather than omit a particular state prayer or two from the formulary, it might be doubted whether it would not be better to shut up the churches, and not pray at all? I trust, sir, I have a sense of religion as well as yourself; and I can assure you I have been shocked at hearing and seeing the weakness and vanity of particular ministers, who have rudely resisted the ordinances respecting the liturgy, and wantonly insulted the established authority of the state, by imposing a prayer on their audience on a subject in which the general doctrines of religion have no concern, and on which they were at liberty to be wholly silent. Congress did not order them to pray for this or that particular ruler, they only enjoined them silence on the subject; and why the ministry should not choose to [be] silent, rather than to provoke their congregations and their governors by a positive disobedience of public orders, I cannot tell, unless, perhaps (which however I will not impute to yourself) they judge it to be more for their purpose to appear meritorious in the eye of a temporal, than of an heavenly tribunal.

You are pleased, Sir, to speak very freely of the members of Congress. They are my masters; and while I can assist the public cause by obedience to their orders, without doing violence to my own sense of moral duty, I will serve them faithfully. Should the time come (which I dare not suppose) when their commands and my sense of duty militate, I will quietly retire, and will be aware how I follow the many examples I have seen, of endeavouring to set the state in an uproar by an ill timed opposition to them.

Your representation of the present state, and future prospect of our affairs, is strong, pathetic, and ornamented with great powers of rhetoric; but it is not founded on fact. The French gentleman you speak of must be an extraordinary character, or must have a very strange opinion of your understanding, to declare to you that he had negociated a treaty with Congress, and at the same time to profess to you that he hoped the Americans would never think of independence. If there is no independency, there can be no Congress; and if there is no Congress, his nego[tia]tion is worth nothing. He would have done more wisely to have staid at home, than to have voyaged to America, to negotiate a treaty with a set of public characters which he hoped would never exist, or to fill the mind of an honest clergyman with his paradoxical politics. You say you are well informed of the state of France; Dr. Franklin too affects to have some knowledge on that subject; but your own account differs so widely from that of Franklin's (whom I believe to be a very honest man) that one or other of you must be duped by your intelligences[.] As Dr. Franklin is on the spot, has lived much in public life, and has been very conversant with men and manners, I am unwilling to disbelieve the intelligence he transmits to us.

What a picture do you draw, my worthy friend, of the present state of Great Britain and America? You say that in Great-Britain, all ranks of men are unanimous. We know the contrary. The large Minorities in both Houses of Parliament; the rank, fortune, and abilities of those who compose the Minorities, are an immediate contradiction to your assertion of unanimity. Besides, we all know that the system of the present government of that country is *Power.* Their Sovereign idolizes that destructive phantom; his Ministers seek to gratify him in it by every means, however dishonest; and he suffers himself to be cajoled by their flattering engagements. He has personally affronted many respectable characters in his dominions, because he suspected they would oppose his aim. These, together with many others who are apprised of his principles, are resolved to stand in the breach between power and liberty; they will steadily oppose every infringement on the balance of the constitution; they consider the present system of British politics respecting America, as founded in tyranny; and they knew that while they support such measures, they support their own liberties.

Whence is it that you have procured your intelligence of the condition of America. I have already told you that your letter was not dictated by any spirit of prophecy. Where is the British army you talk of, as having passed unmolested through a vast extent of country? You surely did not hint at Mr. Burgoyne's expedition: And as to the army under Sir William Howe, you are aware that, not expecting to be allowed to pass unmolested by land, it came by sea to possess itself of Philadelphia, and that it has not made an excursion 15 miles from that city since it first arrived there.

Having made use of your best rhetoric to awaken my fears, you lastly endeavour to make an impression on my vanity. You tell me, that the existence of the army, and the whole support of the present contest on the part of America, depends on me, and you intreat me to use my influence with Congress to procure the resolution of Independency to be rescinded, and to prepare some well digested, constitutional plan of reconciliation for the consideration of the Commissioners. Consider, my good Sir, how this contest began, and how it has been carried on. We on this Continent were quiet, easy, and well affected to our mother country, till we were alarmed with her intention to destroy our constitutional rights. She first injured us. *We* remonstrated. She treated our remonstrances with the most supercilious disdain, and provoked us to appeal to that power who has hitherto graciously supported us. She has passed acts to restrain us from all trade, nay if possible, to starve us; and has so utterly cast us off, that we have been driven by force into a declaration of Independency.

She still persists in requiring from us unconditional submission. I am credibly informed, it was the language of Ministers on the first day of the session of Parliament. I am far from feeling myself to be a person of the consequence you attribute to me: I derive my authority from Congress, and should particular circumstances remove me from the head of the army, I doubt not there are gentlemen of rank and experience to whom the soldiers would readily submit themselves. But suppose I could persuade myself that I had the influence and authority you say I have, what would mankind think of me, who, at the head of three millions of people, bravely withstanding the attempts of their oppressors, and now, in all human probability, on the very point of success, should persuade this people to renounce all their advantages, and to gratify our enemies by first rescinding a resolution taken in a season much more perilous than the present? To what purpose too, shall we rescind it? Are any offers made to us? We have none to make; we only desire to remain unmolested. Have we any assurance that in the moment when we rescind our resolution and forego what little alliance we have with France, we shall again be receiv'd into friendship with Great-Britain? The Commissioners offer us pardon. We want no pardon. We have done nothing wrong. We have only defended our natural political rights. What constitutional plan of reconciliation can we prepare, which is more likely to be accepted, than the plan of independency? The Ministers of Great-Britain who conduct the war against us, are insolent and insidious; are to be controuled only by their fears: 'Till they fear us, they will assume a right to oppose us; and when they fear us, like other tyrants, they will fear us basely, and grant us all we can desire[.] I think that at the hands of these men we shall easily obtain a recognition of Independence, as a full security for the protection of our constitutional liberty. These being my sentiments, I must wait to hear some proffers from the Commissioners before I take any step towards sheathing my sword. I have drawn it in the cause of my country, and by the blessing of God, will employ it faithfully, till my country is restored to peace and security. I am, Sir, your sincere friend,

GEORGE WASHINGTON[20]

CIRCA NOVEMBER 5
TO BRIGADIER GENERAL THOMAS CONWAY

The first sign of potential machinations to install Gates as commander in chief came in the form of an insulting reference to Washington in a letter from Brigadier General Thomas Conway to Gates. Washington's terse announcement that he had become privy to the letter initiated a controversy that would last through the winter.

[Whitemarsh, Pa., ca. 5 November 1777]

Sir,

A Letter which I received last Night, containd the following, paragraph.

In a Letter from Genl Conway to Genl Gates he says—"Heaven has been determind to save your Country; or a weak General and bad Councellors would have ruined it." I am Sir Yr Hble Servt.[21]

DECEMBER 17
GENERAL ORDERS

With the fall of the Delaware River forts to the British in early November, it became evident that Howe's army was in Philadelphia to stay—at least through the winter. Washington next had to decide where his own army would spend the winter. Some of his officers argued in favor of York, Pennsylvania, or Wilmington, Delaware, where the troops could find supplies and shelter from the weather. Washington rejected those options because they were too far away from Philadelphia, and would thus allow the British to take complete control of the countryside of southeast Pennsylvania. Instead, he chose an obscure settlement on the Schuylkill River called Valley

124

Forge—far enough away from Philadelphia to be safe, yet close enough to allow his militia, cavalry, and light infantry to contest the enemy for control of the country-side. It was not a popular decision. Washington attempted to explain his rationale to the army, but most of his men remained skeptical.

Head Quarters, at the Gulph [Pa.] Decr 17th 1777. The Commander in Chief with the highest satisfaction expresses his thanks to the officers and soldiers for the fortitude and patience with which they have sustained the fatigues of the Campaign—Altho' in some instances we unfortunately failed, yet upon the whole Heaven hath smiled on our Arms and crowned them with signal success; and we may upon the best grounds conclude, that by a spirited continuance of the measures necessary for our defence we shall finally obtain the end of our Warfare—Independence—Liberty and Peace—These are blessings worth contending for at every hazard—But we hazard nothing. The power of America alone, duly exerted, would have nothing to dread from the force of Britain—Yet we stand not wholly upon our ground—France yields us every aid we ask, and there are reasons to believe the period is not very distant, when she will take a more active part, by declaring war against the British Crown. Every motive therefore, irresistably urges us—nay commands us, to a firm and manly perseverance in our opposition to our cruel oppressors—to slight difficulties—endure hardships, and contemn every danger—The General ardently wishes, it were now in his power, to conduct the troops into the best winter quarters—But where are these to be found? Should we retire to the interior parts of the State, we should find them crowded with virtuous citizens, who, sacrificing their all, have left Philadelphia and fled thither for protection. To their distresses humanity forbids us to add—This is not all, we should leave a vast extent of fertile country to be despoiled and ravaged by the enemy, from which they would draw vast supplies, and where many of our firm friends would be exposed to all the miseries of the most insulting and wanton depredation—A train of evils might be enumerated, but these will suffice—These considerations make it indispensibly necessary for the army to take such a position, as will enable it most effectually to prevent distress & to give the most extensive security; and in that position we must make ourselves the best shelter in our power—With activity and diligence Huts may be erected that will be warm and dry—In these the troops will be compact, more secure against surprises than if in a divided state and at hand to protect the country. These cogent reasons have determined the General to take post in the neighbourhood of this camp; and influenced by them, he persuades himself, that the officers and soldiers, with one heart, and one mind, will resolve to surmount every difficulty, with a fortitude and patience, becoming their profession, and the sacred cause in which they are engaged: He himself will share in the hardship, and partake of every inconvenience . . .[22]

DECEMBER 20
GENERAL ORDERS

The work of building huts commenced immediately after the troops began arriving at Valley Forge on December 19.

Head Quarters, at the Valley-Forge, Decr 20th 1777.

. . .

The Major Generals accompanied by the Engineers are to view the ground attentively, and fix upon the proper spot and mode for hutting so as to render the camp as strong and inaccessible as possible—The Engineers after this are to mark the ground out, and direct the field Officers appointed to superintend the buildings for each brigade where they are placed.

The soldiers in cutting their firewood, are to save such parts of each tree, as will do for building, reserving sixteen or eighteen feet of the trunk, for logs to rear their huts with—In doing this each regiment is to reap the benefit of their own labour.

All those, who in consequence of the orders of the 18th instant, have turned their thoughts to an easy, and expeditious method of covering the huts, are requested to communicate their plans to Major Generals Sullivan, Greene or Lord Stirling, who will cause experiments to be made, and assign the profer'd reward to the best projector.

The Quarter Master General is to delay no time, but use his utmost exertions, to procure large quantities of straw, either for covering the huts, if it should be found necessary, or for beds for the soldiers—He is to assure the farmers that unless they get their grain out immediately, the straw will be taken with the grain in it, and paid for as straw only.

The Quarter Master General is to collect, as soon as possible, all the tents not now used by the troops, and as soon as they are hutted, all the residue of the tents, and have them washed and well dried, and then laid up in store, such as are good for the next campaign, the others for the uses which shall be directed—The whole are to be carefully preserved—The Colonels and Officers commanding regiments are forthwith to make return to the Qr Mr General, of every tent belonging to their corps.

The army being now come to a fixed station, the Brigadiers and officers commanding brigades, are immediately to take effectual measures, to collect, and bring to camp, all the officers and soldiers at present scattered about the country.

All officers are enjoined to see that their men do not wantonly or needlessly burn and destroy rails, and never fire their sheds, or huts when they leave them.[23]

DECEMBER 23
TO HENRY LAURENS

Supply problems, particularly shortages of food and clothing, plagued Washington's army as soon as it arrived at Valley Forge. A few days after entering camp, many troops mutinied, hooting, whistling, and cawing like crows in protest at the lack of food. The shortages would continue throughout the winter, sometimes bringing the army close to dissolution, and testing all of Washington's skills to keep his men alive. Washington explains his troubles in this letter to Henry Laurens, who had been elected to replace John Hancock as president of Congress.

Valley Forge Decemb. 23d 1777.

Sir

. . . I am now convinced beyond a doubt, that unless some great and capital change suddenly takes place in that line this Army must inevitably be reduced to one or other of these three things. Starve—dissolve—or disperse, in order to obtain subsistence in the best manner they can. rest assured, Sir, this is not an exaggerated picture, and that I have abundant reason to support what I say.

Yesterday afternoon receiving information that the Enemy, in force, had left the City, and were advancing towards Derby, with apparent design to forage and draw subsistence from that part of the Country, I ordered the Troops to be in readiness, that I might give every Opposition in my power; when behold! to my great mortification, I was not only informed, but convinced, that the Men were unable to stir on account of provision, and that a dangerous mutiny, begun the night before and which with difficulty was suppressed by the spirited exertions of some Officers, was still much to be apprehended for want of this Article.

This brought forth the only Commissary in the purchasing line in this Camp, and with him this melancholy and alarming truth, That he had not a single hoof of any kind to slaughter, and not more than 25 Barrells of Flour! From hence form an opinion of our situation, when I add, that he could not tell when to expect any.

All I could do under these circumstances was, to send out a few light parties to watch and harrass the Enemy, whilst other parties were instantly detached different ways to collect, if possible, as much provision as would satisfy the present pressing wants of the Soldiery—But will this answer? No Sir: three or four days bad weather would prove our destruction. What then is to become of the Army this Winter? and if we are as often without Provisions now, as with them, what is to become of us in the Spring, when our force will be collected, with the aid perhaps of Militia, to take advantage of an early campaign before the Enemy can be reinforced? These are considerations of great magnitude—meriting the closest attention, and will, when my own reputation is so intimately connected and to be affected by the event, justify my saying that the present Commissaries are by no means equal to the execution of the Office, or that the disaffection of the people is past beleif. The misfortune however does in my opinion proceed from both causes, and though I have been tender heretofore of giving any opinion or lodging complaints, as the change in that department took place contrary to my Judgement, and the consequences thereof were predicted; yet finding that the inactivity of the Army, whether for want of provisions, Cloaths, or other essentials is charged to my account, not only by the common vulgar, but those in power, it is time to speak plain in exculpation of myself. With truth then I can declare, that no Man in my opinion ever had his measures more impeded than I have, by every department. Since the month of July we have had no assistance from the Quarter Master General, and to want of assistance from this department, the Commissary General charges great part of his deficiency—to this I am to add, that notwithstanding it is a standing order and often repeated, that the Troops shall always have two days provisions by them, that they might be ready at any sudden call, yet no opportunity has scarcely ever offered of taking advantage of the Enemy, that has not been either totally obstructed, or greatly impeded on this account: and this the great & crying evil is not all. Soap—Vinegar and other articles allowed by Congress we see none of, nor have we seen them, I believe, since the battle of Brandywine. The first indeed we have now little occasion for, few men having more than one shirt—many only the moiety of one, and some none at all. In addition to which, as a proof of the little benefit received from a Cloathier General, and at the same time, as a farther proof of the inability of an Army under the circumstances of this, to perform the common duties of Soldiers, besides a number of Men confined to Hospitals for want of Shoes, & others in Farmers Houses on the same account, we have by a Field return this day made, no less than 2898 Men now in Camp unfit for duty, because they are barefoot and otherwise naked; and by the same return it appears, that our strength in continental Troops, including the Eastern Brigades which have joined since the surrender of Genl Burgoyne, exclusive of the Maryland Troops sent to Wilmington, amount to no more than 8200—in Camp fit for duty. Notwithstanding which, and that since the 4th Instant our numbers fit for duty from the hardships and exposures they have undergone, particularly on account of Blankets (numbers having been obliged and still are, to set up all night by fires, instead of taking comfortable rest in a natural and common way) have decreased near 2000 Men, we find Gentlemen without knowing whether the Army was really going into Winter Quarters or not (for I am sure no Resolution of mine would warrant the Remonstrance) reprobating the measure as much, as if they thought the Soldiery were made of Stocks or Stones, and equally insensible of Frost and Snow; and moreover, as if they conceived it easily practicable for an inferior Army, under the disadvantages I have described ours to be, which is by no means exaggerated, to confine a Superior one, in all respects well appointed and provided for a Winters Campaign, within the City of Philadelphia, and to cover from depredation and waste the States of pensylvania, Jersey, &ca. But what makes this matter still more extraordinary in my eye is, that these very Gentlemen, who were well apprized of the nakedness of the Troops from occular demonstration, who thought their own Soldiers worse clad than others and advised me near a month ago, to postpone the execution of a plan I was about to adopt in consequence of a Resolve of Congress for seizing Cloaths, under strong assurances, that an ample supply would be collected in ten days agreable to a decree of the State (not one article of which, by the bye, is yet come to hand) should think a Winters Campaign, and the covering these States from the invasion of an Enemy so easy and practicable a business. I can assure those Gentlemen, that it is a much easier and less distressing thing, to draw Remonstrances in a comfortable room by a good fire side, than to occupy a cold, bleak hill, and sleep under frost & snow without Cloaths or Blankets: However, although they seem to have little feeling for the naked and distressed Soldier, I feel superabundantly for them, and from my soul pity those miseries, which it is neither in my power to releive or prevent. It is for these reasons therefore, I have dwelt upon the subject, and it adds not a little to my other difficulties and distress, to find that much more is expected of me, than is possible to be performed; and, that upon the ground of safety and policy, I am obliged to conceal the true state of the Army from public view, and thereby expose myself to detraction & calumny.

. . . In fine every thing depends upon the preparation that is made in the Several departments in the course of this Winter and the success or misfortunes of next Campaign will more than probably originate with our activity or Supineness this Winter. I have the Honor to be Sir Your Most Obedt Servant

Go: Washington[24]

———

DECEMBER 31
TO MAJOR GENERAL LAFAYETTE

From being just another French volunteer officer, Lafayette had by the winter of 1777 become Washington's devoted friend and trusted adviser.

Head Quarters Decr 31st 1777

My Dear Marquis,

Your favour of Yesterday conveyed to me fresh proof of that friendship and attachment which I have happily experienced since the first of our acquaintance, and for which I entertain sentiments of the purest affection. It will ever constitute part of my happiness to know that I stand well in your opinion, because I am satisfied that you can have no views to answer by throwing out false colours, and that you possess a Mind too exalted to condescend to dirty Arts and low intrigues to acquire a reputation. Happy, thrice happy, would it have been for this Army and the cause we are embarked in, if the same generous spirit had pervaded all the Actors in it. But one Gentleman [General Thomas Conway], whose name you have mentioned, had, I am confident, far different views. His ambition and great desire of being puffed off as one of the first Officers of the Age, could only be equalled by the means which he used to obtain them; but finding that I was determined not to go beyond the line of my duty to indulge him in the first, nor, to exceed the strictest rules of propriety, to gratify him in the second, he became my inveterate Enemy; and has, I am persuaded, practised every Art to do me an injury, even at the expense of reprobating a measure, which did not succeed, that he himself advised to. How far he may have accomplished his ends, I know not, and, but for considerations of a public nature, I care not: For it is well known, that neither ambitious, nor lucrative, motives led me to accept my present appointments; in the discharge of which, I have endeavoured to observe one steady and uniform conduct, which I shall invariably pursue, while I have the honour to command, regardless of the Tongue of slander or the powers of detraction.

The fatal tendency of disunion is so obvious, that I have, in earnest terms, exhorted such officers as have expressed their dissatisfaction at General Conway's promotion [to inspector general], to be cool and dispassionate in their decision upon the matter; and I have hopes that they will not suffer any hasty determination to injure the service. At the same time, it must be acknowledged that Officers' feelings upon these occasions are not to be restrained, although You may controul their actions.

The other observations contained in your Letter, have too much truth in them, and it is much to be lamented that things are not now as they formerly were; but we must not in so great a contest, expect to meet with nothing but Sun shine. I have no doubt but that every thing happens so for the best; that we shall triumph over all our misfortunes, and shall, in the end, be ultimately happy; when, My Dear Marquis, if you will give me your Company in Virginia, we will laugh at our past difficulties and the folly of others; where I will endeavour, by every civility in my power, to shew you how much and how sincerely, I am, Your Affectionate and Obedient servant,

G. Washington[25]

1778

JANUARY 2–3
TO THE BOARD OF WAR

The army's desperate need for supplies caused some officers to call for the forcible sei-
zure of food and clothing from civilians. Washington, seeing the makings of disaster
in the proposal, refused.

Valley forge January 2[–3] 1778

Gentlemen

. . .

I shall use every exertion that may be expedient & practicable for sub-
sisting the Army & keeping it together: But I must observe, that this never
can be done by coercive means. Supplies of provision and Cloathing must
be had in Another way, or it cannot exist. The small seizures that were
made of the former, some days ago, in consequence of the most pressing
and Urgent necessity—When the alternative was, to do that or dissolve,
excited the greatest alarm & uneasiness imaginable, even among some of
Our best & Warmest Friends—Such procedures may relieve for an instant—but eventually will prove of the most pernicious consequence—Besides spreading disaffection & jealousy in the people, they never fail even
in the most veteran Armies under the most rigid & exact discipline to raise
in the Soldiery a disposition to licentiousness—plunder and Robbery,

which has ever been found exceedingly difficult to suppress and which has not only proved ruinous to the Inhabitants, but in many instances to Armies themselves. . .

G.W.[1]

JANUARY 2

TO NICHOLAS COOKE

Among the many problems besetting the army in the winter of 1777–1778 was a manpower crisis. Brigadier General James Mitchell Varnum of Rhode Island wrote to Washington on this date suggesting that his state might, among other measures, recruit a battalion of free blacks. Washington did not address Varnum's suggestion directly, but forwarded Varnum's letter to Rhode Island state legislature president Nicholas Cooke. While hardly an endorsement, it is closest Washington ever came to supporting the enlistment of blacks in the military. Rhode Island enlisted black soldiers for four months in the spring of 1778 before returning to its previous policy of recruiting whites only.

Head Quarters [Valley Forge] 2d January 1778.

Sir.

Inclosed you will receive a Copy of a Letter from General Varnum to me, upon the means which might be adopted for completing the Rhode Island Troops to their full proportion in the Continental Army—I have nothing to say in addition to what I wrote the 29th of last month on this important subject, but to desire that you will give the Officers employed in this business all the assistance in your power. I am with great respect Sir Your most obedt Servt

Go: Washington[2]

JANUARY 2

TO HENRY LAURENS

On December 31, 1777, Thomas Conway, just promoted to major general and in-spector general of the army and still feuding with the commander in chief, wrote a letter to Washington in which he sarcastically compared him to Prussia's King Frederick the Great. It was, wrote Washington's aide Tench Tilghman, a letter for which Conway "deserved to be kicked"; another aide, John Laurens, claimed that it would have resulted in a duel were it not for Washington's public responsibilities as commander in chief. Under the circumstances, Washington could only send the letter to Congress, hoping that the delegates would chastise the insubordinate general. Henry Laurens—John's father—considered Conway's conduct "unpardonable," but Congress, which had just appointed Conway inspector general, had no grounds for deposing him. Eventually, however, Washington's allies in the army and Congress, encouraged by his aides, would make Conway's position so uncomfortable that he had no choice but to resign and leave for Europe.[3]

Valley Forge January 2d 1778

Sir

I take the liberty of transmitting to you the Inclosed Copies of a Letter from me to Genl Conway since his return from York to Camp, and of Two Letters from him to me, which you will be pleased to lay before Congress. I shall not in this Letter animadvert upon them, but after making a single observation submit the whole to Congress.

If General Conway means by cool receptions mentioned in the last paragraph of his Letter of the 31st Ulto, that I did not receive him in the language of a warm and cordial Friend, I readily confess the charge. I did not, nor shall I ever, till I am capable of the arts of dissimulation. These I despise, and my feelings will not permit me to make professions of friend-ship to the man I deem my Enemy, and whose system of conduct forbids it. At the same time, Truth authorises me to say, that he was received & treated with proper respect to his Official character, and that he has had no cause to justifye the assertion, that he could not expect any support for fulfilling the duties of his Appointment. I have the Honor to be with great respect Sir Your Most Obedt Servt

Go: Washington[4]

JANUARY 4
TO MAJOR GENERAL HORATIO GATES

Meanwhile, tensions between Washington and Gates, to whom Conway had written a letter insulting to the commander in chief the previous November, continued.

Valley forge Jany 4th 1778

Sir,

Your Letter of the 8th Ulto came to my hands a few days ago; and, to my great surprize informed me, that a copy of it had been sent to Congress—for what reason, I find myself unable to account; but, as some end doubtless was intended to be answered by it, I am laid under the disagreeable necessity of returning my answer through the same channel, lest any member of that honorable body, should harbour an unfavourable suspicion of my having practiced some indirect means, to come at the contents of the confidential Letters between you & General Conway.

I am to inform you then, that Colo. Wilkenson, in his way to Congress in the Month of October last, fell in with Lord Stirling at Reading; and, not in confidence that I ever understood, inform'd his Aid de Camp Majr McWilliams that Genl Conway had written thus to you "Heaven has been determined to save your Country; or a weak General and bad Counsellors would have ruined it"—Lord Stirling, from motives of friendship, transmitted the account with this remark—"The inclosed was communicated by Colo. Wilkenson to Majr McWilliams, such wicked duplicity of conduct I shall always think it my duty to detect."

In consequence of this information, and without having any thing more in view than merely to shew that Gentleman that I was not unapprized of his intrieguing disposition, I wrote him a Letter in these words. "Sir—A Letter which I received last night contained the following paragraph.

"In a Letter from Genl Conway to Genl Gates he says 'Heaven has been determined to save your Country; or a weak Genl and bad Counsellors would have ruined it—I am Sir & ca."

Neither this Letter, nor the information which occasioned it, was ever, directly, or indirectly, communicated by me to a single Officer in this army (out of my own family) excepting the Marquis de la Fayette, who having been spoken to on the subject by Genl Conway, applied for, and saw, under injunctions of secrecy, the Letter which contained Wilkensons informa-

tion—so desirous was I, of concealing every matter that could, in its consequences, give the smallest Interruption to the tranquility of this army, or,
afford a gleam of hope to the enemy by dissensions therein.

Thus Sir, with an openness and candour which I hope will ever characterize and mark my conduct, have I complied with your request. the
only concern I feel upon the occasion (finding how matters stand) is, that
in doing this, I have necessarily been obliged to name a Gentleman whom
I am perswaded (although I never exchanged a word with him upon the
subject) thought he was rather doing an act of Justice, than committing an
act of infidility; and sure I am, that, till Lord Stirlings Letter came to my
hands, I never knew that Genl Conway (who I viewed in the light of a
stranger to you) was a corrispondant of yours, much less did I suspect that
I was the subject of your confidential Letters—pardon me then for adding,
that so far from conceiving, that the safety of the States can be affected, or
in the smallest degree injured, by a discovery of this kind; or, that I should
be called upon in such solemn terms to point out the author, that I considered the information as coming from yourself; and given with a friendly
view to forewarn, and consequently forearm me, against a secret enemy; or,
in other words, a dangerous incendiary; in which character, sooner or later,
this Country will know Genl Conway. But—in this, as in other matters of
late, I have found myself mistaken. I am Sir yr Most Obedt Servt

Go: Washington[5]

JANUARY 20
TO CAPTAIN HENRY LEE JR.

*The partisan exploits of Captain Henry "Light-Horse Harry" Lee Jr.—father of
Confederate leader Robert E. Lee—provided Washington with a ray of hope in the
difficult winter of 1777–1778.*

Valley forge Jany 20th 1778

My dear Lee,

Altho I have given you my thanks in the general Orders of this day for
the late instance of your gallant behaviour I cannot resist the Inclination I
feel to repeat them again in this manner. I needed no fresh proof of your

merit, to bear you in remembrance—I waited only for the proper time and season to shew it—these I hope are not far off. I shall also think of & will reward the merit of Lindsay when an opening presents as far as I can consistently & shall not forget the corporal whom you have recommended to my notice. Offer my sincere thanks to the whole of your gallant party and assure them that no one felt pleasure more sensibly, or rejoiced more sincerely for yours & their escape than Yr Affectionate

G. Washington[6]

JANUARY 23
TO WILLIAM GORDON

In this letter to his friend William Gordon, Washington reflects on the intrigues seemingly forming against him; this time, to appoint Major General Charles Lee, still held captive by the British, to command of the Continental Army.

I have attended to your information and remark, on the supposed intention of placing General L——, at the head of the army: whether a serious design of that kind had ever entered into the head of a member of C—— or not, I never was at the trouble of enquiring. I am told a scheme of that kind is now on foot by some, in behalf of another gentleman—but whether true or false, whether serious, or merely to try the pulse, I neither know nor care; neither interested nor ambitious views led me into the service—I did not solicit the command, but accepted it after much entreaty, with all that diffidence which a conscious want of ability and experience equal to the discharge of so important a trust, must naturally create in a mind not quite devoid of thought; and after I did engage, pursued the great line of my duty, and the object in view (as far as my judgement could direct) as pointedly as the needle to the pole. So soon then as the public gets dissatisfied with my services, or a person is found better qualified to answer her expectation, I shall quit the helm with as much satisfaction, and retire to a private station with as much content, as ever the wearied pilgrim felt upon his safe arrival in the Holy-land, or haven of hope; and shall wish most devoutly, that those who come after may meet with more prosperous gales than I have done, and less difficulty. If the expectation of the public has not been answered by my endeavours, I have more reasons than one to regret it; but at present shall only add, that a day may come when the public cause is no longer to be benefited by a concealment of our circumstances; and till that period arrives, I shall not be among the first to disclose such truths as may injure it.[7]

FEBRUARY 6

TO JONATHAN TRUMBULL SR.

The army's worst crisis came in February 1778, as a logistical collapse led to the virtual disappearance of provisions from camp. Several regiments mutinied, and were only with the greatest difficulty prevented from leaving camp.

Valley Forge the 6th February 1778

Sir

I must take the liberty of addressing you on a subject, which, though out of your sphere, I am fully persuaded, will have every possible attention in your power to give—It is the alarming situation of the Army on account of provision—Shall not undertake minutely to investigate the Causes of this, but there is the strongest reason to believe, that its existence cannot be of long duration, unless more constant, regular and larger supplies of the meat kind are furnished, than have been for some time past. We have been once on the brink of a dissolution in the course of the present year for want of this Article, and our condition now is but little better. What is still more distressing, I am assured by Coll Blaine, Deputy Commissary in the middle District, comprehending the States of Jersey—Pensylvania & Maryland, that they are nearly exhausted in this instance; and the most vigorous and active exertions on his part will not procure more than sufficient to supply the Army during this Month if so long. This being the case, and as any relief that can be obtained from the more Southern States will be but partial, trifling and of a day, we must turn our views to the Eastward and lay our account of support from thence—Without it we cannot but disband— I must therefore, Sir, intreat you, in the most earnest terms, and by that zeal which has so eminently distinguished your character in the present arduous struggle, to give every countenance to the person or persons employed in the purchasing line in your State, and to urge them to the most vigorous efforts to forward supplies of Cattle from time to time; and thereby prevent such a melancholy and alarming Catastophre—As I observed before, this subject is rather out of your province; yet I know your wishes to promote the service in every possible degree, will render any apology unnecessary, and that the bare state of facts will be admitted as a full and ample justification for the trouble it is like to occasion you—I have the Honor to be with great Respect and Esteem Sir Your most obedient Servant

Go: Washington[8]

FEBRUARY 10

TO BRIGADIER GENERAL GEORGE WEEDON

The disappearance from camp of many of Washington's field officers severely complicated his task of managing the army. It especially upset him that so many of his "country men"—by which he meant Virginians—were among the missing. Weedon disregarded Washington's appeal and went home anyway.

Valley forge Feby 10th 1778.

Dear Sir,

It is matter of no small grief to me, to find such an unconquerable desire in the Officers of this Army to be absent from Camp, as every day exhibits; and my feelings upon the occasion are not a little wounded by perceiving that this passion is more prevalent among my country men, than in any other Troops in the whole Army—[Peter] Mulenberg is now gone—you think it the hardest case imaginable that you are here—Woodford & [Charles] Scott are also applying—the field Officers of all your Brigades are, in a manner, absent; a new arrangement of the army is taking place, and important changes (to effect which properly, the aid of every officer of Rank is necessary) is on the Carpet; and yet, I must attempt (for it can be no more than an attempt) to do all these duties myself, and perform the part of a Brigadier—a Colonel—&c. (because in the absence of these every thing relative to their business comes directly to me) or, I must incur displeasure by the denial—I can see clearly that instead of having the proper Officers to assist in organizing, training, and fitting the Troops for the field against the next Campaign, that we shall be plunged into it as we were last year heels over head without availing ourselves of the advantages which might be derived from our present situation & prospects, if every Officer would lay his hands properly to the work, & afford those aids which I have a right to expect, and the Service requires instead of longing, & hankering after their respective homes. But I shall say no more, nor will I oppose your Inclination any longer than to request that you, Woodford & Scott, will, before you go give me your Sentiments of the Officers to be retaind, if a reduction should take place, with some other matters of a local nature which I cannot come at without assistance. . .

Go: Washington[9]

FEBRUARY 12

TO MAJOR GENERAL NATHANAEL GREENE

Major General Nathanael Greene frequently proved a savior during times of crisis. On September 11, 1777, Greene commanded the rear guard that allowed Washington's army to escape destruction at the Battle of Brandywine. In February 1778, as described in this letter, Washington ordered Greene to scour the countryside for food, resulting in the procurement of just enough provisions to keep the army alive. In March, Greene would take over the all-but-defunct Quartermaster Department, reforming it and returning the army to a more even logistical keel. And in 1780–1781, Greene would save the American cause from collapse in the southern states.

Sir,

The good People of the State of Pennsylvania living in the vicinity of Philadelphia & near the Delaware River having suffered much by the Enemy carrying off their property without allowing them any Compensation, thereby distressing the Inhabitants—supplying their own Army & enabling them to protract the cruel & unjust war that they are now waging against these States—And whereas by recent intelligence I have reason to expect that they intend making another grand Forage into this Country, it is of the utmost Consequence that the Horses Cattle Sheep and Provender within Fifteen or Twenty miles west of the River Delaware between the

Schuylkil and the Brandywine be immediately removed, to prevent the Enemy from receiving any benefit therefrom, as well as to supply the present Emergencies of the American Army.

I do therefore Authorise impower & Command you forthwith to take Carry off & secure all such Horses as are suitable for Cavalry or for Draft and all Cattle & Sheep fit for Slaughter together with every kind of Forage that may be found in possession of any of the Inhabitants within the Aforesaid Limits Causing Certificates to be given to each person for the number value & quantity of the horses Cattle Sheep & Provender so taken.

Informing them that notice will be given to the holders of such Certificates by the Commissaries & Quarter master General when & where they may Apply for Payment that they may not be disappointed in calling for their money.

All Officers civil and military, Commissaries, Quarter masters &ca, are hereby Orderd to obey and assist you in this necessary business.

All the Provinder on the Islands between Philadelphia and Chester which may be difficult of Access or too hazardous to attempt carrying off, you will immediately Cause to be destroyed, giving Direction, to the Officer or Officers to whom this Duty is assign'd, to take an account of the Quantity together with the Owners Names, as far as the nature of the Service will admit. Given under my hand at head Quarters this 12th day of Feby 1778.

Go: Washington[10]

FEBRUARY 15
TO WILLIAM GORDON

Although under increasing criticism from detractors, Washington denied rumors that he was preparing for resignation.

Valley-forge Feby 15th 1778.
Dear Sir,

Since my last to you about the end of January I have been favoured with your Letter of the 12th of that Month, which did not reach my hands till within these few days. The question there put, was, in some degree, solved in my last—But to be more explicit, I can assure you that no person ever heard me drop an expression that had a tendency to resignation. the same principles that led me to embark in the opposition to the arbitrary claims of Great Britain operate with additional force at this day; nor is it my desire to withdraw my Services while they are considered of importance in the present contest—but to report a design of this kind is among the Arts wch those who are endeavouring to effect a change, are practicing, to bring it to pass. I have said, & I still do say, that there is not an Officer in the Service of the United States that would return to the sweets of domestic life with more heart-felt joy than I should; but I would have this declaration, accompanied by these Sentiments, that while the public are satisfied with my endeavours I mean not to shrink in the cause—but, the moment her voice, not that of faction, calls upon me to resign, I shall do it with as much pleasure as ever the weary traveller retired to rest. This my dear Doctor you are at liberty to assert, but in doing it, I would have nothing formal—all things will come right again & soon recover their proper tone as the design is not only seen thro but reprobated. . .

Go: W——n.[11]

FEBRUARY 28

TO LIEUTENANT COLONEL JOHN FITZGERALD

The zeal of Washington's aides, including John Fitzgerald, for finding and rooting out secret enemies led them, and the commander in chief, nearly to the verge of paranoia. In this letter, "C" and "G" are Conway and Gates; "M" is an old associate, Thomas Mifflin.

Valley-forge Feby 28th 1778

Dear Sir,

. . .

I thank you sincerely for the part you acted at York respecting C—y's Letter; & believe with you, that matters have, & will, turn out very different to what that Party expected. G—s has involved himself in his Letters to me, in the most absurd contradictions—M. has brought himself into a scrape he does not know how to get out of, with a Gentleman of this state—& C—, as you know, is sent upon an expedition which all the world knew—& the event has proved, was not practicable. In a word, I have a good deal of reason to believe that the Machinations of this Junto will recoil upon their own heads, & be a means of bringing some matters to light which by getting me out of the way some of them thought to conceal . . .

Go: Washington[12]

MARCH I
GENERAL ORDERS

Head-Quarters V. Forge Sunday March 1st 1778. The Commander in Chief again takes occasion to return his warmest thanks to the virtuous officers and soldiery of this Army for that persevering fidelity and Zeal which they have uniformly manifested in all their conduct; Their fortitude not only under the common hardships incident to a military life, but also under the additional sufferings to which the peculiar situation of these States have exposed them, clearly proves them worthy the enviable privelege of contending for the rights of human nature, the Freedom & Independence of their Country; The recent Instance of uncomplaining Patience during the scarcity of provisions in Camp is a fresh proof that they possess in an eminent degree the spirit of soldiers and the magninimity of Patriots—The few refractory individuals who disgrace themselves by murmurs it is to be hoped have repented such unmanly behaviour, and resolved to emulate the noble example of their associates upon every trial which the customary casualties of war may hereafter throw in their way—Occasional distress for want of provisions and other necessaries is a spectacle that frequently occurs in every army and perhaps there never was one which has been in general so plentifully supplied in respect to the former as ours; Surely we who are free Citizens in arms engaged in a struggle for every thing valuable in society and partaking in the glorious task of laying the foundation of an Empire, should scorn effeminately to shrink under those accidents & rigours of War which mercenary hirelings fighting in the cause of lawless ambition, rapine & devastation, encounter with cheerfulness and alacrity, we should not be merely equal, we should be superior to them in every qualification that dignifies the man or the soldier in proportion as the motive from which we act and the final hopes of our Toils, are superior to theirs. Thank Heaven! our Country abounds with provision & with prudent management we need not apprehend want for any length of time. Defects in the Commissaries department, Contingencies of weather and other temporary impediments have subjected and may again subject us to a deficiency for a few days, but soldiers! American soldiers! will despise the meaness of repining at such trifling strokes of Adversity, trifling indeed when compared to the transcendent Prize which will undoubtedly crown their Patience and Perseverence, Glory and Freedom, Peace and Plenty to themselves and the Community; The Admiration of the World, the Love of their Country and the Gratitude of Posterity! Your General unceasingly employs his thoughts on the means of relieving your distresses, supplying your wants and bringing your labours to a speedy and prosperous issue—Our Parent Country he hopes will second his endeavors by the most vigorous exertions and he is convinced the faithful officers and soldiers associated with him in the great work of rescuing our Country from Bondage and Misery will continue in the display of that patriotic zeal which is capable of smoothing every difficulty & vanquishing every Obstacle. . . .[13]

MARCH I

TO BRYAN FAIRFAX

Washington's zeal for the American cause and contempt for Tories did not cause him to reject old friends, like Bryan Fairfax, who remained loyal to King George III.

Head Qrs Valley-forge Mar. 1st 1778.

Dear Sir,

Your favor of the 8th of Decr came safe to my hands—after considerable delay in its passage.

The Sentiments you have expressed of me in this Letter are highly flattering—meriting my warmest acknowledgements, as I have too good an opinion of your sincerity and candour, to believe that you are capable of unmeaning professions—& speaking a language foreign from your heart—The friendship I ever professed, & felt for you, met with no diminution from the difference in our political sentiments—I knew the rectitude of my own intentions & believing in the sincerity of yours, lamented, though I did not condemn, your renunciation of the creed I had adopted—nor do I think any person, or power ought to do it whilst your conduct is not opposed to the general Interest of the People, & the measures they are pursuing—The latter, that is our actions, depending on ourselves may be controuled, while the powers of thinking originating from higher causes, cannot always be moulded to our wishes.

The determinations of Providence are always wise—often inscrutable—and, thô its decrees appear to bear hard upon us at times, is, nevertheless meant for gracious purposes—In this light I cannot help viewing your late disappointment; for if you had been permitted to have gone to England, unrestrained even by the rigid Oaths which are administred upon those occasions, your feelings as a husband, parent, &ca must have been considerably wounded in the prospect of a long—perhaps lasting seperation from your nearest relatives—what then must they have been if the obligation of an Oath had left you without a Will?

Your hope of being instrumental in restoring peace, would prove as unsubstantial as mist before a Noon day Sun; and would as soon dispel; for believe me Sir, G. Britain understood herself perfectly well in this dispute, but did not comprehend America—She meant as Lord Cambden in his late speech in Parliament clearly, & explicitly declares, to drive America into rebellion, that her own purposes might be more fully answered by it; but take this along with it, that this plan originating in a firm belief founded on mis-information, that no effectual opposition would, or could be made, they little dreamt of what has happened, and are disappointed in their views.

Does not every act of Administration from the Tea act to the present Sessions of Parliament declare this in plain & selfevident characters? Had the Commissioners any powers to treat with America? If they meant peace, would Lord Howe have been detained in England five Months after passing the Act? Would the powers of these Commissioners have been confined to mere acts of grace upon condition of absolute submission? No—surely No! they meant to drive us into what they termed rebellion, that they might be furnished with a pretext to disarm, and then strip us of the rights & previledges of Englishmen—If they were actuated by principles of Justice, why did they refuse, indignantly to accede to the terms which were humbly supplicated before hostilities commenced, and this Country deluged in blood, & now make their principal officers, and even the Commissioners themselves, say that these terms are just & reasonable; nay, that more will be granted than we have yet asked, if we will relinquish our claim to Independancy—what name does such conduct as this deserve? and what punishment is there in store for the Men who have distressed Millions—Involved thousands in ruin—and plunged numberless families in inextricable woe! Could that which is just & reasonable now have been unjust four years ago? If not, upon what principles I repeat, does Administration act? they must either be wantonly wicked & cruel or (which is only another mode of expressing the same thing) under false colours are now endeavouring to deceive the great body of the People by industriously propagating an Idea, that G. Britain is willing to offer any, & that we will accept of no terms; thereby hoping to poison, & disaffect the minds of those who wish for Peace, & create feuds and dissentions in consequence—In a word, having less dependance now on their Arms than their Arts, they are practicing such low, & dirty tricks, that Men of Sentiment and honor must blush for their fall. among other manœuvres in this way, they are forging Letters and publishing them as intercepted ones of mine, to prove that I am an enemy to the present measures of this Continent; having been deceived, & led on by Congress in hopes that at length, they would recede from their claims & withdraw their opposition to G. Britain. . .

Go: Washington[14]

———

MARCH 18
TO CATHARINE WILHELMINA LIVINGSTON

Washington had a few enemies, but also numerous admirers—including many young women. Twenty-six-year-old Catharine "Kitty" Livingston was the daughter of William Livingston, the governor of New Jersey.

Camp—Valley-forge 18th Mar. 1778.
General Washington having been informed, lately, of the honor done him by Miss Kitty Livingston in wishing for a lock of his Hair, takes the liberty of inclosing one, accompanied by his most respectful compliments.[15]

MARCH 27
TO PATRICK HENRY

Many anonymous letters critical of Washington turned up in the winter and spring of 1778, including one written to the governor of Virginia, Patrick Henry. Henry forwarded the letter to Washington, who decided that it had been written by Dr. Benjamin Rush, a dedicated patriot who frequently assured Washington of his admiration and respect.

Valley Forge March 27th 1778
Dr Sir
About eight days ago I was honored with your favor of the 20th Ulto.

Your friendship, Sir, in transmitting me the anonymous Letter you had received, lays me under the most grateful obligations, and if my acknowledgements can be due for any thing more, it is for the very polite and delicate terms, in which you have been pleased to communicate the matter.

I have ever been happy in supposing that I had a place in your esteem, and the proof you have afforded upon this occasion makes me peculiarly so. The favourable light in which you hold me, is truly flattering, but I should feel much regret, if I thought the happiness of America so intimately connected—with my personal welfare, as you so obligingly seem to consider it. All I can say is, that she has ever had, and I trust she ever will have, my honest exertions to promote her interest. I cannot hope that my services have been the best—But my Heart tells me—they have been the best that I could render.

That I may have erred in using all the means in my power for accomplishing the objects of the arduous exalted station with which I am honored, I cannot doubt; nor do I wish my conduct to be exempted from reprehension farther than it may deserve. Error is the portion of humanity, and to censure it, whether committed by this or that public character, is the prerogative of freemen. However, being intimately acquainted with the man, I conceive the Author of the Letter transmitted; and having always received from him the strongest professions of attachment and regard, I am constrained to consider him, as not possessing, at least, a great degree of candor and honest sincerity, though his views in addressing you, should have been the result of conviction and founded in motives of public good. This is not the only secret, insidious attempt, that has been made to wound my reputation. There have been others equally base, cruel and ungenerous, because conducted with as little frankness, and proceeding from views perhaps as personally interesting. I am Dr Sir with great esteem & regard Yr Much obliged friend & Servant

Go: Washington[16]

APRIL 30
TO HENRY LAURENS

The appearance in camp of Friedrich Wilhelm von Steuben, a former officer in the Prussian army who claimed (falsely) the rank of baron, provided Washington with an opportunity to correct the army's abysmal discipline and drill. Steuben, who Congress appointed inspector general with the rank of major general in place of the disgraced Conway, may not have been all that he claimed to be, but he was a superb drill instructor, and a major reason why Washington's army emerged from Valley Forge stronger than it had ever been before.

Head Quarters 30th April 1778.

Sir

The extensive ill consequences arising from a want of uniformity in discipline and manœuvres throughout the Army—have long occasioned me to wish for the establishment of a well organised inspectorship, and the concurrence of Congress in the same views has induced me to set on foot a temporary institution, which from the success that has hitherto attended it, gives me the most flattering expectations, and will I hope obtain their approbation.

Baron de Steubens length of service in the first military School in Europe, and his former rank pointed him out as a person peculiarly qualified to be at the head of this department; this appeared the least exceptionable way of introducing him into the army and one that would give him the most ready opportunity of displaying his talents—I therefore proposed to him to undertake the office of Inspector General which he agreed to with the greatest chearfulness, and has performed the duties of it with a zeal and intelligence equal to our wishes—he has two ranks of Inspectors under him, the lowest are officers charged with the inspection of brigades, with the title of brigade-inspectors—the others superintend several of these—they have written instructions relative to their several functions—and the manœuvres which they are to practice are illustrated by a company which the Baron has taken the pains to train himself.

. . .

I should do injustice if I were to be longer silent with regard to the merits of the baron de Steuben, his knowledge of his profession added to the zeal which he has discovered since he began upon the functions of his office, lead me to consider him as an acquisition to the service and to recommend him to the attention of Congress—his expectations with regard to rank extend to that of Major General—his finances he ingenuously confesses will not admit of his serving without the incident emoluments—and Congress I presume from his Character and their own knowledge of him, will without difficulty gratify him in these particulars.

The Baron is sensible that our situation requires a few variations in the duties of his office, from the general practice in Europe, and particularly that they must necessarily be more comprehensive—in which as well as in his instructions he has skilfully yielded to circumstances.

The Success which has hitherto attended the plan, enables me to request with confidence the ratification of Congress, and is I think a pledge of the establishment of a well combined general System, which insurmountable obstacles have hitherto opposed. I have the honor to be with great respect Sir Your most obedt Servt

Go: Washington[17]

MAY 5
GENERAL ORDERS

In early May, Washington received word that the event for which so many in America had been waiting—but on which he had long ago given up hope—had come true: France had signed a treaty of alliance and commerce with the United States. This alliance heralded the intervention of France in the war with Great Britain, and in an instant entirely transformed the conflict. Washington made certain that his troops understood the importance of the moment.

Head-Quarters V. Forge Tuesday May 5th 1778.
. . .

It having pleased the Almighty ruler of the Universe propitiously to defend the Cause of the United American-States and finally by raising us up a powerful Friend among the Princes of the Earth to establish our liberty and Independence upon lasting foundations, it becomes us to set apart a day for gratefully acknowledging the divine Goodness & celebrating the important Event which we owe to his benign Interposition.

The several Brigades are to be assembled for this Purpose at nine ôClock tomorrow morning when their Chaplains will communicate the Intelligence contain'd in the Postscript to the Pennsylvania Gazette of the 2nd instant and offer up a thanksgiving and deliver a discourse suitable to the Occasion—At half after ten ôClock a Cannon will be fired, which is to be a signal for the men to be under Arms—The Brigade Inspectors will then inspect their Dress and Arms, form the Battalions according to instructions given them and announce to the Commanding Officers of Brigades that the Battalions are formed: The Brigadiers or Commandants will then appoint the Field Officers to command the Battalions, after which each Battalion will be ordered to load & ground their Arms.

At half after eleven a second Cannon be fired as a signal for the march upon which the several Brigades will begin their march by wheeling to the right by Platoons & proceed by the nearest way to the left of their ground in the new Position; this will be pointed out by the Brigade Inspectors—A third signal will be given upon which there will be discharge of thirteen Cannon; When the thirteen has fired a running fire of the Infantry will begin on the right of Woodford's and continue throughout the whole front line, it will then be taken on the left of the second line and continue to the right—Upon a signal given, the whole Army will *Huzza!* "Long Live the King of France"—The Artillery then begins again and fires thirteen rounds, this will be succeded by a second general discharge of the Musquetry in a running fire—*Huzza!*—"And long live the friendly European Powers"—Then the last discharge of thirteen Pieces of Artillery will be given, followed by a General runing fire and Huzza! "To the American States."

There will be no Exercise in the morning and the guards of the day will not parade 'till after the feu de joie is finished, when the Brigade Major will march them out to the Grand Parade: The Adjutants then will tell off their Battalions into eight Platoons and the commanding officer will reconduct them to their Camps marching by the Left.

Major General Lord Stirling will command on the right, the Marquis De la fayette on the left and Baron De Kalb the second line—Each Major General will conduct the first Brigade of his Command to its ground, the other Brigades will be conducted by their commanding Officers in separate Columns—The Posts of each Brigade will be pointed out by Baron De Steuben's Aids—Majr Walker will attend Lord Stirling—Major De Eponsieu the Marquis De la Fayette and Captain Lanfant the Baron De Kalb—The line is to be formed with the Interval of a foot between the files.

Each man is to have a Gill of rum—The Quarter-Masters of the several Brigades are to apply to the Adjutant General for an order on the Commissary of Military stores for the number of blank Cartridges that may be wanted.[18]

JUNE 18
TO HENRY LAURENS

The French alliance bore early fruit on June 18 when the British, choosing to concentrate their forces in New York and the West Indies, evacuated Philadelphia. To escape capture, the British garrison would have to march across New Jersey to Sandy Hook, where transport ships awaited them; Washington set his army in motion to pursue.

Head Qrs
½ after 11 A. M. June 18th 1778

Sir

I have the pleasure to inform Congress, that I was this minute advised by Mr Roberts that the Enemy evacuated the City early this morning. He was down at the Middle ferry on this side, where he received the intelligence from a number of the Citizens, who were on the opposite shore. They told him, that about Three Thousand of the Troops had embarked on board Transports. The destruction of the Bridge prevented him crossing. I expect every moment Official accounts on the subject. I have put Six Brigades in motion, and the rest of the Army are preparing to follow with all possible dispatch. We shall proceed towards Jersey & govern ourselves according to circumstances. As yet I am not fully ascertained of the Enemy's destination, nor are there wanting a variety of Opinions as to the route they will pursue, whether it will be by Land or Sea, admitting it to be New York. Some think it probable in such case, that the part of their Army, which crossed the Delaware, will march down the Jersey shore some distance and then embark. There is other intelligence corroborating Mr Roberts's, but none Official is yet come. I have the Honor to be with great respect & esteem Sir yr Most Obedt servant

Go: Washington[19]

JULY 1
TO HENRY LAURENS

Washington describes the ensuing campaign, which culminated on June 28 in the Battle of Monmouth, in this letter to the president of Congress. Major General Charles Lee commanded the first elements of the American army to encounter the British at Monmouth, and after a short engagement led them back in disorderly retreat. Washington confronted Lee on the battlefield, dismissed him, and took personal command. This time, unlike at Kip's Bay in 1776, the commander in chief was able to halt the retreat and rally the troops, who cheered his arrival at the front and then turned and held the line against the attacking redcoats. Although the battle's results were inconclusive and the British reached their transport ships at Sandy Hook in safety, the Americans had fought bravely and well.

English Town [N.J.] 1st July 1778

Sir

I embrace this first moment of leisure, to give Congress a more full and particular account of the movements of the Army under my command, since its passing the Delaware, than the situation of our Affairs would heretofore permit.

I had the honor to advise them, that on the appearances of the enemy's intention to march thro' Jersey becoming serious, I had detatched General Maxwells Brigade, in conjunction with the Militia of that State, to interrupt and impede their progress, by every obstruction in their power; so as to give time to the Army under my command to come up with them, and take advantage of any favorable circumstances that might present themselves. The Army having proceeded to Coryell's ferry and crossed the Delaware at that place, I immediately detatched Colo. Morgan with a select Corps of 600 Men to reinforce General Maxwell, and marched with the main Body towards princetown.

The slow advance of the Enemy had greatly the air of design, and led me, with others, to suspect that General Clinton desirous of a general Action was endeavouring to draw us down into the lower Country, in order by a rapid movement to gain our Right, and take possession of the strong Grounds above us. This consideration, and to give the troops time to repose and refresh themselves from the fatigues they had experienced from rainy and excessive hot Weather, determined me to halt at Hopewell Township, about five Miles from princetown, where we remained till the Morning of the 25th On the preceding day I made a second detatchment of 1500 chosen troops under Brigadier Genl Scott, to reinforce those already in the vicinity of the Enemy, the more effectually to annoy and delay their march. The next day the Army moved to Kingston, and having received intelligence that the Enemy were prosecuting their Rout towards Monmouth Court House, I dispatched a thousand select men under Brigadier General Wayne, and sent the Marquis de la Fayette to take the command of the whole advanced Corps, including Maxwells Brigade and Morgans light Infantry; with orders to take the first fair opportunity of attacking the Enemy's Rear. In the evening of the same day, the whole Army marched from Kingston where our Baggage was left, with intention to preserve a proper distance for supporting the advanced Corps, and arrived at Cranberry early the next morning. The intense heat of the Weather, and a heavy storm unluckily coming on made it impossible to resume our march that day without great inconvenience and injury to the troops. Our advanced Corps being differently circumstanced, moved from the position it had held the night before, and took post in the evening on the Monmouth Road, about five Miles from the Enemy's Rear, in expectation of attacking them next morning on their march. The main Body having remained at Cranberry, the advanced Corps was found to be too remote, and too far upon the Right to be supported either in case of an attack upon, or from the Enemy, which induced me to send orders to the Marquis to file off by his left towards English Town, which he accordingly executed early in the Morning of the 27th.

The Enemy in marching from Allen Town had changed their disposition and placed their best troops in the Rear, consisting of all the Grenadiers, Light Infantry, and Chasseurs of the line. This alteration made it necessary to increase the number of our advanced Corps; in consequence of which I detatched Major General Lee with two Brigades to join the Marquis at English Town, on whom of course the command of the whole devolved, amounting to about five thousand Men. The main Body marched the same day and encamped within three Miles of that place. Morgans Corps was left hovering on the Enemy's right flank, and the Jersey Militia, amounting at this time to about 7 or 800 Men under General Dickinson on their left.

The Enemy were now encamped in a strong position, with their right extending about a Mile and an half beyond the Court House, in the parting of the Roads leading to Shrewsbury and Middletown, and their left along the Road from Allen Town to Monmouth, about three miles on this side the Court House. Their Right flank lay on the skirt of a small wood, while their left was secured by a very thick one, a Morass running towards their Rear, and their whole front covered by a wood, and for a considerable extent towards the left with a Morass. In this situation they halted till the morning of the 28th.

Matters being thus situated, and having had the best information, that if the Enemy were once arrived at the Heights of Middletown, ten or twelve Miles from where they were, it would be impossible to attempt any thing against them with a prospect of success I determined to attack their Rear the moment they should get in motion from their present Ground. I communicated my intention to General Lee, and ordered him to make his disposition for the attack, and to keep his Troops constantly lying upon their Arms, to be in readiness at the shortest notice. This was done with respect to the Troops under my immediate command.

About five in the Morning General Dickinson sent an Express, informing, that the Front of the Enemy had began their march. I instantly put the Army in motion, and sent orders by one of my Aids to General Lee to move on and attack them, unless there should be very powerful Reasons to the contrary; acquainting him at the same time, that I was marching to support him, and for doing it with the greater expedition and convenience, should make the Men disencumber themselves of their packs and Blankets.

After marching about five Miles, to my great surprize and mortification, I met the whole advanced Corps retreating, and, as I was told, by General Lee's orders without having made any opposition, except one fire given by a party under the command of Colo. Butler, on their being charged by the Enemy's Cavalry, who were repulsed. I proceeded immediately to the Rear of the Corps, which I found closely pressed by the Enemy, and gave directions for forming part of the retreating troops, who by the brave and spirited conduct of the Officers, aided by some pieces of well served Artillery, checked the Enemy's advance, and gave time to make a disposition of the left Wing and second line of the Army upon an eminence, and in a wood a little in the Rear, covered by a morass in front. On this were placed some Batteries of Cannon by Lord Stirling, who commanded the left Wing, which played upon the Enemy with great effect, and seconded by parties of Infantry detached to oppose them, effectually put a stop to their advance.

General Lee being detatched with the advanced Corps, the command of the Right Wing, for the occasion, was given to General Greene. For the expedition of the march, and to counteract any attempt to turn our Right, I had ordered him to file off by the new Church two Miles from English Town, and fall into the Monmouth Road, a small distance in the Rear of the Court House, while the rest of the Column moved directly on towards the Court House. On intelligence of the Retreat, he marched up and took a very advantagious position on the Right.

The Enemy, by this time, finding themselves warmly opposed in front made an attempt to turn our left Flank; but they were bravely repulsed and driven back by detached parties of Infantry. They also made a movement to our Right, with as little success, General Greene having advanced a

Body of Troops with Artillery to a commanding peice of Ground, which not only disappointed their design of turning our Right, but severely enfiladed those in front of the left Wing. In addition to this, General Wayne advanced with a Body of Troops and kept up so severe and well directed a fire that the Enemy were soon compelled to retire behind the defile, where the first stand in the beginning of the Action had been made.

In this situation, the Enemy had both their Flanks secured by thick Woods and Morasses, while their front could only be approached thro 'a narrow pass. I resolved nevertheless to attack them, and for that purpose ordered General [Enoch] Poor with his own and the Carolina Brigade, to move round upon their Right, and General Woodford upon their left, and the Artillery to gall them in front: But the impediments in their way prevented their getting within reach before it was dark. They remained upon the Ground, they had been directed to occupy, during the Night, with intention to begin the attack early the next morning, and the Army continued lying upon their Arms in the Feild of Action, to be in readiness to support them. In the mean time the Enemy were employed in removing their wounded, and about 12 OClock at Night marched away in such silence, that tho 'General Poor lay extremely near them, they effected their Retreat without his Knowledge. They carried off all their wounded except four Officers and about Forty privates whose wounds were too dangerous to permit their removal.

The extreme heat of the Weather—the fatigue of the Men from their march thro 'a deep sandy Country almost entirely destitute of Water, and the distance the Enemy had gained by marching in the Night, made a pursuit impracticable and fruitless. It would have answered no valuable purpose, and would have been fatal to numbers of our Men, several of whom died the preceding day with Heat.

Were I to conclude my account of this days transactions without expressing my obligations to the Officers of the Army in general, I should do injustice to their merit, and violence to my own feelings. They seemed to vie with each other in manifesting their Zeal and Bravery. The Catalouge of those who distinguished themselves is too long to admit of particularizing individuals: I cannot however forbear mentioning Brigadier General Wayne whose good conduct and bravery thro 'the whole action deserves particular commendation.

The Behaviour of the troops in general, after they recovered from the first surprize occasioned by the Retreat of the advanced Corps, was such as could not be surpassed.

All the Artillery both Officers and Men that were engaged, distinguished themselves in a remarkable manner.

Inclosed Congress will be pleased to receive a Return of our killed, wounded and missing. Among the first were Lieut. Colo. Bunner of Penna and Major Dickinson of Virginia both Officers of distinguished merit and much to be regretted. The Enemy's slain left on the Feild and buried by us, according to the Return of the persons assigned to that duty were four Officers and Two hundred and forty five privates. In the former number was the Honble Colo. Monckton. Exclusive of these they buried some themselves, as there were several new Graves near the feild of Battle. How many Men they may have had wounded cannot be determined; but from the usual proportion the number must have been considerable. There were a few prisoners taken.

The peculiar Situation of General Lee at this time, requires that I should say nothing of his Conduct. He is now in arrest. The Charges against him, with such Sentence as the Court Martial may decree in his Case, shall be transmitted for the approbation or disapprobation of Congress as soon as it shall have passed. . .

Go: Washington[20]

JULY 11

TO ELIZABETH WATKINS

Whether Washington publicly wore the laurel wreath that he received from Elizabeth Watkins (d. 1846) of Paramus, New Jersey, has never been determined.

[Paramus, N.J.] Saturday July 11th 1778. Genl Washington presents his respectful compliments to Miss Watkins, and offers his grateful thanks for her curious present of a laurel wreath, which he shall wear, with great pleasure in remembrance of the fair giver.

The Genl was not honored with the receipt of Miss Watkinss favor till yesterday afternoon which will apologize for his delay in the acknowledgment.[21]

JULY 17

TO VICE ADMIRAL D'ESTAING

The arrival of a French fleet under Vice Admiral Charles-Hector d'Estaing off the coast of New Jersey seemed to presage the beginning of the end for Great Britain. Washington, already sensitive to the possibility of dissension among the new allies, treated the testy d'Estaing with exceptional delicacy.

Camp at Haverstraw Bay [N.Y.] July 17: 1778.

Sir

. . .

The arrival of a fleet, belonging to his most Christian majesty [King Louis XVI] on our coast, is an event that makes me truly happy; and permit me to observe, that the pleasure I feel on the occasion is greatly increased, by the command being placed in a Gentleman of such distinguished talents, experience and reputation as the Count D'Estaing. I am fully persuaded that every possible exertion will be made by you to accomplish the important purposes of your destination, and you may have the firmest reliance, that my most strenuous efforts shall accompany you in any measure, which may be found eligible.

I esteem myself highly honored by the desire you express, with a frankness which must always be pleasing, of possessing a place in my friendship; At the same time allow me to assure you, that I shall consider myself peculiarly happy, if I can but improve the prepossessions you are pleased to entertain in my favour, into a cordial and lasting amity. . . . With the most ardent desire for your Success and with the greatest respect & esteem I have the Honor to be Sir Yr Most Obedt & most Hble servt

Go: Washington[22]

––––––

AUGUST 4

TO MAJOR CALEB GIBBS

By August, with d'Estaing's fleet preparing for a coordinated attack with an American army under Major General John Sullivan on British-held Newport, Rhode Island, Washington and others were looking forward to the first steps in the ex-

pulsion of the British from North America. Washington had a few other potential benefits of victory in mind as well.

WHITE PLAINS, Aug. 4th, 1778.

Dear Gibbs:—

If your attempt upon Rhode Island should prove [fortunate], and I think there is scarce a possibility of its failure, unless a superior Fleet should compel Count d' Estaing to quit his station; you will have it much in your power to provide for the use of this family, many articles of which you know we stand in much need—as also some things which I should be glad to procure for my own use—among which I find myself in want of a genteel cutting sword.—I do not mean a true horseman's sword; and yet one fit for riding. Many things among the officer's baggage, if it should happen to fall into the hands of our troops, or should be sold by themselves, might be convenient for me; such as table and other camp equipage, properly assorted and contrived for stowage.

To be particular in the recital of my wants I cannot, not having time for recollection.—Your knowledge of them, reminded by what you may see, will prove more adequate than vague directions. Tea equippage, plates and dishes, bowls, basins, camp stools, are essentially necessary;—such of them as can be procured, of materials not liable to break, should be preferred.

The money necessary for the purchase of these things will be advanced by General Greene, upon showing him this letter. I most sincerely wish success to the enterprize, and much honor and reputation to yourself, being with great truth and sincerity Your affectionate,

GEO. WASHINGTON.[23]

———

AUGUST 28

TO MAJOR GENERAL WILLIAM HEATH

The failure of the Rhode Island expedition because of the French fleet's abrupt departure from the coast created such anger among the Americans that it threatened to derail the alliance before it had a chance to operate in any meaningful manner.

Washington looked beyond the immediate failure at Rhode Island—which, though disappointing, had no serious long-term consequences for the American cause—to the possibly disastrous implications of a breach with France. Washington did not believe d'Estaing's reasons for deserting Sullivan, but suggested that the American public should not be given any reason for questioning the Frenchman's conduct.

Head Quarters White plains 28th Augt 1778

Dear Sir

The unfortunate circumstance of the French Fleet having left Rhode Island at so critical a moment, I am apprehensive, if not very prudently managed, will have many injurious consequences, besides merely the loss of the advantages we should have reaped from succeeding in the Expedition. It will not only tend to discourage the people, and weaken their confidence in our new alliance, but may possibly produce prejudices and resentments, which may operate against giving the Fleet such Zealous and effectual assistance in its present distress, as the exigence of affairs and our true interest demand. It will certainly be sound policy to combat these effects, and whatever private opinions may be entertained, to give the most favorable construction, of what has happened, to the public, and at the same time to put the French Fleet, as soon as possible, in condition to defend itself and be useful to us.

The departure of the Fleet from Rhode Island is not yet publicly announced here, but when it is, I intend to ascribe it to necessity, from the damage suffered in the late storm. This, it appears to me, is the Idea which ought to be generally propagated. As I doubt not the force of these Reasons will strike you equally with myself, I would recommend to you to use your utmost influence to palliate and soften matters, and induce those, whose business it is to provide succours of every kind for the fleet, to employ their utmost zeal and activity in doing it. It is our duty to make the best of our misfortune, and not to suffer passion to interfere with our interest and the public good.

. . .

Go: Washington[24]

SEPTEMBER 1
TO MAJOR GENERAL NATHANAEL GREENE

Anti-French sentiment in New England became so strong that Lafayette feared he would be lynched. Washington asked Greene, who was on the spot in his native state of Rhode Island, to try to settle things down.

Head Quarters White plains 1st Sepr 1778

Dear Sir

 . . . I have not now time to take notice of the several arguments that were made use of, for and against the Counts quitting the Harbour of New-port and sailing for Boston. Right or wrong, it will probably disappoint our sanguine expectations of success, and what I esteem a still worse consequence, I fear it will sow the seeds of dissention and distrust between us and our new allies, except the most prudent measures are taken to suppress the feuds and jealousies that have already arisen. I depend much upon your temper and influence to conciliate that animosity which I plainly perceive, by a letter from the Marquis, subsists between the American Officers and the French in our service. This you may depend will extend itself to the Count and the officers and men of his whole Fleet, should they return to Rhode Island, except upon their arrival there, they find a reconciliation has taken place. The Marquis speaks kindly of a letter from you to him upon this subject. He will therefore take any advice coming from you, in a friendly light, and if he can be pacified, the other French Gentlemen will of course be satisfied as they look up to him as their Head. The Marquis grounds his complaint upon a general order of the 24 Augt the latter part of which is certainly very impolitic and upon the universal clamor that prevailed against the french Nation. I beg you will take every measure to keep the protest entered into by the General Officers, from being made public. The Congress, sensible of the ill consequences that will flow from the World's knowing of our differences, have passed a resolve to that purpose—Upon the whole, my dear Sir, you can conceive my meaning better than I can express it, and I therefore fully depend upon your exerting yourself to heal all private animosities between our principal Officers and the french, and to prevent all illiberal expressions and reflections that may fall from the Army at large . . .[25]

OCTOBER 12

TO REVEREND ALEXANDER MCWHORTER

In this letter, Washington asks a chaplain, the Reverend Alexander McWhorter, to extract information from two men convicted to death. They were executed on November 3.

Head Qrs Fredericksburg 12th Otbr 1778

Sir.

    There are now under sentance of death, in the provost, a Farnsworth and Blair, convicted of being spies from the enemy, and of publishing counterfeit Continental currency. It is hardly to be doubted but that these unfortunate men are acquainted with many facts respecting the enemys affairs, and their intentions which we have not been able to bring them to acknowlege. Besides the humanity of affording them the benefit of your profession, it may in the conduct of a man of sense answer another valuable purpose—And While it serves to prepare them for the other world, it will naturally lead to the intelligence we want in your inquiries into the condition of their spiritual concerns. You will therefore be pleased to take the charge of this matter upon yourself, and when you have collected in the course of your attendance such information as they can give you will transmit the whole to me. I am Sir &c.

G. W——n[26]

NOVEMBER 14

TO HENRY LAURENS

In the autumn of 1778, Congress became infatuated with a plan for joining forces with the French for an invasion of Canada. On November 11, Washington wrote to Congress and advanced a number of arguments against the planned invasion, most of them having to do with the difficulty of supplying a large army and sending it across hundreds of miles of wilderness against well-defended enemy positions. In this private letter to Henry Laurens written three days later, Washington suggests that his reasons for opposing the plan arose more from his suspicions of French motives.

Dear Sir

This will be accompanied by an Official Letter on the subject of the proposed Expedition against Canada—You will perceive I have only considered it in a Military light—indeed I was not authorized to consider it in any other, and I am not without apprehensions, that I may be thought in what I have done, to have exceeded the limits intended by Congress—But my sollicitude for the public welfare which I think deeply interested in this affair, will I hope justify me in the eyes of all those who view things through that just medium.

I do not know Sir what may be your Sentiments in the present case— but whatever they are, I am sure I can confide in your honor & friendship, and shall not hesitate to unbosom myself to you on a point of the most delicate and important nature. The question of the Canadian expedition in the form it now stands appears to me one of the most interesting that has hitherto agitated our national deliberations. I have one objection to it untouched in my public letter, which is in my estimation insurmountable—and alarms all my feelings for the true and permanent interests of my Country. This is the introduction of a large body of French Troops into Canada, and putting them in possession of the Capitol of that Province—attached to them by all the ties of blood, habits, manners, religion & former Connixion of Government. I fear this would be too great a temptation to be resisted by any power actuated by the common maxims of national policy.

Let us realize for a moment the striking advantages France would derive from the possession of Canada, the acquisition of an extensive territory abounding in supplies for the use of her Islands—the opening a vast source of the most beneficial commerce with the Indian Nations which she might then monopolise—she having ports of her own on the Continent independant on the precarious good will of an Ally—the engrossing the whole trade of Newfoundland whenever she pleased (the finest nursery of Seamen in the world)—the security afforded to her Islands—and finally of awing & controuling these States, the natural and most formidable rival of every Maratime power in Europe. Canada would be a solid acquisition to France on all these accts and because of the Numerous inhabitants, subjects to her by inclination, who would aid in preserving it under her power against the attempt of every other.

France acknowledged for some time past the most powerful Monarchy in Europe by land able now to dispute the empire of the Sea with Britain, and if joined with Spain, I may say certainly superior, in possession of Canada on our left, and the extensive territory anciently comprehended within its limits—while the other branch of the House of Bourbon possesses New Orleans—the Key of the Mississippi—on our right—seconded by the numerous tribes of Indians on our rear from one extremity to the other, a people so generally friendly to her, and whom she knows so well to conciliate—would it is much to be apprehended, have it in her power to give law to these States.

Let us suppose that, when the five thousand French Troops, (and under the idea of that number twice as many may be sent) were entered the City of Quebec, they should declare an intention to hold Canada as a pledge & security for the debt due to France from the United States—or under other specious pretences hold the place till they can find a bond for contention—and, in the Mean while, should excite the Canadians to engage in supporting their pretences & claims, what should we be able to say with only four or five thousand Men to carry on the dispute? It may be supposed that France would not choose to renounce our friendship by a step of this kind, as the consequence would probably be a reunion with England on some terms or other, and the loss of what she had acquired in so violent and unjustifiable a manner, with all the advantages of an alliance with us. This, in my opinion, is too slender a security against the Measure, to be relied on. The truth of the position will entirely depend on Naval Events—If France and Spain should unite, and obtain a decided superiority by Sea—a reunion with England would avail very little, and might be set at defiance—France with a numerous Army at command, might throw in what number of land forces she thought proper to support her pretensions, and England without Men, without Money, and inferior on her favourite element could give no effectual aid to oppose them, Resentment, reproaches, and submission seem to be all that would be left us. Men are very apt to run into extremes, hatred to England may carry some into an excess of confidence in France, especially, when motives of gratitude are thrown into the scale—Men of this description would be unwilling to suppose France capable of acting so ungenerous a part. I am heartily disposed to entertain the most favourable sentiments of our New Ally, and to cherish them in others, to a reasonable degree, but it is a maxim founded on the universal experience of Mankind, that no Nation is to be trusted farther than it is bound by its interest, And no prudent Statesman or politician will venture to depart from it. In our circumstances, we ought to be particularly cautious for we have not yet attained sufficient vigor and maturity to recover from the shock of any false step, into which we may unwarily fall.

If France should even engage in the scheme in the first instance with the purest intentions, there is the greatest danger that in the progress of the business, invited to it by circumstances perhaps urged on by the solicitations & wishes of the Canadians, she would alter her views. As the Marquis cloathed his proposition when he spoke of it to me, it would seem to originate wholly with himself, but it is far from impossible that it had its birth in the Cabinet of France, & was put into this artful dress, to give it the readier currency. I fancy, I read in the countenances of some people on this occasion, more than the disinterested zeal of Allies—I hope I am mistaken and my fears of mischief, make me refine too much and awaken jealousies that have no sufficient foundation.

But upon the whole, Sir, to waive every other consideration, I do not like to add to the number of National obligations—I would wish as much as possible, to avoid giving a foreign power new claims of merit for services performed to the United States, and would ask No assistance that is not indispensible. I am with the truest attachment, & most perfect Confidence, Dr Sir Yr Most Obed. & Obliged

Go: Washington[27]

DECEMBER 18–30
TO BENJAMIN HARRISON

By the winter of 1778–1779, the military situation had become reasonably static; but new dangers to American independence had appeared in the form of political indecisiveness and economic weakness. Never, as Washington declared in this letter, did the country stand more in need of talented, public-spirited men.

Head Qrs Middle Brook [N.J.] Decr 18th[–30th] 1778.
My dear Sir,

. . .

I can assign but two causes for the enemys continuance among us, and these balance so equally in my Mind, that I scarce know which of the two preponderates—The one is, that they are waiting the ultimate determination of Parliament—the other, that of our distresses; by which I know the Commissioners went home not a little buoyed up—and sorry I am to add, not without cause. What may be the effect of such large & frequent emissions—of the dissentions—Parties—extravigance—and a general lax of public virtue Heaven alone can tell! I am affraid even to think of It but it appears as clear to me as ever the Sun did in its meredian brightness, that America never Stood in more eminent need of the wise—patriotic—& spirited exertions of her Sons than at this period and if it is not a sufficient cause for genl lamentation, my misconception of the matter impresses it too strongly upon me, that the States seperately are too much engaged in their local concerns and have too many of their ablest men with-drawn from the general Council for the good of the common weal—in a word, I think our political system may, be compared to the mechanism of a Clock—and that our conduct should derive a lesson from it for it answers no good purpose to keep the smaller Wheels in order if the greater one which is the support & prime mover of the whole is neglected. How far the latter is the case does not become me to pronounce but as their can be no harm in a pious wish for the good of ones Country I shall offer it as mine that each State would not only choose, but absolutely compel their ablest Men to attend Congress—that they would instruct them to go into a thorough investigation of the causes that have produced so many disagreeable effects in the Army & Country—in a word that public abuses should be corrected—& an entire reformation worked without these it does not, in my Judgment, require the spirit of divination to foretell the consequences of the present Administration, nor to how little purpose the States, individually, are framing constitutions—providing laws—and filling Offices with the abilities of their ablest men. These, if the great whole is mismanaged must sink in the general wreck & will carry with it the remorse of thinking that we are lost by our own folly and negligence, or the desire perhaps of living in ease & tranquility during the expected accomplishment of so great a revolution in the effecting of which the greatest abilities & the honestest men our (i.e. the American) world affords ought to be employed. It is much to be feared my dear Sir that the States in their seperate capacities have very inadequate ideas of the present danger. removed (some of them) far distant from the scene of action & seeing, & hearing such publications only as flatter their wishes they conceive that the contest is at an end and that to regulate the government & police of their own State is all that remains to be done—but it is devoutly to be wished that a sad reverse of this may not fall upon them like a thunderclap that is little expected. I do not mean to designate particular States—I wish to cast no reflections upon any one—The Public believes (and if they do believe it, the fact might almost as well be so) that the States at this time are badly represented—and that the great & important concerns of the nation are horribly conducted for want either of abilities or application in the Members—or through discord & party views of some individuals. that they should be so, is to be lamented more at this time, than formerly, as we are far advanced in the dispute & in the opinn of many drawg to a happy period—have the eyes of Europe upon us—& I am perswaded many political Spies to watch—discover our situation—& give information of our weaknesses & wants. . . . adieu my dear Sir I am Sincerely & Affecly Yrs

Go: Washington
Phila[dephia] 30th

P.S. This Letter was to have gone by Post from Middle brook but missed that conveyance, since which I have come to this place at the request of Congress whence I shall soon return.

I have seen nothing since I came here (on the 22d Instant) to change my opinion of Men or measures but abundant reason to be convinced, that our Affairs are in a more distressed, ruinous—& deplorable condition than they have been in Since the commencement of the War—By a faithful labourer then in the cause. By a Man who is daily injuring his private Estate without even the smallest earthly advantage not common to all, in case of a favourable Issue to the dispute—By one who wishes the prosperity of America most devoutly and sees or thinks he sees it, on the brink of ruin, you are beseeched most earnestly my dear Colo. Harrison to exert yourself in endeavouring to rescue your Country by (let me add) sending your ablest & best Men to Congress—these characters must not slumber, nor sleep at home, in such times of pressing danger—they must not content themselves in the enjoyment of places of honor or profit in their own Country while the common interests of America are mouldering & sinking into irretrievable (if a remedy is not soon applied) ruin, in which theirs also must ultimately be involved. If I was to be called upon to draw A picture of the times—& of Men—from what I have Seen, heard, & in part know I should in one word say that idleness, dissipation & extravigance seems to have laid fast hold of most of them. That speculation— peculation—& an insatiable thirst for rishes seems to have got the better of every other consideration and almost of every order of Men. That party disputes & personal quarrels are the great business of the day whilst the momentous concerns of an empire—a great & accumulated debt—ruined finances—depreciated money—& want of credit (which in their consequences is the want of every thing) are but secondary considerations & postponed from day to day—from week to week as if our affairs wore the most promising aspect—after drawing this picture, which from my Soul I beleive to be a true one I need not repeat to you that I am alarmed and wish to see my Country men roused. I have no resentments, nor do I mean to point at any particular characters, this I can declare upon my honor for I have every attention paid me by Congress that I can possibly expect & have reason to think that I stand well in their estimation but in the present situation of things I cannot help asking—Where is Mason—Wythe—Jefferson—Nicholas—Pendleton—Nelson—& another I could name—& why, if you are sufficiently impressed with your danger, do you not (as New York has done in the case of Mr Jay) send an extra Member or two for at least a certain limited time till the great business of the Nation is put upon a more respectable & happy establishment. Your Money is now sinking 5 pr Ct a day in this City and I shall not be surprized if in the course of a few months a total stop is put to the currency of it. And yet an assembly—a Concert—a Dinner, or Supper (that will cost three or four hundred pounds) will not only take Men off from acting in but even from thinking of this business while a great part of the Officers of yr army from absolute necessity are quitting the Service and the more virtuous few rather than do this are sinking by sure degrees into beggery & want. I again repeat to you that this is not an exagerated acct—that it is an alarming one I do not deny, & confess to you that I feel more real distress on acct of the present appearances of things than I have done at any one time since the commencement of the dispute—but it is time to bid you, once more adieu. Providence has heretofore taken us up when all other means & hope seemed to be departing from us in this I will confide. Yrs &ca

G. W——n[28]

1779

MARCH 20

TO HENRY LAURENS

Continued talk—much of it coming from Washington's former aide John Laurens, son of the former president of Congress, Henry Laurens—of arming slaves and even of forming them into Continental regiments left Washington unimpressed, except with the dangers of giving arms to blacks.

Dear Sir

. . .

The policy of our arming Slaves is in my opinion a moot point, unless the enemy set the example, for should we begin to form Battalions of them I have not the smallest doubt (if the war is to be prosecuted) of their following in it, and justifying the measure upon our own ground. The upshot then must be who can Arm fastest—and where are our Arms? besides I am not clear that a descrimination will not render Slavery more irksome to those who remain in it—Most of the good and evil things of this life are judged of by comparison, and I fear comparison in this Case will be productive of Much discontent in those who are held in servitude—but as this is a subject that has never employed much of my thoughts, these are no more than the first crude Ideas that have struck me upon the occasion.

. . .

Go: Washington[1]

Nathanael Greene;
portrait by Charles Willson Peale (1793)

Henry Knox;
portrait by Charles Willson Peale (c.1794)

Henry Lee, Jr.;
portrait by William Edward West (c.1838)

Alexander Hamilton;
portrait by John Trumbull (1792)

George Washington crossing the Delaware River, December 1776;
painting by Emanual Leutze (1851)

attention also to such things as you shall con
ceive fit subjects for Communication on that
occasion, and noting them as they occur
that you would be so good as to furnish me
with them in time to be prepared, and engraf
ted with others for the opening of the Session. —
With very sincere and
Affectionate regard
I am . ever Yours
G.ᵗ Washington

James Madison Junᵗ Esq

Sample of Washington's handwriting

Lafayette;
portrait by Charles Willson Peale (1780)

Benedict Arnold,
engraving after John Trumbull (1879)

New York Fire of September 1776;
by Franz Xaver Habermann (c. 1778, DLC)

Joseph Reed, Washington's aide and
President of Pennsylvania (DLC)

Rochambeau reviews his troops, satirical British print (1780, DLC)

John Hancock;
portrait by John Singleton Copley (1765)

Steuben;
engraving (1857)

Washington and Lafayette at Valley Forge, 1778; lithograph (1843, DLC)

Surrender of Cornwallis at Yorktown, October 1781;
painting by John Trumbull (1820)

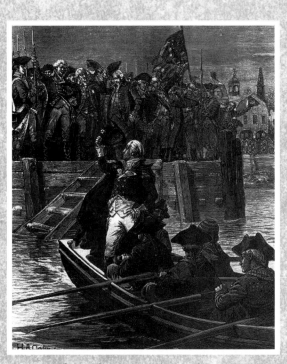

Washington leaves New York, December 4, 1783;
Harper's Weekly *engraving (1883)*

Washington resigns his commission, 1783;
painting by John Trumbull (1824)

expectations & prospects—for this purpose an intimacy with some well informed Refugee may be political & advantageous. highly so will it be, to contract an acquaintance with a person in the Naval department, who may either be engaged in the business of providing Transports for the imbarkation of Troops, or in victualling of them. Many other things will occur upon reflection with out an inumeration of them; I shall therefore only add my wishes that the whole may be placed on such a footing as to answer the end most effectually, & that I am Sir Yr Very Hble Servt

Go: Washington

P.S. I wish, merely for curiosity, and that I may be prepared with sufficient knowledge for any future favourable contingency, to know the depth of Water through Hell gate? the largest Ship of War that has ever passed it? & the largest that can pass it?

G. W——n[2]

MAY 12

MESSAGE TO THE DELAWARE NATION

Washington's role as diplomat extended not just to the French, but also to Native Americans, who frequently sent delegations to his camp.

Head Qrs Middle Brook May the 12: 1779

To the Chief Men, Deputies from the Delaware Nation—

Brothers—

I am happy to see you here. I am glad the long Journey you have made, has done you no harm; and that you are in good health. I am glad also you left All our friends of the Delaware Nation well.

Brothers—

I have read your paper. The things you have said are weighty things, and I have considered them well. The Delaware Nation have shewn their good will to the United States. They have done wisely and I hope they will never repent. I rejoice in the new assurances you give of their friendship. The things you now offer to do to brighten the chain, prove your sincerity.

I am sure congress will run to meet you—and will do every thing in their power to make the friendship between the people of those States—and their Brethren of the Delaware nation, last for ever.

Brothers—

I am a Warrior. My words are few and plain; but I will make good what I say. 'Tis my business to destroy all the Enemies of these States and to protect their friends. You have seen how we have withstood the English for four years; and how their great Armies have dwindled away and come to very little; and how what remains of them in this part of our great Country, are glad to stay upon two or three little Islands—where the Waters and their Ships hinder us from going to destroy them. The English, Brothers, are a boasting people—They talk of doing a great deal; but they do very little. They fly away on their Ships from one part of our Country to another; but as soon as our Warriors get together they leave it and go to some other part. They took Boston & philadelphia—two of our greatest Towns; but when they saw our Warriors in a great body ready to fall upon them—they were forced to leave them.

Brothers.

We have till lately fought the English all alone. Now the Great King of France is become our Good Brother and Ally. He has taken up the Hatchet with us, and we have sworn never to bury it, till we have punished the English and made them sorry for All the wicked things they had in their Hearts to do against these States. And there are other Great Kings and Nations on the other side of the big Waters, who love us and wish us well—and will not suffer the English to hurt us.

Brothers.

Listen well to what I tell you and let it sink deep into your Hearts. We love our Friends—and will be faithful to them—as long as they will be faithful to us. We are sure our Good brothers the Delawares will alaways be so. But we have sworn to take vengeance on our Enemies—and on false friends. The other day, a handful of our young men destroyed the settlement of the Onondagas. They burnt down all their Houses—destroyed their grain and Horses and Cattle—took their Arms away—killed several of their Warriors and brought off many prisoners and obliged the rest to fly into the woods. This is but the beginning of the troubles which those Nations, who have taken up the Hatchet against us, will feel.

Brothers.

I am sorry to hear that you have suffered for want of Necessaries—or that any of our people have not dealt justly by you. But as you are going to Congress, which is the great Council of the Nation and hold all things in their hands, I shall say nothing about the supplies you ask. I hope you will receive satisfaction from them. I assure you—I will do every thing in my power to prevent your receiving any further injuries and will give the strictest orders for this purpose. I will severely punish any that shall break them.

Brothers.

I am glad you have brought three of the Children of your principal Chiefs to be educated with us. I am sure Congress will open the Arms of love to them—and will look upon them as their own Children and will have them educated accordingly. This is a great mark of your confidence and of your desire to preserve the friendship between the Two Nations to the end of time—and to become One people with your Brethren of the United States. My ears hear with pleasure the other matters you mention. Congress will be glad to hear them too. You do well to wish to learn our arts and ways of life and above all—the religion of Jesus Christ. These will make you a greater and happier people than you are. Congress will do every thing they can to assist you in this wise intention; and to tie the knot of friendship and union so fast—that nothing shall ever be able to loose it.

Brothers—

There are some matters about which I do not open my Lips, because they belong to Congress, and not to us warriors—You are going to them— they will tell you all you wish to know.

Brothers.

When you have seen all you want to see, I will then wish you a good Journey to Philadelphia. I hope you may find there every thing your hearts can wish, that when you return home you may be able to tell your Nation good things of us—And I pray god he may make your Nation wise and Strong, that they may always see their own true interest and have courage to walk in the right path; and that they never may be deceived by lies to do any thing against the people of these States, who are their Brothers and ought always to be one people with them.

Go: Washington
Commander in chief
of all the armies in the
United States of America[3]

MAY 28

TO NICHOLAS ROGERS

Nicholas Rogers (1753–1822), a prominent Baltimore merchant who dabbled in painting, prepared several portraits of George and Martha Washington during the war, including a ring-sized depiction of Martha in Elizabethan ruff and hood. Washington, who did not enjoy posing, nevertheless expressed his appreciation of the artist's efforts.

Head Qrs Middlebrook May 28th 1779.

Dear Sir,

A few days ago I was honored with your polite and obliging favor of the 6th Instt accompanied by a miniature picture of Mrs Washington—I wish it was in my power to express as forcably as I feel, the lively sense I have of the repeated instances of your polite attention to her and myself—such tribute as unfeigned thanks afford, is presented to you with much sincerity; & if I knew how to make a more acceptable offering it should not be wanting.

Difficult as it is to strike a likeness on so small a scale, it is the opinion of many that you have not failed in the present attempt. The dress is not less pleasing for being a copy of antiquity, it would be happy for us, if in these days of depravity the imitation of our ancestors were more extensively adopted—their virtues wd not hurt us.

Mrs Washington joins me in a tender of best wishes for you and with much esteem & regard—I am Dr Sir Yr most obedt & obliged Hble Servt

Go: Washington[4]

MAY 31

TO MAJOR GENERAL JOHN SULLIVAN

Continuing Indian depredations on the frontier convinced Washington that the time had come to put an end to them once and for all, and by any means—however ruthless.

[Middle Brook]

Sir,

The expedition you are appointed to command is to be directed against the hostile tribes of the six nations of Indians, with their associates and adherents. The immediate objects are the total destruction and devastation of their settlements and the capture of as many prisoners of every age and sex as possible.

. . .

I would recommend that Some post in the center of the Indian Country should be occupied with all expedition with a sufficient quantity of provision—whence parties should be detached to lay waste all the settlements around, with instructions to do it in the most effectual manner that the country may not be merely *overrun* but *destroyed.*

I beg leave to suggest as general rules that ought to govern your operations—to make rather than receive attacks, attended with as much impetuosity, shouting and noise as possible, and to make the troops act in as loose and dispersed a way as is consistent with a proper degree of government concert and mutual support—It should be previously impressed upon the minds of the men, wherever they have an opportunity, to rush on with the war hoop and fixed bayonet—Nothing will disconcert and terrify the indians more than this.

I need not urge the necessity of using every method in your power to gain intelligence of the enemy's strength motions and designs; nor need I suggest the extraordinary degree of vigilance and caution which will be necessary to guard against surprises from an adversary so secret desultory and rapid as the Indians.

If a detachment operates on the Mohock River the Commanding officer should be instructed to be very watchful that no troops come from Oswegatchie and Niagara to Oswego without his knowlege; and for this purpose he should keep trusty spies at those three places to advertise him instantly of the movement of any party and its force. This detachment should also endeavour to keep up a constant intercourse with the main body.

More than common care will be necessary of your arms and ammunition from the nature of the service—They should be particularly inspected after a rain or the passage of any deep water.

After you have very thoroughly completed the destruction of their

Settlements; if the indians should show a disposition for peace, I would have you to encourage it, on condition that they will give some decisive evidence of their sincerity by delivering up some of the principal instigations of their past hostility into our hands—[John] Butler, [Joseph] Brandt, the most mischievous of the tories that have joined them or any other they may have in their power that we are interested to get into ours—They may possibly be engaged, by address, secrecy and strategam, to surprise the garrison of Niagara and the shipping on the lakes and put them into our possession. This may be demanded as a condition of our friendship and would be a most important point gained—If they can render a service of this kind you may stipulate to assist them in their distress with supplies of provisions and other articles of which they will stand in need, having regard in the expectations you give them to our real abilities to perform. I have no power, at present to authorise you to conclude a treaty of peace with them but you may agree upon the terms of one, letting them know that it must be finally ratified by Congress and giving them every proper assurance that it will. I shall write to Congress on the subject and endeavour to obtain more ample and definitive authority.

But You will not by any means, listen to any overture of peace before the total ruin of their settlements is effected—It is likely enough their fears if they are unable to oppose us, will compel them to offers of peace, or policy may lead them to endeavour to amuse us in this way to gain time and succour for more effectual opposition. Our future security will be in their inability to injure us the distance to which they are driven—and in the terror with which the severity of the chastisement they receive will inspire them. Peace without this would be fallacious, and temporary—New presents and an addition of force from the enemy, would engage them to break it the first fair opportunity and all the expence of our extensive preparations would be lost.

When we have effectually chastised them we may then listen to peace and endeavour to draw further advantages from their fears. But even in this case great caution will be necessary to guard against the snares which their treachery may hold out—They must be explicit in their promises give substantial pledges for their performance and execute their engagements with decision and dispatch. Hostages are the only kind of security to be depended on.

. . .

When you have completed the objects of your expedition, unless otherwise directed in the mean time, you will return to form a junction with the main army by the most convenient expeditious & secure route according to circumstances—The Mohock River, if it can be done without too great risk, will perhaps be most elegible on several accounts—Much should depend on the relative position of the main army at the time . . . Relying perfectly upon your Judgment, prudence and activity, I have the highest expectation of success, equal to our Wishes; and I beg leave to assure you, that I anticipate with great pleasure, the honor which will redound to yourself and the advantage to the common cause, form a happy Termination of this important enterprise. . .

G. Washington[5]

JULY 10

TO BRIGADIER GENERAL ANTHONY WAYNE

Late in 1778, a British expedition dispatched by General Henry Clinton captured Savannah, Georgia, heralding the beginning of an all-out campaign to conquer the southern states. In the north, Clinton held on to New York but did not attempt to challenge the main American army. Washington was never the one to stand pat, however, and he searched carefully for British posts vulnerable to attack. He found one at Stony Point, New York, where a sizable British garrison lay out of reach of immediate support. Washington's instructions to the leader of the attacking force, Brigadier General Anthony Wayne, left nothing to chance. Wayne attacked on July 16 and was brilliantly successful, capturing 472 British prisoners.

New Windsor [N.Y.] 10th July 1779

Dr Sir,

. . .

My ideas of the enterprise in contemplation are these.

That it should be attempted by the light Infantry only, which should march under cover of night and with the utmost secrecy to the enemys lines, securing every person they find to prevent discovery.

Between one and two hundred chosen men and officers I conceive fully sufficient for the surprise, and apprehend the approach should be along the water on the south side crossing the Beach & entering at the abbatis.

This party is to be preceded by a van guard of prudent and determined men, well commanded who are to remove obstructions—secure the Sentries & drive in the guard—They are to advance (the whole of them) with fixed Bayonets and muskets unloaded. The officers commanding them are to know precisely what batteries or particular parts of the line they are respectively to possess that confusion and the consequences of indecision may be avoided.

These parties should be followed by the main body at a small distance for the purpose of support and making good the advantages which may be gained—or to bring them off in case of repulse & disappointment. other parties may advance to the works (but not so as to be discovered till the conflict is begun) by the way of the causay & River on the north if practicable as well for the purpose of distracting the enemy in their defence as to cut off their retreat. These parties may be small unless the access and approaches should be very easy and safe.

The three approaches here mentioned should be well reconnoitered before hand & by persons of observation. single men in the night will be more likely to ascertain facts than the best glasses in the day.

A white feather or cockade or some other visible badge of distinction for the night should be worn by our troops, and a watch word agreed on to distinguish friends from foes.

If success should attend the enterprise, measures should be instantly taken to prevent if practicable the retreat of the garrison by water or to annoy them as much as possible if they attempt it—and the guns should be immediately turned against the shipping & Verplanks point and covered if possible from the enemy's fire.

Secrecy is so much more essential to these kind of enterprises than numbers, that I should not think it adviseable to employ any other than the light troops—If a surprise takes place they are fully competent to the business—if it does not numbers will avail little.

As it is in the power of a single deserter to betray the design—defeat the project—& involve the party in difficulies & danger, too much caution cannot be used to conceal the intended enterprise to the latest hour from all but the principal officers of your Corps and from the men till the moment of execution—Knowledge of your intention, ten minutes previously obtained, blasts all your hopes; for which reason a small detachment composed of men whose fidelity you can rely on under the care of a judicious officer should guard every avenue through the marsh to the enemy's works by which our deserters or their spies can pass, and prevent all intercourse.

The usual time for exploits of this kind is a little before day for which reason a vigilant officer is then more on the watch, I therefore recommend a midnight hour.

I had in view to attempt Verplanks point at the same instant that your operations should commence at stoney point, but the uncertainty of co-operating, in point of time and the hazard thereby run of defeating the attempt on stoney point, which is infinitely most important—the other being dependent—has induced me to suspend that operation.

These are my general ideas of the plan for a surprise, but you are at liberty to depart from them in every instance where you think they may be improved or changed for the better. A dark night and even a rainy one if you can find the way will contribute to your success—The officers in these night marches should be extremely attentive to keep their men together as well for the purpose of guarding against desertion to the enemy as to prevent skulking.

As it is a part of the plan, if the surprise should succeed to make use of the enemy's cannon against their shipping & their post on the other side, it will be well to have a small detachment of Artillery with you to serve them—I have sent an order to the Park for this purpose and to cover the design have ordered down, a couple of light field pieces—When you march you can leave the pieces behind.

So soon as you have fixed your plan and the time of execution I shall be obliged to you to give me notice. . .

Go: Washington[6]

JULY 29
TO JOSEPH REED

A series of articles by the disgraced former general Charles Lee, critical of Washington's military leadership, was the occasion of this candid letter on the burdens and duties of command. Reed, once Washington's aide, had by now become president of Pennsylvania's supreme executive council.

West-point [N.Y.] July 29th 1779

Dear Sir,

. . .

If I had ever assumed the character of a military genius and the Officer of experience—If under these false colours I had sollicited the command I was honoured with—or if, after my appointment, I had presumptuously driven on under the sole guidance of my own judgment & self-will—& misfortunes the result of obstinacy & misconduct—not of necessity—had followed, I should have thought myself a proper object for the lash, not only of his, but the pen of every other writer; and a fit subject of public resentment. But when it is well known that the command, in a manner, was forced upon me—That I accepted it with the utmost diffidence, from a consciousness that it required greater abilities, and more experience than I possessed, to conduct a great military machine embarrassed as I knew ours must be, by a variety of complex circumstances, and as it were but little better than a mere Chaos. and when nothing more was promised on my part than has been most inviolably performed, it is rather grating to pass over in silence charges, which may impress the uninformed, the others know that these charges have neither reason nor truth to support them, and that a Simple narrative of facts would defeat all his assertions notwithstanding they are made with an effrontery which few men do, and for the honor of human nature none ought, to possess.

If this gentleman is envious of my station, and conceives that I stand in his way to preferment; I can assure him, in most solemn terms, that the first wish of my Soul is to return to that peaceful retirement, and domestick ease and happiness from whence I came—To this end all my labours have been directed; and for this purpose have I been more than four years a perfect Slave; endeavouring under as many embarrassing circumstances as ever fell to one Mans lott to encounter and as pure motives as ever man was influenced by, to promote the cause, & service I had embarked in. . .

Go: Washington[7]

AUGUST 16

TO JOHN COCHRAN

Although he dined humbly by the standards of the day, Washington knew how to entertain guests at headquarters, especially ladies.

West-point Augt 16th 79

Dr Doctr,

I have asked Mrs Cockran & Mrs Livingston to dine with me to morrow; but ought I not to apprize them of their fare? As I hate deception, even where the imagination only is concerned—I will.

It is needless to premise that my table is large enough to hold the ladies—of this they had occular proof yesterday—To say how it is usually covered is rather more essential, & this, shall be the purport of my Letter.

Since our arrival at this happy spot, we have had a Ham (sometimes a shoulder) of Bacon, to grace the head of the table—a piece of roast Beef adorns the foot—and, a small dish of Greens or Beans (almost imperceptable) decorates the center. When the Cook has a mind to cut a figure (and this I presume he will attempt to do to morrow) we have two Beef-stake Pyes, or dishes of Crabs in addition, one on each side the center dish, dividing the space, & reducing the distance between dish & dish to about Six feet, which without them, would be near twelve a part—Of late, he has had the surprizing luck to discover, that apples will make pyes; and its a question if, amidst the violence of his efforts, we do not get one of apples instead of having both of Beef.

If the ladies can put up with such entertainment, and will submit to partake of it on plates—once tin but now Iron—(not become so by the labor of scowering) I shall be happy to see them. I am Dr Doctor Yr Most Obedt Sert

Go: Washington[8]

AUGUST 21

TO MAJOR GENERAL STIRLING

Another surprise attack on an isolated British garrison, this time by Major Henry Lee Jr., against Paulus Hook, New Jersey, on August 19, netted 158 British prisoners.

August 21st 1779

My Lord.

I have been duly favored with your letter of the 19th written at 9 O'clock A.M. and that of the same date of one O'clock P.M. containing the agreeable information of Major Lees having succeeded against Powles Hook. I join my congratulations with your Lordships on this occasion and thank you for the effectual assistance afforded Major Lee in completing the enterprise. The increase of confidence which the army will derive from this affair and that of Stoney point, I flatter myself tho great will be among the least of the advantages resulting from these events.

As the enemy must feel himself disgraced by these losses he may endeavor to lessen it by a retaliation in kind. It is natural to expect his attempts on such parts of the army as lye most exposed. This sentiment I make no doubt has occurred to your Lordship, and will of course proportion your vigilance to the nature of your situation, and the danger which may be apprehended. . . . Your Lordship will be pleased to give my thanks to the officers and troops concerned in the capture of the garrison at Powles Hook for their good conduct and gallant behaviour on the occasion. The commissary of prisoners is directed to attend to receive the British prisoners. . .

G. Washington[9]

SEPTEMBER 12

TO MAJOR GENERAL LAFAYETTE

Major General John Sullivan successfully cleared the Iroquois Indians from the Mohawk River Valley during the summer and early autumn of 1779; but although his merciless destruction of native settlements caused severe hardships, it did not prevent further frontier raids as Washington had intended. Thirsty for revenge, the Iroquois would return in 1780 and beyond.

West Point Septr 12th 1779

My Dear Marquis,

. . .

Most sincerely my dear Marquis do I congratulate you on the great & glorious exploits of Count D'Estaing in the West Indies—the bright prospect of European affairs—& our little successes in America the last of which though small on the great scale will nevertheless weigh in the ballance by our little successes I mean the storming of Stony point & surprize of Paules hook (within Cannon shott of the City of New York) and capture of the Garrisons—the first amounting to Six hundred Men—the other to two hundred. driving the enemy out of South Carolina & defeat of the Indians which last event I have within these few days received an Account of from General Sullivan who is now in the heart of their Country with 4000 Men and informs me that on the 29th Ultimo he advanced to their Intrenchments at a place called Newtown, where the Warriors of Seven Nation's some regulars—& Tories commanded by the two Butlars—Brandt—& a Captn McDonald had been assembled eight days to oppose him. the position was well chosen and their dispositon well made but on finding themselves hard pushed in front and their left flank in danger of being turned they fled in great confusion & disorder, & with much precipitation leaving their packs, Camp kettles, Trinkets, & many arms on the ground & eleven Warriors which they could not get off dead. The prisoners of which a few were taken, say that their slain & wounded were carried off during the action on horses & in Canoes—our loss was trifling—in the whole to the date of his Letter under a hundred killed & wounded although he had advanced to & destroyed 14 Towns large & most flourishing Crops of Corn, pulse &ca. He was proceeding in his plan of chastisement & will convince them it is to be hoped of two things—first, that their cruelties are not to pass with impunity—& secondly that they have been instigated to arms, & acts of Barbarizm by a Nation which is unable to protect them & of consequence has left them to that correction which is due to their villainy.

. . .

G. Washington[10]

SEPTEMBER 24

TO MAJOR BENJAMIN TALLMADGE

As the war progressed, Washington became increasingly savvy with secret methods of communication.

Head Quarters West-point 24th Sepr 1779.

Sir

. . .

It is not my opinion that Culper Junr should be advised to give up his present employment. I would imagine that with a little industry he will be able to carry on his intelligence with greater security to himself, and greater advantages to us—under cover of his usual business, than if he were to dedicate himself wholly to the giving of information. It may afford him opportunities of collecting intelligence, that he could not derive so well in any other manner. It presents also those suspicians which would become natural should he throw himself out of the line of his present employment. He may rest assured of every proper attention being paid to his services.

One thing appears to me deserving of his particular consideration; as it will not only render his communication less exposed to detection, but relieve the fears of such persons as may be entrusted with its conveyance to the second link in the chain—and of course very much facilitate the subject we have in view. I mean that he should occasionally write his information on the blank leaves of a pamphlet—on the first second &c. pages of a common pocket book—on the blank leaves at each end of registers for the year—almanacks, or any new publication—or book of small value. He should be determined in the choice of these books, principally by the goodness of the blank paper as the ink is not easily legible unless it is on paper of a good quality. Having settled a plan of this kind with his friend, he may forward them without risque of search, or the scrutiny of the enemy—as this is chiefly directed against paper made up in the form of letters.

I would add a further hint on this subject. Even letters may be made more subservient to his communications, than has been yet practiced. He may write a familiar letter on domestic affairs, or on some little matters of business to his friend at Satuket or elsewhere, interlining with the stain his secret intelligence, or writing it on the opposite blank side of the letter. But that his friend may know how to distinguish these from letters addressed solely to himself—he may always leave such as contain secret information without a date or place (dating it with the stain); or fold them up in particular manner, which may be concerted between the parties. This last appears to be the best mark of the two, and may be the signal for their being designed for me.

The first mentioned mode however, or that of the books, appears to me the one least liable to detection. . .

Go: Washington[11]

SEPTEMBER 30

TO MAJOR GENERAL LAFAYETTE

The extent of the friendship that had formed between Washington and Lafayette appears in this letter, along with the commander in chief's sense of humor. Thier friendship was not so deep, however, as to convince Washington to agree to visit France after the war. Nor did Washington, even in private correspondence with his closest friend, admit any parallel between British raids on civilian property in New England and American destruction of Indian villages in the Mohawk Valley.

West Point Septr 30th 1779.

My Dear Marquis,

. . .

It gave me infinite pleasure to hear from your self of the favourable reception you met with from your Sovereign, & of the joy which your safe arrival in France had diffused among your friends—I had no doubt but that this wou'd be the case—to hear it from yourself adds pleasure to the account. & here My dear friend let me congratulate you on your new, honourable & pleasing appointment in the Army commanded by the Count de Vaux which I shall accompany with an assurance that none can do it with more warmth of Affection, or sincere joy than my self. Your forward Zeal in the cause of liberty—Your singular attachment to this infant World—Your ardent & persevering efforts, not only in America but since your return to France to serve the United States. your polite attention to

Americans—and your strict & uniform friendship for *me,* has ripened the first impressions of esteem & attachment which I imbibed for you into such perfect love & gratitude that neither time nor absence can impair which will warrant my assuring you, that whether in the character of an Officer at the head of a Corps of gallant French (if circumstances should require this)—whether as a Major General commanding a division of the American Army—Or whether, after our Swords & Spears have given place to the plough share & pruning hook, I see you as a private Gentleman—a friend & Companion—I shall welcome you in all the warmth of friendship to Columbias shore; & in the latter case, to my rural Cottage, where homely fare & a cordial reception shall be substituted for delicacies & costly living. this from past experience I know *you* can submit to—& if the lovely partner of your happiness will consent to participate with *us* in such rural entertainment & amusements I can undertake in behalf of Mrs Washington that she will do every thing in her power to Make Virginia agreeable to the Marchioness—My inclination & endeavours to do this can not be doubted when I assure you that I love every body that is dear to you. consequently participate in the pleasure you feel in the prospect of again becoming a parent & do most Sincerely congratulate you and your Lady on this fresh pledge she is about to give you of her love.

. . .

You are pleased My dear Marquis to express an earnest desire of seeing me in France (after the establishment of our independancy) & do me the honour to add, that you are not singular in your request. let me entreat you to be perswaded, that to meet you any where after the final accomplishment of so glorious an event would contribute to my happiness—& that, to visit a country to whose generous aid we stand so much indebted, would be an additional pleasure—but remember my good friend, that I am unacquainted with your language. that I am too far advanced in years to acquire a knowledge of it. and that to converse through the medium of an interpreter upon common occasions, especially with the *Ladies* must appear so extremely aukward—insipid—& uncouth—that I can scarce bear it in idea. I will therefore hold myself disengaged for the *present* and when I see you in Virginia—we will talk of this matter & fix our Plans.

. . .

The Operations of the enemy this campaign have been confined to the establishment of works of defence. taking a post at Kings ferry—& burning the defenceless towns of New haven—Fairfield—Norwalk, &ca on the sound within reach of their shipping where little else was, or could be opposed to them than the cries of distressed Women and helpless children— but these were offered in vain—since these notable exploits they have never stepped out of their Works or beyond their lines—How a conduct of this kind is to effect the conquest of America the wisdom of a North—a Germaine—or Sandwich best can tell. it is too deep & refined for the comprehension of common understandings & general run of politicians.

. . .

By my last advices from General Sullivan of the 9th Instant I am led to conclude that 'ere this he has completed the entire destruction of the whole Country of the Six Nations, excepting so much of it as is inhabited by the Oneidas who have always lived in amity with us; and a few towns belonging to the Cayugas and Onondago's who were disposed to be friendly—At the time these advices came away he had penentrated to the heart of their settlements after having defeated in a general engagement the united force of Indians—Tories—and regulars from Niagara—Burnt between 15 & 20 Towns—destroyed their Crops & every thing that was to be found—He was then advancing to the exterior Towns with a view to complete the desolation of the whole Country, & Remove the cruel inhabitants of it to a greater distance, who were then fleeing in the utmost confusion, consternation and distress towards Niagara, distant 100 Miles through an uninhabited wilderness—experiencing a little of that distress, but nothing of those cruelties which they have exercised on our unhappy frontier Settlers, who (Men, Women & Children) have been deliberately Murdered, in a Manner shocking to humanity.

But to conclude—you requested from me a long letter—I have given you one—but methinks my Dear Marquis, I hear you say there is reason in all things—that this is too long—I am clearly in Sentiment with you, & will have Mercy on you in my next—But at present must pray your patience a while longer, till I can make a tender of my most respectful compliments to the Marchioness. Tell her (if you have not made a Mistake, & offered your *own love* instead of *hers* to me) that I have a heart susceptable of the tenderest passion, & that it is already so strongly impressed with the most favourable ideas of her, that she must be cautious of putting loves torch to it; as you must be in fanning the flame. But here again methinks I hear you say, I am not apprehensive of danger—My wife is young—you are growing old & the atlantic is between you—All this is true, but know my good friend that no distance can keep *anxious* lovers long asunder, and that the Wonders of former ages may be revived in this—But alas! will you not remark that amidst all the wonders recorded in holy writ no instance can be produced where a young Woman from *real inclination* has prefered an old Man—This is so much against me, that I shall not be able *I fear* to contest the prize with you—yet, under the encouragement you have given me I shall enter the list for so inestimable a jewell.

I will now reverse the scene, & inform you, that Mrs Washington (who set out for Virginia when we took the field in June) often has in her letters to me, enquired if I had heard from you, and will be much pleased at hearing that you are well, & happy. In her name (as she is not here) I thank you for your polite attention to her—and shall speak her sense of the honor confered on her by the Marchioness.

When I look back to the length of this letter I am so much astonished & frightned at it my self, that I have not the courage to give it a careful reading for the purpose of correction—You must therefore receive it with all its imperfections—accompanied with this assurance that though there may be many incorrections in the letter, there is not a single defect in the friendship of my dear Marquis Yr Most Obedt—& Affecte Servt

Go: Washington[12]

————

DECEMBER 16
CIRCULAR TO THE STATES

The winter of 1779–1780 was one of the coldest in recorded history, with snowdrifts at the American encampments around Morristown nine to ten feet deep. Unfortunately, the brutal weather coincided with yet another failure of the Continental Army's supply network, along with rampant inflation that reduced the value of the Continental currency to almost nothing. As at Valley Forge, Washington appealed to the state and local authorities, along with humble farmers, to help keep his soldiers alive; but the poor grain harvest of 1779 severely limited their resources. The crisis would continue well into the spring of 1780, provoking mutinies and once again bringing Washington's army to the brink of dissolution.

Head Quarters Morristown 16th Decemr 1779.

Sir

The situation of the Army with respect to supplies is beyond description alarming, it has been five or six Weeks past on half allowance, and
we have not three days Bread or a third allowance on hand nor any where
within reach. When this is exhausted we must depend on the precarious gleanings of the neighbouring country. Our Magazines are absolutely
empty every where and our Commissaries intirely destitute of money or
credit to replenish them. We have never experienced a like extremity at
any period of the War. We have often felt temporary want from acciden-
tal delays in forwarding supplies, but we always had something in our
Magazines and the means of procuring more. Neither one nor the other
is at present the case. This representation is the result of a minute examination of our resources. Unless some extraordinary exertions be made by
the States from which we draw our supplies there is every appearance
that the Army will infallibly disband in a fortnight. I think it my duty to
lay this candid view of our situation before your Excellency, and to intreat
the vigorous interposition of the State to rescue us from the danger of an
event, which if it did not prove the total ruin of our affairs, would at least
give them a shock from which they would not easily recover, and plunge
us into a train of new and still more perplexing embarrassments than any
we have hitherto felt. . .

Go: Washington[13]

1780

JANUARY 22
TO MAJOR GENERAL NATHANAEL GREENE

Washington was willing to, and often did, share his soldiers' hardships; but there were limits to the inconveniences he would accept in his winter lodgings in the Jacob Ford mansion in Morristown, N.J.

Head Qrs Jany 22d 1780

Dear Sir,

Appearances & facts must speak for themselves—to these I appeal—I have been at my present quarters since the first day of Decr & have not a Kitchen to cook a dinner in, altho 'the Logs have been put together some considerable time by my own Guard—nor is there a place at this moment in which a servant can lodge, with the smallest degree of comfort. Eighteen belonging to my family, & all Mrs [Jacob] Fords are crouded together in her Kitchen, & hardly one of them able to speak for the colds they have caught.

I have repeatedly taken notice of this inconveniency to Majr Gibbs, & have as often been told that boards were not to be had. I acquiesced—and believe you will do me the justice to acknowledge, that it never has been my practice to involve the public in any expence I could possibly avoid, or derive benefits which would be inconvenient, or prejudicial to others—To share a common lot—& participate the inconveniences which the army (from the peculiarity of our circumstances are obliged to undergo) has, with me, been a fundamental principle; and while I conceived this to be the case—universally—I was perfectly content—That it is not so, I appeal to your own observation; tho 'I never intended to make the remark, nor should I have done it, but for the question which involuntarily drew from me the answer, which has been the subject of your Letter.

Equally opposed is it to my wishes & expectation, that you should be troubled in matter respecting my accomodation, further than to give the necessary orders, & furnish materials; without which, orders are nugatory.

From what you have said, I am fully satisfied that the persons to whom you have entrusted the execution of my work, are alone to blame; for certain I am they might, by attention, have obtained (equally with others) as many boards as would have answered my purposes, long 'ere this.

Far, very far is it from me, to censure any measures you have adopted for your own accomodation, or for the more immediate convenience of Mrs Greene—at all times I think you are entitled to as good, as circumstances will afford; and in the present condition of your Lady, conceive that no delay could be admitted—I should therefore with great willingness have made my conveniency yield to hers, if the point had lain there, being very sincerely Yr obedt & affecte Servt

Go: Washington[1]

APRIL 2
TO MAJOR GENERAL STEUBEN

The feelings of foreboding that oppressed Washington in the spring of 1780—particularly with regard to Charleston, South Carolina, where a large force under Major General Benjamin Lincoln had gathered to defend the city from advancing British forces—would prove all too justified.

Morristown April 2d 1780.

My Dear Baron,

. . .

Your anxiety on the score of Southern affairs cannot exceed mine. The measure of collecting the whole force for the defence of Charles town ought no doubt to have been well considered before it was determined. It is putting much to the hazard—but at this distance we can form a very imperfect judgment of its propriety or necessity. I have the greatest reliance on General Lincoln's prudence; but I cannot forbear dreading the event. Ill as we can afford a diminution of our force here and nothwithstanding the danger we run from the facility with which the enemy can concenter their force at our weak points besides other inconveniences I have recommended it to Congress to detach the Maryland division to reinforce the Southern States. Though this detachment cannot in all probability arrive, in season, to be of any service to Charles Town it may assist to check the progress of the enemy & save the Carolinas.

My sentiments concerning public affairs correspond too much with yours—The prospect my Dear Baron is gloomy and the storm threatens. Not to have the anxieties you express at the present juncture would be not to feel that zeal and interest in our cause, by which all your whole conduct shows you to be actuated. But I hope we shall extricate ourselves, and bring every thing to a prosperous issue. I have been so inured to difficulties in the course of this contest that I have learned to look upon them with more tranquillity than formerly—those which now present themselves no doubt require vigorous exertions to overcome them—& I am far from dispairing of doing it. . . . I am very sensible my Dear Baron to the obliging assurances of your regard; and I entreat you, to believe there is a perfect reciprocity of sentiments and that I am with great consideration and the truest esteem Your most Obedt servt

G. Washington[2]

———

MAY 28
TO JOSEPH REED

By the spring of 1780, Washington's assessment of the overall situation had become as bleak as at any time during the war, despite France's continuing efforts—with Spanish help—against Great Britain. Washington's understanding of European political and economic affairs, as demonstrated in this letter, was deep.

Morris-Town May 28th 1780

Dear Sir,

I am much obliged to you for your favor of the 23d—Nothing could be more necessary than the aid given by your State towards supplying us with provision. I assure you every idea you can form of our distresses will fall short of the reality. There is such a combination of circumstances to exhaust the patience of the soldiery that it begins at length to be worn out—and we see in every line of the Army the most serious features of mutiny and sedition—All our departments—all our operations are at a stand—and unless a system very different from that wch has for a long time prevailed be immediately adopted throughout the States our affairs must soon become desperate—beyond the possibility of recovery.

If you were on the spot my dear Sir, if you could see what difficulties surround us on every side—how unable we are to administer to the most ordinary calls of the service—you wd be convinced that these expressions are not too strong, and that we have almost ceased to hope. The Country in general is in such a state of insensibility and indifference to its inter-est, that I dare not flatter myself with any change for the better. . . . The present juncture is so interesting that if it does not produce corrispondent exertions, it will be a proof that motives of honor public good & even self preservation have lost their influence upon our minds—This is a decisive moment—one of the most (I will go further & say *the most*) important America has seen. The Court of France has made a glorious effort for our deliverance, and if we disappoint its intentions by our supineness we must become contemptible in the eyes of all Mankind; nor can we after that ven-ture to confide that our allies will persist in an attempt to establish what it will appear we want inclination or ability to assist them in.

Every view of our own circumstances ought to determine us to the most vigorous efforts; but there are considerations of another kind that should have equal weight—The combined fleets of France & Spain last year were greatly superior of those of the enemy—The enemy nevertheless sustained no material damage & at the close of the Campaign have given a very important blow to our allies—This Campaign the difference between the fleets from every account I have been able to collect will be inconsider-able—indeed it is far from clear that there will not be an equality—What are we to expect will be the case if there should be another Campaign? In all probability the advantage will be on the side of the English, and then what will become of America? We ought not to deceive ourselves. The Maritime resources of Great Britain are more substantial and real than those of France & Spain united—Her commerce is more extensive than that of both her rivals; and it is an axiom that the Nation which has the most extensive commerce will always have the most powerful marine— Were this argument less convincing the fact speaks for itself—her progress in the course of the last year is an incontestible proof.

It is true France in a manner created a Fleet in a very short space & this may mislead us in the judgment we form of her naval abilities. But if they bore any comparison with those of great Britain how comes it to pass that with all the force of Spain added she has lost so much ground in so short a time, as now to have scarcely a superiority. We should consider what was done by France as a violent and unnatural effort of the government which for want of sufficient foundation cannot continue to operate proportionable effects.

In modern wars the longest purse must chiefly determine the event—I fear that of the enemy will be found to be so—though the Government is deeply in debt & of course poor, the nation is rich and their riches afford a fund which will not be easily exhausted. Besides, their system of public credit is such that it is capable of greater exertions than that of any other nation—Speculatists have been a long time foretelling its downfall, but we see no Symptoms of the catastrophe being very near. I am perswaded it will at least last out the war, and then in the opinion of many of the best politicians it will be a national advantage. If the war should terminate successfully the crown will have acquired such influence & power that it may attempt any thing—and a bankruptcy will probably be made the ladder to climb to absolute authority. Administration may perhaps wish to drive matters to this issue—at any rate they will not be restrained by an apprehension of it from forcing the resources of the state. It will promote their present purposes on which their all is at stake and it may pave the way to triumph more effectually over the constitution. With this disposition I have no doubt that ample means will be found to prosecute the war with the greatest vigor.

France is in a very different position. The abilities of her present financier has done wonders—By a wise administration of the revenues aided by advantageous loans he has avoided the necessity of additional taxes. But I am well informed—if the war continues another Campaign he will be obliged to have recourse to the taxes usual in time of war which are very heavy—and which the people of France are not in condition to indure for any duration. When this necessity commences France makes war on ruinous terms; and England from her individual wealth will find much greater facility in supplying her exigencies.

Spain derives great wealth from her mines, but not so great as is generally imagined—Of late years the profit to government is essentially diminished—Commerce and industry are the best means of a nation; both which are wanting to her—I am told her treasury is far from being so well filled as we have flattered ourselves—She also much divided on the propriety of the war—there is a strong party against it—The temper of the nation is too sluggish to admit of great exertions—and though the Courts of the two Kingdoms are closely linked together, there never has been in any of their wars a perfect harmony of measures, nor has it been the case in this; which has already been no small detriment to the common cause.

I mention these things to show that the circumstances of our allies as well as our own call for peace; to obtain which we must make one great effort this Campaign. The present instance of the friendship of the Court of France is attended with every circumstance that can render it important and agreeable; that can interest our gratitude or fire our emulation. If we do our duty we may even hope to make the campaign decisive on this Continent. But we must do our duty in earnest—or disgrace & ruin will attend us—I am sincere in declaring a full perswasion, that the succour will be fatal to us, if our measures are not adequate to the emergency. . .

Go: Washington[3]

JUNE 14
TO JAMES BOWDOIN

The surrender of Charleston on May 12, with 2,500 Continentals, including the entire Virginia line, falling into British captivity, cast a dark pall on American affairs; but Washington, despite his earlier pessimism, had recovered at least some measure of hope, as revealed in this letter to the future governor of Massachusetts.

Head Qurs Springfield in Jersey
June 14. 1780

Dr Sir

. . .

With respect to Charles Town—although I have received no Official advices of it on our part—the loss of it seems placed beyond doubt. The Articles of Capitulation are published in a York Gazette Extraordinary by Authority, which were signed the 12 of May, with all the preliminary negotiations between the Commanders. The Garrison, at least the part denominated Continental, are prisoners of War. This is a very severe blow; but not such as will ruin us, if we exert ourselves virtuously and as we are able. Something like it seems to have been necessary, to rouse us from the more than thrice unaccountable state of security in which we were sunk. Heaven Grant the blow may have this effect. If it should, the misfortune may prove a benefit and the means of saving us.

. . .

G: Washington[4]

JULY 16

TO LIEUTENANT GENERAL ROCHAMBEAU

On July 10, a French fleet bearing 5,500 troops under the command of the Comte de Rochambeau arrived in Newport, Rhode Island, which the British had evacuated. The military potential of this force was not to be realized immediately, for the British navy blockaded the port, making it difficult for Rochambeau to deploy outside Rhode Island. Washington did not allow the next several months to go to waste, however, and forged a close working relationship with the French general—initially via an intermediary, Lafayette—that would bear glorious fruit a little over a year later.

Head Quarters in New Jersey
July 16th 1780

Sir,

I hasten to impart to you the happiness I feel at the welcome news of your arrival; and as well in the name of the american army as in my own name to present you with an assurance, of our warmest sentiments for Allies, who have generously come to our Aid.

As a citizen of the United States and as a Soldier in the cause of liberty, I thankfully acknowledge this new mark of friendship from his Most Christian Majesty—and I feel a most grateful sensibility for the flattering confidence he has been pleased to honor me with on this occasion.

Among the obligations we are under to your Prince, I esteem it one of the first that he has made choice for the command of his Troops of a Gentleman whose high reputation and happy union of social qualities & military abilities promise me every public advantage & private satisfaction.

I beg Sir, you will be the interpreter of my Sentiments to the Gentlemen under your command. Be pleased to assure them that to the pleasure I anticipate of an acquaintance with them, I join the warmest desire to do every thing that may be agreeable to them and the Soldiers under their command. But in the midst of a War, the nature and difficulties of which are peculiar & uncommon, I cannot flatter myself in any way to attone for the sacrifice they have made; but by giving them such oppertunities in the field of glory as will enable them to display that gallantry and those talents which we shall always be happy to acknowledge with applause.

The Marquis De La Fayette has been by me desired from time to time to communicate such intelligence and make such propositions as circumstances dictated. I think it so important immediately to fix our plan of operations and with as much secrecy as possible, that I have requested him to go himself to New London, where he will probably meet you. As a Genl Officer I have the greatest confidence in him—as a friend he is perfectly acquainted with my sentiments & opinions—He knows all the circumstances of our Army & the Country at large; All the information he gives and all the propositions he makes, I entreat you will consider as coming from me. I request you will settle all arrangements whatsoever with him; and I shall only add, that I shall exactly conform to the intentions of His Most Christian Majesty as explained in the several papers put into my hand by his order & signed by his Ministers.

Permit me to refer you to the Marquis De La Fayette, for more particular assurances of what I feel on this occasion; which I the more readily do from a knowledge of his peculiar affection and regard for you. Impatiently waiting for the time when our operations will afford me the pleasure of a personal acquaintance with you—I have the honor to be with the most perfect consideration and attachment, Your most Obedient & humble Servant

Go: Washington[5]

————

JULY 20
GENERAL ORDERS

Head Quarters Pracaness [N.J.] Thursday July 20th 1780 The Commander in Chief has the pleasure to Congratulate the Army on the Arrival of a large Land and Naval Armament at Rhode Island sent by his most Christian Majesty to Co'operate with the Troops of these States against the Common Enemy accompanied with every Circumstance that can render it honorable and useful.

The Generosity of this succour and the manner in which it is given is a new Tie between France and America The Lively concern which our Allies manifest for our Safety and Independence has a Claim to the Affection of every Virtuous Citizen. The General with confidence assures the Army that the Officers and Men of the French Forces come to our Aid animated with a Zeal founded in Sentiment for us as well as in Duty to their Prince and that they will do every thing in their Power to promote Harmony and cultivate Friendship He is equally persuaded that on our Part we shall vie with them in their good dispositions to which we are excited by Gratitude as well as by a common Interest; and that the only contention between the two Armies will be to excel each other in good offices and in the display of every Military Virtue—This will be the Pledge of the most solid advantages to the common Cause and of a glorious Issue to the Campaign. . . .[6]

————

SEPTEMBER 15

TO SAMUEL HUNTINGTON

American fortunes in the South reached a nadir on August 16 with the Battle of Camden, South Carolina, in which a British army under Lord Charles Cornwallis demolished a hodgepodge force of militia and Continentals under the hero of Saratoga, Horatio Gates. The disaster opened the way for a British invasion of North Carolina. Washington gives his view of the strategic outlook in this letter to the president of Congress.

Head Quarters New Bridge [N.J.]
Sept. 15th 1780

Sir,

I am honored with your letters of the 6th and 8th instant with their enclosures—happy to find that the late disaster in Carolina has not been so great as its first features indicated—This event however, adds itself to many others to exemplify the necessity of an army—the fatal consequences of depending on militia. Regular Troops alone are equal to the exigences of modern war, as well for defence as offence, and whenever a substitute is attempted it must prove illusory and ruinous—*No Militia* will ever acquire the habits necessary to resist a regular force—Even those nearest the seat of War are only valuable as light Troops to be scattered in the woods and plague rather than do serious injury to the Enemy—The firmness requisite for the real business of fighting is only to be attained by a constant course of discipline and service. I have never yet been witness to a single instance that can justify a different opinion; and it is most earnestly to be wished the liberties of America may no longer be trusted in any material degree to so precarious a dependence.

I cannot but remark that it gives me pain to find—the measures pursuing to the Southward still turn upon accumulating large bodies of militia instead of once for all making a decided effort to have a permanent force. In my ideas of the true system of war to the Southward—the object ought to be to have a good army rather than a large one. Every exertion should be made by North Carolina Virginia Maryland and Delaware to raise a permanent force of Six Thousand men exclusive of Horse and Artillery—These with the occasional aid of the Militia in the vicinity of the scene of action, will not only suffice to prevent the further progress of the

Enemy; but, if properly supplied to oblige them to compact their force and relinquish a part of what they may now hold. To expel them from the Country intirely is what we cannot aim at—till we derive more effectual support from abroad; and by attempting too much, instead of going forward, we shall go backward. Could such a force be once on foot it would immediately make an inconceivable change in the face of our affairs—in the opposition to the Enemy, expence, consumption of provision, waste of arms stores &ca—No magazines can be equal to the demands of an army of militia—and none ever needed œconomy more than ours. . .

Go: Washington[7]

SEPTEMBER 25
TO COLONEL NATHANIEL WADE

On September 23, three militiamen stopped and questioned a man traveling on a road near Tarrytown, New York. Their suspicions aroused by the man's apparently desperate desire to get through, the militiamen searched him and discovered some papers hidden in his stocking. The papers revealed the man's identity—he was Major John André, adjutant general of the British army—and his mission, which was to conspire with Major General Benedict Arnold for the betrayal of West Point to the British. Had the plot succeeded, almost the entire Hudson River would have come under British control; but André's capture allowed the Americans to foil the plot in the nick of time. Arnold escaped to a British ship, HMS Vulture, *but Washington rushed reinforcements to the Hudson, including Massachusetts militia under Colonel Nathaniel Wade, and West Point remained in American hands. The wounds left by the treason of Arnold, who despite his vanity and frequent imbroglios remained one of Washington's favorite generals—took longer to heal.*

Head Quarters Robinson's House [N.Y.]
Septr 25th 1780

Sir

General Arnold is gone to the Enemy. I have just now received a line from him, inclosing one to Mrs Arnold dated on board the Vulture. From this circumstance & Colo. Lamb's being detached on some business, the command of the Garrison for the present devolves on you. I request you will be as vigilant as possible & as the Enemy may have it in contemplation to attempt some enterprise even to night against these Posts, I wish you to make immediately after receipt of this, the best disposition you can of your force, so as to have a proportion of Men in each work on the West side of the River. You will see or hear from me further tomorrow. I am Sir Your Mo. Obet Servt

Go: Washington[8]

SEPTEMBER 26
TO SAMUEL HUNTINGTON

Robinson's house in the Highlands [N.Y.]
Septr 26th 1780

Sir

I have the honor to inform Congress that I arrived here yesterday about 12 o'clock on my return from Hartford. Some hours previous to my arrival Major Genl Arnold went from his quarters which were at this place, and as it was supposed over the river to the garrison at West-point, whither I proceeded myself in order to visit the post. I found General Arnold had not been there during the day, and on my return to his quarters, he was still absent. In the mean time a packet had arrived from Lt Colonel Jamison, announcing the capture of a John Anderson who was endeavouring to go to New-York, with the several interesting and important papers mentioned below, all in the hand writing of General Arnold. This was all accompanied with a letter from the prisoner avowing himself to be Major John André Adjt General of the British army, relating the manner of his capture, and endeavouring to shew that he did not come under the description of a spy. From these several circumstances, and information that the General seemed to be thrown into some degree of agitation on receiving a letter a little time before he went from his quarters, I was led to conclude immediately that he had heard of Major Andre's captivity, and that he would if possible escape to the enemy, and accordingly took such measures as appeared the most probable to apprehend him. But he had embarked in a barge, and proceeded down the river under a flag to the vulture ship of war, which lay at some miles below Stoney and Verplank's points. He wrote me after he got on board a letter, of which the inclosed is a copy. Major André is not arrived yet, but I hope he is secure & that he will be here to-day. I have been, and am taking precautions, which I trust will prove effective, to prevent the important consequences which this conduct on the part of General Arnold was intended to produce. I do not know the party that took Major André, but it is said, that it consisted only of a few militia, who acted in such a manner upon the occasion as does them the highest honor and proves them to be men of great virtue. They were offered, I am informed, a large sum of money for his release, and as many goods as they would demand, but without any effect. Their conduct gives them a just claim to the thanks of their country, and I also hope they will be otherwise rewarded. As soon as I know their names I shall take pleasure in transmitting them to Congress.

I have taken such measures with respect to the Gentlemen of General Arnolds family [his aides] as prudence dictated; but from every thing that has hitherto come to my knowledge, I have the greatest reason to believe that they are perfectly innocent. I early secured Joshua Smith, the person mentioned in the close of General Arnolds letter, and find him to have had a considerable share in this business. I have the honor to be, with regard, Sir your Excellency's most obt & hble Sert

Go: Washington[9]

SEPTEMBER 30
TO GENERAL HENRY CLINTON

Major André's youth and good manners endeared him to his captors, but they could not save him from being executed as a spy despite a personal appeal for clemency from General Henry Clinton. Washington sincerely regretted the execution, but felt that he had no choice but to approve it.

Head Quarters [Tappan, N.Y.]
Septemr 30th 1780

Sir
In answer to Your Excellency's letter of the 26th instant, which I have had the honor to receive, I am to inform you, that Major André was taken

under such circumstances, as would have justified the most summary proceedings against him. I determined, however, to refer his case to the examination and decision of a Board of General Officers, who have, on his
free and voluntary confession and letters, reported—First. "That he came
on shore from the Vulture Sloop of War in the night of the twenty first
of September last on an interview with General Arnold in a private and
secret manner. Secondly—that he changed his dress within our lines, and
under a feigned name and in a disguised Habit, passed our Works at Stony
and Verplanks points the evening of the twenty second of September last,
and was taken the morning of the twenty third of September last, at Tarry
Town, in a disguised Habit, being then on his way to New York, and when
taken, he had in his possession several papers which contained intelligence
for the Enemy. The Board having maturely considered these facts do also
report to his Excellency Genl Washington that Major André Adjutant General to the British Army ought to be considered as a Spy from the Enemy,
and that agreeable to the law and usage of Nations it is their opinion he
ought to suffer death."

From these proceedings it is evident Major André was employed in the
execution of Measures, very foreign to the objects of Flags of Truce, and
such as they were never meant to authorise or countenance in the most
distant degree—and this Gentleman confessed with the greatest candor in
the course of his examination "that it was impossible for him to suppose he
came on shore under the sanction of a Flag." I have the honor to be Your
Excellency's Most obt and most hble Servt

Go: Washington[10]

OCTOBER 9
TO BENJAMIN FRANKLIN

*Benjamin Franklin seconded Lafayette's earlier suggestion that Washington make
a European tour after the war had ended; but by the autumn of 1780 Washington
yearned more than ever for retirement to the comforts of home.*

.

Bergen County in the State of N. Jersey
Oct. 9 1780

Dear Sir,

I was very much obliged by the letter which you did me the honor to write me by our amiable young friend the Marquis De La Fayette, whose exertions to serve this Country in his own are additional proofs of his zealous attachment to our cause, and has endeared him to us still more.

He came out flushed with expectations of a decisive campaign and fired with hopes of acquiring fresh laurels, but in both he has been disappointed; for we have been condemned to an inactivity as inconsistent with the situation of our affairs as with the ardor of his temper.

I am sensible of all I owe you My Dear Sir for your sentiments of me, and while I am happy in your esteem, I cannot but wish for occasions of giving you marks of mine.

The idea of making a tour together, which you suggest after the war, would be one of the strongest motives I could have to postpone my plan of retirement and make a visit to Europe, if my domestic habits which seem to acquire strength from restraint did not tell me, I shall find it impossible to resist them longer than my duty to the public calls for the sacrafice of my inclinations.

I doubt not you are so fully informed by Congress of our political and military State that it would be superfluous to trouble you with any thing relating to either—If I were to speak on topics of the kind it would be to shew that our present situation makes one of two things essential to us—A Peace—or the most vigorous aid of our allies particularly in the article of money. Of their disposition to serve us we cannot doubt; their generosity will do every thing their means will permit.

With my best wishes for the preservation of your useful life and for every happiness that can attend you which a sincere attachment can dictate I am—My Dear Sir—Yr Most Obedt Hble Servt

Go: Washington[11]

OCTOBER 13

TO LIEUTENANT COLONEL JOHN LAURENS

On and off for the remainder of his life, Washington would ponder Arnold's treason, without ever really understanding why it had happened.

Hd Qrs Passaic Falls [N.J.]
13th Oct. 1780.

My dear Laurens. . .

In no instance since the commencement of the War has the interposition of Providence appeared more conspicuous than in the rescue of the Post & Garrison of West point from Arnolds villainous perfidy. How far he meant to involve me in the catastrophe of this place does not appear by any indubitable evidence—and I am rather inclined to think he did not wish to hazard the more important object of his treachery by attempting to combine two events the lesser of which might have marred the greater.

A combination of extraordinary circumstances—an unaccountable deprivation of presence of Mind in a Man of the first abilities—and the virtuous conduct of three Militia Men—threw the Adjutant General of the British forces in America (with full proofs of Arnolds treachery) in to our hands—and but for the egregious folly—or the bewildered conception of Lieutt Colo. Jameson who seemed lost in astonishment and not to have known what he was doing I should as certainly have got Arnold.

André has met his fate—and with that fortitude which was to be expected from an accomplished Man—and gallant Officer—But I am mistaken if at *this time*, Arnold is undergoing the torments of a mental Hell. He wants feeling! From some traits of his character which have lately come to my knowledge he seems to have been so hackneyed in villainy—& so lost to all sense of honor and shame that while his faculties will enable him to continue his sordid pursuits there will be no time for remorse. . . . your Sincere friend and obliged Servant

Go: Washington[12]

OCTOBER 22
TO SAMUEL HUNTINGTON

Once again, Washington called on Nathanael Greene to save the United States from disaster, appointing him to take command of the "Southern Army," which really amounted to nothing more than a few thousand militia scattered across Virginia and North Carolina. Greene, who had spent two and a half years as quartermaster general, was eager to take the field. Within months, he assembled a respectable military force and began a brilliant campaign against Cornwallis that would lead eventually to the siege and capitulation of Yorktown.

Head Quarters Prekaness [N.J.] 22d Octobr 1780

Sir

 I have the honor to inform Congress, that in consequence of their resolution of the 5th instant, I have appointed Major General Greene to the command of the Southern Army, 'till the enquiry into the conduct of Major Genl Gates is completed. I inclose a Copy of my instructions to General Greene, by which and a Copy of my letter to Genl Gates, Congress will perceive the mode I have adopted for the enquiry: I did not perceive any other which could be substituted with equal propriety, but if Congress are of a different opinion, I submit it to them for their further directions.

 I beg leave to mention General Greene, upon this occasion, to Congress as an Officer, in whose abilities, fortitude and integrity, from a long and intimate experience of them, I have the most intire confidence—In the command he is going into he will have every disadvantage to struggle with. The confidence and support of Congress, which it will be his ambition to merit, will be essential to his success. The defect of military resources in the southern department—the confusion in which the affairs of it must for sometime be, require that the Commanding Officer should be vested with extensive powers. I dare say Congress will take their measures in a manner suited to the exigency. General Greene waits upon them for their orders.

 As, in a great measure, a new Army is to be formed to the southward, the presence of the Baron de Steuben will in my opinion be of more essential utility in that quarter than here, where though the ensuing Campaign, we shall have the greatest part of our force raw Recruits, yet as we are organized and in some order, the sub-inspectors will suffice for the purposes of the department. I therefore submit to Congress the propriety of sending the Baron de Steuben to the southern Army. The sooner they are pleased to announce their pleasure on this head the better. I have the honor to be with perfect Respect Your Excellency's most obedt and humble Servt

Go: Washington[13]

———

1781

JANUARY 3
TO CHARLES PETTIT

Pettit, a quartermaster in Philadelphia, had access to the finest American-made articles, as well as items imported from overseas. Among the "much wanted" items listed in the enclosed memorandum were white and buff silk, buff twist, six "Tooth Brushes of the strongest & stiffest hair," and two almanacs for 1781.[1]

New Windsor [N.Y.] Jany 3d 1781

Dear Sir,

. . .

If you will excuse my giving you the trouble of a small Commission I will thank you for the articles contained in the inclosed Memorandum which—tho 'much wanted—are not to be had in this part of the World— If the Money sent is inadequate to the purchase of them, the balance shall be transmitted so soon as known.

I have a more important favour to request of you—It is—to enquire after, and let me know if a good family Steward can be had—I must not stand upon wages if a person properly qualified should offer—because I am well convinced that a sober, honest, & diligent Man by good management, & proper attention to the duties of his Office would save, in the course of a year, the wages of ten indifferent ones.

Besides the qualities just mentioned, if he possessed a knowledge of the order, & Œconomy of a Table, it would add to his usefulness. I need not detail the duties of his Office—a general superintendance of Family matters—providing for its wants—& seeing to the faithful application of what is provided—comprehends the whole. I am—Dr Sir Yr most Obedt Servt

Go: Washington[2]

JANUARY 3D—4

TO BRIGADIER GENERAL ANTHONY WAYNE

At 9:00 P.M. on New Year's Day, 1781, a thousand Continental soldiers from Pennsylvania assembled in their camp at Morristown, New Jersey, and announced that they had had enough. Fed up with insanely rampant inflation—a horse sold for $150,000—and months without receiving any pay, their families impoverished, their farms and businesses collapsed, wearing rags, and eating bad food, they decided that they would march on Philadelphia and present their grievances to Congress, which seemed to have forgotten the men who fought and died for their country's independence. Disregarding their officers and imprisoning their hapless commander, Anthony Wayne, the mutineers marched to Princeton, elected a Board of Sergeants, and opened negotiations with Congress. Washington, fearing that his own Continental contingent at New Windsor, New York, would erupt in mutiny if he left for Princeton, could only await developments from a distance.

Head Quarters New Windsor [N.Y.]
3d[–4] January 1781

My dear Sir

I this day, at Noon, recd yours of the 2d in the Morning, by Major Fishbourn, who has given me a full account of the unhappy and alarming defection of the Pennsylvania line. The Officers have given convincing proofs that every thing possible was done by them to check the Mutiny upon its first appearance, and it is to be regretted that some of them have fallen sacrifices to their Zeal. I very much approve of the determination of yourself—Colo. Butler and Colo. Stewart to keep with the troops, if they will admit of it, as, after the first transports of passion, there may be some favorable intervals which may be improved. I do not know where

220

this may find you, or in what situation. I can therefore only advise what seems to me most proper at this distance and upon a consideration of all circumstances.

Opposition, as it did not succeed in the first instance, cannot be effectual while the Men remain together, but will keep alive resentment and will tempt them to turn about and go in a body to the enemy, who by their Emissaries will use every Argument and mean in their power to persuade them that it is their only Asylum, which, if they find their passage stopped at the Delaware, and hear that the Jersey Militia are collecting in their rear, they may think but too probable. I would therefore recommend it to you to cross the Delaware with them—draw from them what they conceive to be their principal Grievances and promise to represent faithfully to Congress and to the State the substance of them and to endeavour to obtain a redress. If they could be stopped at Bristol or Germantown the better—I look upon it, that if you can bring them to a negociation, matters may afterwards be accommodated, but that an attempt to reduce them by force will either drive them to the Enemy, or dissipate them in such a manner that they will never be recovered.

Major Fishbourn informs me that General Potter and Colo. Johnston had gone forward to apprise Congress of this unhappy event, and to advise them to go out of the way to avoid the first burst of the Storm. It was exceedingly proper to give Congress and the State notice of the Affair that they might be prepared, but the removal of Congress, waving the indignity, might have a very unhappy influence. The Mutineers finding the Body, before whom they were determined to lay their Grievances, fled, might take a new turn, and wreak their vengeance upon the persons and properties of the Citizens, and in a town of the size of Philadelphia there are numbers who would join them in such a business. I would therefore wish you, if you have time, to recall that advice, and rather recommend it to them to stay and and hear what propositions the Soldiers have to make.

Immediately upon the receipt of your letter I took measures to inform myself of the temper of the Troops in this quarter, and have sent into the Country for a small Escort of Horse to come to me, and if nothing alarming appears here and I hear nothing further from you, I shall, tomorrow Morning, set out towards Philadelphia by the Route of Chester—Warwick. Colo. Sewards. Davenports Mill Morris Town. Somerset. Princeton. Trenton on which you will direct any dispatches for me. As I shall be exceedingly anxious to hear what turn matters have taken, or in what situation they remain, you will be pleased to let me hear from you. I am with very great Regard Dear Sir Your most obt & hble Servt

Go: Washington

P.S. 4th Jany 7 OClock A.M. Upon second thoughts, I am in doubt whether I shall come down, because the Mutineers must have returned to their duty or the business be in the hands of Congress before I could reach you, and because I am advised by such of the General Officers as I have seen not to leave this post in the present situation of things—temper of the troops—and distress of the Garrison for want of Flour—Cloathing and in short every thing.[3]

JANUARY 15
TO JOHN LAURENS

Washington could never have too many pictures of Martha around.

New Windsor 15 Jany 1781
Colonel Laurens will be so good as to have Mrs Washington's picture herewith given handsomely [set in] a button for the Shirt collar—a [*mutilated text*] the bosom—a ring for the finger (of [the] size of his own)—a locket for a Wa[tch]—or any thing else his fancy may think better.

Go: Washington[4]

JANUARY 30
GENERAL ORDERS

The Pennsylvania mutiny lasted until January 10, when an agreement was struck granting the soldiers amnesty and honorable discharges from military service. Washington did nothing to punish the mutineers; but when a few hundred New Jersey Continentals mutinied at Pompton, N.J., on the twentieth, he ordered the rebellion to be put down ruthlessly lest the whole army disintegrate. Five hundred picked troops under Major General Robert Howe surrounded the mutineers and forced them to surrender, after which the ringleaders were executed. Tensions did not disappear, however, but remained just below the service; one spark, Washington knew, could ignite an army-wide mutiny and leave the American cause in ruins.

Head Quarters New Windsor Tuesday January 30th 1781 The General returns his thanks to Major General Howe for the judicious measures he pursued and to the officers and men under his command for the good conduct and alacrity with which they executed his orders for suppressing the late Mutiny in a part of the New Jersey line—It gave him inexpressible pain to have been obliged to employ their arms upon such an occasion and convinced that they themselves felt all the Reluctance which former Affection to fellow Soldiers could inspire—He considers the patience with which they endured the fatigues of the march through rough and mountainous roads rendered almost impassable by the depth of the Snow and the cheerfulness with which they performed every other part of their duty as the strongest proof of their Fidelity, attachment to the service, sense of subordination and abhorrence of the principles which actuated the Mutineers in so daring and atrocious a departure from what they owed to their Country, to their Officers to their Oaths and to themselves.

The General is deeply sensible of the sufferings of the army. He leaves no expedient unessayed to relieve them, and he is persuaded Congress and the several states are doing every thing in their power for the same purpose—But while we look to the public for the fullfilment of its engagements we should do it with proper allowance for the embarrassments of public affairs—We began a Contest for Liberty and Independence ill provided with the means for war—relying on our own Patriotism to supply the deficiency—We expected to encounter many wants and distresses and We should neither shrink from them when they happen nor fly in the face of Law and Government to procure redress—There is no doubt the public will in the event do ample justice to men fighting and suffering in its defence—But it is our duty to bear present Evils with Fortitude looking forward to the period when our Country will have it more in its power to reward our services.

History is full of Examples of armies suffering with patience extremities of distress which exceed those we have suffered—and this in the cause of ambition and conquest not in that of the rights of humanity—of their country—of their families of themselves—shall we who aspire to the distinction of a patriot army—who are contending for every thing precious in society against everything hateful and degrading in slavery—shall We who call ourselves citizens discover less Constancy and Military virtue than the mercenary instruments of ambition? Those who in the present instance have stained the honor of the American soldiery and sullied the reputation of patient Virtue for which they have been so long eminent can only atone for their pusillanimous defection by a life devoted to a Zealous and examplary discharge of their duty—Persuaded that the greater part were influenced by the pernicious advice of a few who probably have been paid by the enemy to betray their Associates; The General is happy in the lenity shewn in the execution of only two of the most guilty after compelling the whole to an unconditional surrender—and he flatters himself no similar instance will hereafter disgrace our military History—It can only bring ruin on those who are mad enough to make the attempt; for lenity on any future occasion would be criminal and inadmissible. . . .[5]

FEBRUARY 20
TO MAJOR GENERAL LAFAYETTE

Benedict Arnold had left—but not for good. Commissioned a brigadier general in the British army, he commanded a force of 1,500 British troops that occupied Portsmouth, Virginia, sacked Richmond, and raided along the coast in January 1781. Washington sent his friend, Lafayette, to stop the raids and bring Arnold to justice.

Head Quarters New Windsor Feby 20th 81

Sir,

I have ordered a detachment to be made at this post to rendezvous at Peeks Kill the 19th instant, which together with another to be formed at Morris Town from the Jersey troops will amount to about twelve hundred Rank & file.

The destination of this detachment is to act against the corps of the enemy now in Virginia in conjunction with the Militia and some ships from the fleet of the Chevalier Des touches, which he informs me sailed the 9th instant from New Port.

You will take the command of this detachment, which you will in the first instance march off by batalions towards Pompton there to rendezvous and afterwards proceed with all possible dispatch to the Head of Elk.

. . .

When you arrive at your destination, you must act as your own judgment and the circumstances shall direct.

You will open a correspondence with the Baron De Steuben who now commands in Virginia informing him of your approach and requesting him to have a sufficient body of Militia ready to act in conjunction with your detachment. It will be adviseable for him to procure persons in whom he can confide well acquainted with the Country at Portsmouth and in the Vicinity, some who are capable of giving you a military idea of it and others to serve as guides.

You should give the earliest attention to acquiring a knowlege of the different rivers but particularly James 'River, that you may know what harbours can best afford shelter and security to the cooperating Squadron, in case of blockade by a superior force.

You are to do no act whatever with Arnold that directly or by implication may skreen him from the punishment due to his treason and desertion, which if he should fall into your hands, you will execute in the most summary way.

. . .

You will keep me regularly advised of your movements & progress; & when the object of the detachment is fulfilled (or unfortunately disappointed) you will return with it by the same rout, if circumstances admit of it and with as much expedition as possible to this Post.

I wish you a successful issue to the enterprise and all the glory which I am persuaded you will deserve.[6]

MARCH 21
TO BENJAMIN HARRISON

With the dispatch of Lafayette to Virginia, the duel between Greene and Cornwallis raging through North Carolina, and talk of the arrival of a large French fleet off the coast, military events were heating up; but at this moment an unwelcome distraction came from Washington's aged mother, Mary Ball Washington, with whom he had an often tense relationship. Her appeal to the Virginia legislature for a pension implied—as she no doubt intended—that Washington had neglected her.

New Windsor 21st March 1781.

My Dr Sir,

Upon my return to this place last night, I met your private & friendly letter of the 25th of February. I do not delay a moment to thank you for the interesting matter contained in it, and to express my surprize at that part which respects a pension for my Mother.

True it is, I am but little acquainted with her *present* situation, or distresses, if she is under any. As true it is, a year or two before I left Virginia (to make her latter days comfortable, & free from care) I did, at her request but at my own expence, purchase a commodious house, Garden & Lotts (of her own choosing) in Fredericksburg, that she might be near my Sister Lewis, her only daughter—and did moreover agree to take her Land & Negroes at a certain yearly rent, to be fixed by Colo. Lewis & others (of her own nomination,) which has been an annual expence to me ever since, as the Estate never raised one half the rent I was to pay—Before I left Virginia, I answered all her calls for money; and since that period, have directed my Steward to do the same. Whence her distresses can arise therefore, I know not, never having received any complaint of his inattention or neglect on that head; tho 'his inability to pay my own taxes, is such I know, as to oblige me to sell negroes for this purpose—the taxes being the most unequal (I am told) in the world—some persons paying for things of equal value, four times, nay ten times, the rate that others do. But putting these things aside, which I could not avoid mentioning, in exculpation of a presumptive want of duty on my part; confident I am that she has not a child that would not divide the last sixpence to relieve her from *real* distress. This she has been repeatedly assured of by me: and all of us, I am certain, would feel much hurt, at having our mother a pensioner, while we had the means of supporting her; but in fact she has an ample income of her own.

I lament exceedingly that your letter, which conveyed the first hint of this matter, did not come to my hands sooner; but I request, in pointed terms if the matter is now in agitation in your assembly, that all proceedings on it may be stopped—or in case of a decision in her favor, that it may be done away, & repealed at my request. . .

G: Washington[7]

APRIL 7

TO MAJOR GENERAL WILLIAM HEATH

Washington's lack of regard for his own safety was well known, and earned the respect of his officers and troops.

New Windsor 7th Apl 1781

Dear Sir,

I have received and thank you for your information of this date. To guard against Assassination (which I neither expect, nor dread) is impossible—but I have not been without my apprehensions of the other attempt—Not from the enemy at New York—but the Tories & disaffected of this place; who might, in the Night, carry me off in my own Boat; and all be ignorant of it till the Morning. If the Water at Night is well guarded, I shall be under no apprehension of attempts of this kind. I am Dr Sir Yr most Obedt Sert

Go: Washington[8]

APRIL 18

TO MAJOR GENERAL NATHANAEL GREENE

On March 15, Greene fought Cornwallis at the Battle of Guilford Courthouse. Greene's troops relinquished the field, but inflicted twice as many casualties as they suffered and forced the British to march for Wilmington, North Carolina, in search

of rest and reinforcement. Daniel Morgan, meanwhile, had won a significant victory over British and loyalist forces at Cowpens, South Carolina, on January 17.

New Windsor April 18th 1781

My dear Sir,

Your private letter of the 18th Ulto came safe to hand—although the honors of the field did not fall to your lot, I am convinced you deserved them. The chances of War are various—and the best concerted measures, and the most flattering prospects may, & often do deceive us, especially while we are in the power of Militia. The motives which induced you to seek an Action with Lord Cornwallis are supportable upon the best Military principles—and the consequences, if you can prevent the dissipation of your Troops, will, no doubt be fortunate—Every support that is in my power to give you from this Army shall cheerfully be afforded—But if I part with any more Troops I must accompany them, or have none to command, as there is not, at this moment, more than a Garrison for West point—nor can I tell when there will.

. . .

I am truly sensible of the merit & fortitude of the veteran Bands under your command, & wish the sentiments I entertain of their worth could be communicated with the warmth I feel them. It was my full intention to have requested you, to thank Morgan and the gallant Troops under his command, for their brilliant victory; but the hurry with which my letters are often written, occasioned the omission at the time I acknowledged the official acct of that Action.

. . .

I have the pleasure to tell you, that as far as I am acquainted with the opinion of Congress with respect to your conduct, it is much in your favor—That this is the judgement of all the Southern Delegates I have great reason to believe, because I have it declared to me in explicit terms by some of them.* I hope the disorder of which you complained in your letter of the 18th was no more than the effect of over fatigue and that you are now perfectly recovered—That success equal to your merits & worth may attend you, is the ardent desire of Dr Sir, Yr Affecte friend and obedt Hble Servt

Go: Washington

P.S. Mrs Washington & the rest of the family present their best wishes to you—and I have the pleasure to tell you that Mrs Greene and your Children were well lately, Your letters to her, under cover to me, are regularly forwarded by the Post.

*Since writing the above I have received a letter from Mr Custis dated the 29th Ulto in which are these words "General Greene has by his conduct gained universal esteem, and possesses in the fullest degree the confidence of all ranks of People"—He had then just returned from the Assembly at Richmond.[9]

APRIL 30
TO LUND WASHINGTON

The appearance of a British war sloop on the Potomac River below Mount Vernon seemed to presage what many assumed would have happened much earlier in the war: the sack and destruction of Washington's estate. Lund Washington, Mount Vernon's farm manager, attempted to conciliate the British—much to Washington's annoyance and distress.

New Windsor 30th April 1781

Dear Lund,

Your letter of the 18th came to me by the last Post. I am very sorry to hear of your loss—I am a little sorry to hear of my own—but that which gives me most concern, is, that you should go on board the enemys vessels, & furnish them with refreshments. It would have been a less painful circumstance to me, to have heard, that in consequence of your non compliance with their request, they had burnt my House, & laid the Plantation in ruins. You ought to have considered yourself as my representative, and should have reflected on the bad example of communicating with the enemy, and making a voluntary offer of refreshment to them with a view to prevent a conflagration.

It was not in your power, I acknowledge, to prevent them from sending a flag on shore—and you did right to meet it—but you should, in the same instant that the business of it was unfolded, have declared, explicitly, that it was improper for you to yield to the request—after which, if they had proceeded to help themselves, *by force,* you could but have submitted (and being unprovided for defence) this was to be prefered to a feeble opposition which only serves as a pretext to burn and destroy.

I am thoroughly perswaded that you acted from your best judgment—and believe, that your desire to preserve my property; and rescue the buildings from impending danger, were your governing motives—But to go on board their Vessels—carry them refreshments—commune with a parcel of plundering Scoundrels—and request a favor by asking the surrender of my Negroes was exceedingly ill-judged—and 'tis to be feared—will be unhappy in its consequences, as it will be a precedent for others, and may become a subject of animadversion.

I have no doubt of the enemys intention to prosecute the plundering plan they have begun—and, unless a stop can be put to it by the arrival of a superior naval force, I have as little doubt of its ending in the loss of all my Negroes—and in the destruction of my Houses—but I am prepared for the event—under the prospect of which, if you could deposit, in safety, at some convenient distance from the Water, the most valuable & least bulky articles, it might be consistent with policy & prudence, and a mean of preserving them for use hereafter. such, & so many things as are necessary for common, & present use must be retained & run their chance through the firy trial of this summer.

Mrs Washington joins me in best and affectionate regard for you, Mrs Washington & Milly Posey; & does most sincerely regret your loss—I do not know what Negros they may have left you—and as I have observed before, I do not know what number they will have left me by the time they have done—but this I am sure of, that you shall never want assistance, while it is in my power to afford it. I am sincerely & affectionately yrs

Go: Washington[10]

MAY 22

CONFERENCE AT WETHERSFIELD WITH ROCHAMBEAU

The spring of 1781 saw the first of a series of remarkable events that would culminate in the siege and capitulation of Yorktown. At Portsmouth, Virginia, Arnold had been reinforced by 2,600 British troops under Major General William Phillips, who took

command and sent raiding parties to Petersburg and elsewhere. Lafayette's timely arrival saved Richmond from destruction, but his force was too small to attack the British. Cornwallis, meanwhile, marched north from Wilmington, North Carolina, joining Phillips and Arnold at Petersburg on May 20. The combined British force in Virginia now amounted to about 7,200, compared to Lafayette's 3,000; Greene, after chasing Cornwallis out of North Carolina, had moved back to South Carolina to destroy the British strongholds there.

In the North, meanwhile, Washington learned that a powerful French fleet under Admiral de Grasse had left Europe for the West Indies, from whence it might sail to North America around the end of the summer. Once he arrived, de Grasse might be able to achieve complete, though temporary, naval dominance off some portion of the the American coast. Washington refused to count on de Grasse's arrival; instead, he focused on the benefits that might arise from uniting his army with that of Rochambeau, whose 5,500 troops had remained at Newport since the previous July. Meeting at Wethersfield, Connecticut, on May 22 to consider their plans for the coming campaign, Washington and Rochambeau agreed to unite their forces on the Hudson River and prepare to assault the British garrison at New York City. Rochambeau then asked what they should do if de Grasse's fleet arrived off the coast in time to coordinate operations with the combined Franco-American army.

. . .

Rochambeau: In this last case, and that of the arrival in these Seas of the West Indies Squadron, which in all probability would be announced beforehand by a Frigate, what are the operations that might have in view at that Epocha—General Washington, upon the combination of his forces being united to the french Army.

Washington: The Enemy by several detachments from New York having reduced their force at that Post to less than half of the number which they had at the time of the former conference at Hartford in September last—it is thought advisable to form a junction of the French & American Armies upon the North river as soon as possible, and move down to the vicinity of New York to be ready to take advantage of any oppertunity which the weakness of the enemy may afford. Should the West India Fleet arrive upon this Coast—the force thus combined may either proceed in the operation against New York, or may be directed against the enemy in some other quarter, as circumstances shall dictate—The great waste of Men (which we have found from experience) in the long Marches to the

Southern States—the advanced Season now to commence there in—and the difficulties and expence of Land transportation thither, with other considerations too well known to His Excellency Count de Rochambeau to need detailing, point out the preference which an operation against New York seems to have, in present circumstances, to attempt sending a force to the Southward. . . .[11]

JUNE 13
TO LIEUTENANT GENERAL ROCHAMBEAU

Rochambeau accepted Washington's preference for attacking New York. Privately, however, he thought more could be gained by moving against Cornwallis in Virginia, and wrote to the admiral—unbeknownst to Washington—suggesting that he would do better to make for the Chesapeake. In Washington's letter below, the words enclosed in brackets were originally written in code.

Head Quarters New Windsor 13th June 1781

Sir

I am honored by your Excellency's favors of the 9th and 10th instants, and with their very interesting communications, which you may be assured will be kept perfectly secret. I flatter myself that the whole Convoy will arrive in safety at some of the Eastern ports, as I believe all the British Ships are cruising off the Hook.

. . .

Your requisitions to the [Count de Grasse] go to every thing I could wish. You cannot, in my opinion, too strongly urge the necessity of bringing [a body of troops] with him, more especially, as I am very dubious whether our force can be drawn together by the time he proposes to be here. Now [4000] or [5000 men] in addition to what we shall certainly have by that time, would, almost beyond a doubt, enable us with the Assistance of the [fleet] to carry our object. It is to be regretted that the [Count's] stay upon this [coast] will be [limited]. That consideration is an additional reason for wishing a force equal to giving a speedy determination to the operation.

Your Excellency will be pleased to recollect that [N. York] was looked upon by us as the only practicable object under present circumstances; but should we be able to secure a [naval superiority] we may perhaps find others more practicable and equally advisable. If the [frigate] should not have [sailed] I wish you to explain this matter to [Count Grasse], as, if I understand you, you have in your communication to him, confined our views to [N. York] alone. And instead of advising him to run immediately into [chesapeak], will it not be best to leave him to judge from the information he may from time to time receive of the situation of the [enemys fleet] upon this [coast], which will be the most advantagious quarter for him to make his appearance in. In the letter which was written to the Minister from Wethersfeild, in which he was requested to urge the [Count] to come this way with his [Whole fleet], [Sandy hook] was mentioned as the most desirable point. Because by coming suddenly there he would certainly [block] up any [fleet] which might be [within] and he would even have a very good chance of [forcing] the [entrance] before dispositions could be made to [oppose] him. Should the [British fleet] not be there, he could follow them to [Chesapeak] which is always accessible to a superior force. . .

Go: Washington[12]

JUNE 27
GENERAL ORDERS

The American and French armies linked near White Plains, New York, on July 6.

[Peekskill, N.Y.]
Wednesday June 27th 1781
The Commander in Chief has the pleasure of announcing to the Army the approach of the troops of his most Christian Majesty under the Command of his Excellency Lieutenant General Count de Rochambeau.

The General assures himself that it would be needless to recommend to the officers and Soldiers of the American Army a cultivation of acquaintance and friendship with our generous Allies—policy Strongly dictates the measure but he hopes they will be influenced by a nobler motive— Gratitude.

To the Officers of all ranks the General recommends the strictest attention to their several duties—to those of the day and on guards he particularly enjoins the most pointed observance of the rules and regulations for the establishment of discipline—Independent of the necessity of the utmost care and circumspection at all times, We shall be more than commonly bound to practise them henceforward—We shall be daily under the Eyes of officers of the first distinction improved by long service, and there is nothing which contributes more to establish the military character of a people than a performance of their duties with Alertness precision and uniformity. . . .[13]

JULY 19

TO MAJOR GENERAL CHASTELLUX

Washington got along extremely well with Rochambeau and the other French officers, including the Chevalier de Chastellux—not least because of their shared love of good wine.

Head Quarters [near Dobbs Ferry, N.Y.]
19 July 1781

Dear Sir

you have taken a most effectual method of obliging me to accept your Cask of Claret—as I find, by your ingenious manner of stating the case, that I shall, by a refusal, bring my patriotism into question, and incur a suspicion of want of attachment to the French Nation, and of regard to you which of all things I wish to avoid. I will not enter into a discussion of the point of divinity, as I perceive you are a Master at that Weapon. In short, my dear sir, my only scruple arises from a fear of depriving you of an Article that you cannot conveniently replace in this Country. you can only releive me by promising to partake very often of that hilarity which a Glass of good Claret seldom fails to produce.[14]

JULY 26

TO JOSEPH WEBB

Washington was always a stickler for dressing comfortably and well, all the way down to his boots and shoes. He had asked Webb, who was a leather and shoe manufacturer, for a fine pair of horse-skin boots, and was pleased with the result.

Hd Qrs near Dobbs ferry [N.Y.] 26 July 1781

Dear Sir,

Colo. Wadsworth delivered me your favor of the 30th Ulto and a few days afterwards the Boots came safe. I thank you for your care & attention in forwarding them. the Shoe of the Boot is sufficiently large, and the whole answers very well; but might have been closer drawn as they slip on very easy. herewith you will receive the cost of them in Eleven dollars, £3.6.0.

In behalf of Mrs Washington, I thank you & Mrs Webb in a particular manner, for your kind invitation to spend her time at Weathersfield—as soon as she was able to bear the journey, she left New Windsor for Philadelphia—from whence, by this time, she will have set out for Virginia, having got her health, in a degree, restored; but not quite.

a few days ago I received a neat pair of Shoes from Mr Roger Brown of Weathersfield; but as they came without letter or account, & the card on the package was much defaced I must request the favor of you to ask the price, & let me know to whom I shall pay the money—The stouter Boots, mentioned in the P.S. to your letter, is not yet come to hand. nor am I in any hurry about them. I only mention the matter as it composes part of your letter.

My best respects attend Mrs & Miss Webb—yourself—& the good families around you. I am Dr Sir Yr most obedt & Obliged Servt

Go: Washington[15]

AUGUST 17

ROCHAMBEAU AND WASHINGTON TO ADMIRAL DE GRASSE

On August 14, as Washington and Rochambeau scouted the British defenses around New York, a letter arrived from de Grasse announcing that he had left the West Indies bound not for New York, but Virginia. The admiral warned that he could only remain off the coast until mid-October, after which he must return to France, making it imperative that the Franco-American army should be prepared to cooperate with him from the very moment of his arrival. What followed was probably the most important decision of Washington's entire military career. To his credit, he neither reproached his French allies for disregarding his preference for New York, nor remained stubbornly attached to his original scheme; instead, Washington decided to transfer the majority of his and Rochambeau's force south to Virginia, where Cornwallis had taken post at Yorktown.

Camp at Phillipsbg [N.Y.] 17th Augt 1781.

Sir

In consequence of the dispatches received from your Excellency by the Frigate La Concorde it has been judged expedient to give up for the present the enterprise against New York and to turn our attention towards the South, with a view, if we should not be able to attempt Charles town itself, to recover and secure the States of Virginia—North Carolina—and the Country of South Carolina and Georgia. . . . For this purpose we have determined to remove the whole of the French Army and as large a detachment of the American as can be spared to Chesapeak; to meet Your Excellency there.

The following appear to us the principal Cases which will present themselves, and upon which we shall be obliged ultimately to form our plans—We have therefore stated them, with a few short observations upon each—Your Excellency will be pleased to revolve them in your own mind and prepare your own opinion by the time we shall have the pleasure of meeting you in Virginia.

1st—What shall be done if the Enemy should be found with the greater part of their force in Virginia upon the arrival of the French Fleet?

. . .

Upon the first, it appears to us that we ought without loss of time to attack the enemy with our United Force.

. . .

We would observe to your Excellency that it will be very essential to the dispatch of the business in contemplation for you to send up to Elk River at the Head of Chesapeak Bay all your Frigates—Transports and Vessels proper for the conveyance of the French and American Troops down the Bay. We shall endeavour to have as many as can be found in Baltimore and other ports secured, but we have reason to beleive they will be very few . . .[16]

SEPTEMBER 15
GENERAL ORDERS

On August 19, 4,000 French and 3,000 American troops left New York in three columns and began the long journey south to Yorktown. Washington entered Williamsburg on September 14, rejoining his friend Lafayette. De Grasse, meanwhile, brushed aside a smaller British fleet and entered the Chesapeake, debarking more French troops and assisting in the transport of allied forces from Head of Elk. This incredible alignment of land and naval forces—practically unheard of in the eighteenth century, before the era of modern communications—left Washington in command of about 8,000 French and 11,000 American troops against 9,000 British troops under Cornwallis at Yorktown.

Head Quarters Williamsburgh Saturday Septembr 15th 1781 The Commander in Chief takes the earliest Opportunity of testifying the satisfaction he feels on Joining the Army under the Command of Major General the Marquis de la Fayette with prospects which (under the smiles of Heaven) he doubts not will crown their toils with the most brilliant success—A conviction that the Officers and soldiers of this Army will still be activated by that true Martial spiritt and thirst of Glory which they have already exhibitted on so many trying occasions and under circumstances far less promising than the present affords him the most pleasing sensations.

The arrival of a powerful Fleet and Army under the Command of His Excellency the Count de Grasse and the Marquis de st simon displays a new and striking instance of the generous attention of his most Christian Majesty to the interests of the United states . . .[17]

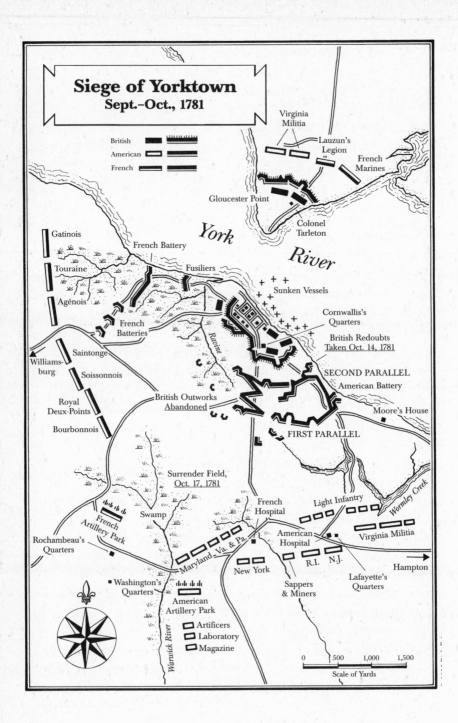

Siege of Yorktown
Sept.–Oct., 1781

British
American
French

Virginia Militia
Lauzun's Legion
French Marines
Gloucester Point
Colonel Tarleton

York
River

Gatinois
French Battery
Touraine
Fusiliers
Agénois
Sunken Vessels
French Batteries
Cornwallis's Quarters
British Redoubts Taken Oct. 14, 1781
Saintonge
Williamsburg
Soissonnois
SECOND PARALLEL
American Battery
Royal Deux-Points
British Outworks Abandoned
Moore's House
Bourbonnois
FIRST PARALLEL

Ravine

Surrender Field, Oct. 17, 1781

French Hospital
Light Infantry
Swamp
French Artillery Park
American Hospital
Virginia Militia
Rochambeau's Quarters
Maryland, Va. & Pa.
New York
R.I. N.J.
Hampton
Washington's Quarters
Sappers & Miners
Lafayette's Quarters
American Artillery Park
Artificers
Laboratory
Magazine

Warwick River

Wormley Creek

0   500   1,000   1,500
Scale of Yards

SEPTEMBER 25

TO ADMIRAL DE GRASSE

Work yet remained to be done—not least the job of convincing de Grasse to maintain his fleet off Yorktown. The French admiral, sensibly fearing the possibility that he might in turn be bottled up if the British, who commanded far greater naval resources, could muster a larger fleet against him, was anxious to depart as soon as possible.

Williamsburg 25th September 1781

Sir,

I cannot conceal from your Excellency the painful anxiety under which I have laboured since the receipt of the letter with which you honored me on the 23rd instt.

the naval movements which your Excellency states there as possible considering the intelligence communicated to you by the Baron de Closen, make it incumbent upon me to represent the consequences that would arise from them—and to urge a perseverance in the plan already agreed upon—Give me leave in the first place to repeat to your Excellency that the enterprise against York[town] under the protection of your Ships, is as certain as any military operation can be rendered by a decisive superiority of strength and means—that it is in fact reducible to calculation—& that the surrender of the british Garrison will be so important in itself and its consequences, that it must necessarily go a great way towards terminating the war, and securing the invaluable objects of it to the Allies.

Your Excellencys departure from the Chesapeake by affording an opening for the succour of York, which the enemy would instantly avail himself of—would frustrate these brilliant prospects—& the consequence would be not only the disgrace and loss of renouncing an enterprise upon which the fairest expectations of the Allies have been founded—after the most expensive preparations & uncommon exertions & fatigues—but the disbanding perhaps the whole Army for want of provisions—the present Theatre of the War is totally deficient in means of land Transportation—being intersected by large rivers—and the whole dependance for interior communication being upon small Vessels—the Country has been so much exhausted besides by the ravages of the enemy and the subsistence of our own Army—that our supplies can only be drawn from a distance and

239

under cover of a fleet Mistress of the Chesapeake—I most earnestly entreat your Excellency farther to consider that if the present opportunity should be missed, that if you should withdraw your maritime force from the position agreed upon, that no future day can restore us a similar occasion—for striking a decisive blow—that the british will be indefatigable in strengthening their most important maritime points—and that the epoch of an honorable peace will be more remote than ever.

The confidence with which I feel myself inspired by the energy of character and the naval talents which so eminently distinguish Your Excellency leaves me no doubt that upon a consideration of the consequences which must follow your departure from the Chesapeake that your Excellency will determine upon the possible measure which the dearest interests of the common cause would dictate.

I had invariably flattered myself from the accounts given me by skilful Mariners, that your Excellencys position moored in the Chesapeake might be made so respectable as to bid defiance to any attempt on the part of the british fleet—at the same time that it would support the operations of the siege—secure the transportation of our supplies by water—and œconomise the most pretious time, by facilitating the debarkation of our heavy Artillery and stores conveniently to the trenches in York River. It is to be observed that the strength of the enemys reinforcement announced under Admiral Digby as we have the intelligence from the british may not only be exaggerated—but altogether a finesse—and supposing the account consistent with truth; their total force it was hoped would not put them in condition to attack with any prospect of success.

If the stationary position which had been agreed upon should be found utterly impracticable, there is an alternative which however inferior considered relatively to the support and facility of our land operations would save our affairs from ruin—this is to cruise with your Excellencys fleet within view of the capes—so as effectually to prevent the entrance of any british Vessels.

Upon the whole I should esteem myself deficient in my duty to the common cause of France & America, if I did not persevere in entreating your Excellency to resume the plans that have been so happily arranged—& if invincible maritime reasons prevent—I depend as a last resource upon your Excellencys pursuing the alternative abovementioned & rendering the Chesapeake inaccessible to any Enemy's Vessel.

However the british Admiral may manœuvre and endeavour to divert your Excellency from the object in view, I can hardly admit a belief that it can be his serious intention to engage in a general action with a fleet whose force will be superior supposing the most flattering accounts for the british to be true—past experience having taught them to engage with caution even upon equal terms—& forced from them acknowledgements, which, prove the respect with which they have been inspired.

Let me add Sir that even a momentary absence of the french fleet may expose us to the loss of the british Garrison at York as in the present state of affairs Lord Cornwallis might effect the evacuation with the loss of his Artillery and baggage & such a sacrifice of men as his object would evidently justify.

The Marquis de la fayette who does me the honor to bear this to your Excellency will explain many peculiarities of our situation which could not well be comprised in a letter—his candour and abilities are well known to your Excellency—and entitle him to the fullest confidence in treating the most important interests—I have earnestly requested him not to proceed any farther than the Capes for fear of accidents should your Excellency have put to sea—in this case he will dispatch a Letter to your Excellency in addition to this. . .

G. Washington[18]

OCTOBER 15
GENERAL ORDERS

The siege of Yorktown began on September 28, as Washington and Rochambeau deployed their army in a six-mile arc around the British positions. On the following two days, Cornwallis abandoned his outer defenses, concentrating his troops in a tight perimeter around the town. This blunder significantly eased the allies' task, bringing much of Yorktown within range of the Franco-American artillery; but two British redoubts, numbered 9 and 10, had to be captured before Cornwallis's position could be made untenable. French and American infantry assaulted these redoubts on the evening of October 14 and captured them, making the British surrender only a matter of time.

Head Quarters Before York[town] Monday October 15th 1781

. . .

The Commander in Chief congratulates the Allied Army on the Success of the Enterprize last evening against the two important works on the left of the enemys line: He requests the Baron Viomenil who commanded the French Grenadiers and Chasseurs and the Marquis de la Fayette who commanded the American Light Infantry to accept his warmest acknowledgements for the excellency of their dispositions and for their own Gallant Conduct upon the occasion and he begs them to present his thanks to every individual officer and to the Men of their respective Commands for the Spirit and Rapidity with which they advanced to the Attacks and for the admirable Firmness with which they supported themselves under the fire of the Enemy without returning a Shot.

The General reflects with the highest degree of pleasure on the Confidence which the Troops of the two Nations must hereafter have in each other—Assured of mutual support he is convinced there is no danger which they will not chearfully encounter—no difficulty which they will not bravely overcome . . .[19]

OCTOBER 17
DIARY ENTRY

With the exception of a weather diary kept during the bitterly cold Morristown winter of 1780, Washington had not kept a diary since June 1775. He resumed it in May 1781, as if in anticipation of the momentous events that would take place later that year.

About ten Oclock the Enemy beat a parley and Lord Cornwallis proposed a cessation of Hostilities for 24 hours, that Commissioners might meet at the house of a Mr. Moore (in the rear of our first parallel) to settle terms for the surrender of the Posts of York and Gloucester. To this he was answered, that a desire to spare the further effusion of Blood would readily incline me to treat of the surrender of the above Posts but previous to the meeting of Commissioners I wished to have his proposals in writing and for this purpose would grant a cessation of hostilities two hours—Within

242

which time he sent out A letter with such proposals (tho' some of them were inadmissable) as led me to believe that there would be no great difficulty in fixing the terms. Accordingly hostilities were suspended for the Night & I proposed my own terms to which if he agreed Commissioners were to meet to digest them into form.[20]

———

OCTOBER 17
TO ADMIRAL DE GRASSE

Head Quarters Before York[town]
17th October 1781

Sir

. . .

I do myself the honor to transmit your Excellency the Copy of a letter which I have just received from Lord Cornwallis. I have informed him in answer thereto that I wish him previous to the meeting of Commissioners to send his proposals in writing to the American lines—for which purpose a cessation of Hostilities for two Hours will be allowed.

I should be anxious to have the honor of your Excellencys participation in the treaty which will according to present appearances shortly take place—I need not add how happy it will make me to welcome your Excellency in the name of America on this shore, and embrace you upon an occasion so advantageous to the interests of the common cause—and on which it is so much indebted to you . . .[21]

———

OCTOBER 18
TO GENERAL CORNWALLIS

Camp before York[town] 18th October 1781
My Lord

To avoid unnecessary discussions and delays, I shall, at once, in answer to your Lordships letter of yesterday, declare the general Basis upon which a definitive Treaty of Capitulation may take place.

243

The Garrisons of York, and Gloucester, including the seamen, as you propose shall be received prisoners of War—The condition annexed, of sending the British and German Troops, to the parts of Europe to which they respectively belong is inadmissible. Instead of this, they will be marched to such parts of the Country as can most conveniently provide for their subsistence, and the benevolent treatment of prisoners which is invariably observed by the Americans will be extended to them. The same honors will be granted to the surrendering Army as were granted to the Garrison of Charlestown.

The Shipping and Boats in the two Harbors with all their Guns—Stores—Tackling—Furniture and Apparel shall be delivered in their present State to an Officer of the Navy, appointed to take possession of them.

The Artillery—Arms—Accoutrements, Military Chest and public Stores of every denomination shall be delivered, unimpaired, to the Heads of departments to which they respectively belong.

The Officers shall be indulged in retaining their side Arms and the Officers and Soldiers may preserve their Baggage and Effects—with this reserve, that property taken in the Country will be reclaimed.

With regard to the Individuals in civil Capacities, whose interests your Lordship wishes may be attended to, untill they are more particularly described, nothing definitive can be settled.

I have to add, that I expect the sick and wounded will be supplied with their own Hospital Stores and be attended by British Surgeons particularly charged with the care of them.

Your Lordship will be pleased to signify your determination either to accept or reject the proposals now offered, in the course of two Hours from the delivery of this letter, that Commissioners may be appointed to digest the Articles of Capitulation, or a renewal of Hostilities may take place. I have the honor to be My Lord Your Lordships Most obedient and humble servant

Go: Washington[22]

OCTOBER 19
TO THOMAS MCKEAN

The Articles of Capitulation were signed on the morning of October 19, leaving Cornwallis and his entire garrison prisoners in American hands. Washington describes the British surrender in this letter to the president of Congress.

Head Quarters near York[town] 19th Octo. 1781

Sir

I have the Honor to inform Congress, that a Reduction of the British Army under the Command of Lord Cornwallis, is most happily effected—The unremitting Ardor which actuated every Officer & Soldier in the combined Army on this Occasion, has principally led to this Important Event, at an earlier period than my most sanguine Hopes had induced me to expect.

The singular Spirit of Emulation, which animated the whole Army from the first Commencement of our Operations, has filled my Mind with the highest pleasure & Satisfaction—and had given me the happiest presages of Success.

On the 17th instant, a Letter was received from Lord Cornwallis, proposing a Meeting of Commissioners, to consult on Terms for the Surrender of the Posts of York & Gloucester—This Letter (the first which had passed between us) opened a correspondence, a copy of which I do myself the Honor to inclose. that Correspondence was followed by the Definitive Capitulation, which was agreed to, & Signed on the 19th Copy of which is also herewith transmitted—and which, I hope, will meet the Approbation of Congress.

I should be wanting in the feelings of Gratitude, did I not mention on this Occasion, with the warmest Sense of Acknowlegments, the very chearfull & able Assistance, which I have received in the Course of our Operations, from his Excellency the Count de Rochambeau, and all his Officers of every Rank, in their respective Capacities. Nothing could equal this Zeal of our Allies, but the emulating Spirit of the American Officers, whose ardor would not suffer their Exertions to be exceeded.

The very uncommon Degree of Duty & Fatigue which the Nature of the Service required from the officers of Engineers & Artillery of both

Armies, obliges me particularly to mention the Obligations I am under to the Commanding & other Officers of those Corps.

I wish it was in my Power to express to Congress, how much I feel myself indebted to The Count de Grasse and the Officers of the Fleet under his Command, for the distinguished Aid and Support which has been afforded by them; between whom, & the Army, the most happy Concurrence of Sentiments & Views have subsisted, and from whom, every possifble Co-operation has been experienced, which the most harmonious Intercourse could afford.

Returns of the Prisoners, Military Stores, Ordnance, Shipping & other Matters, I shall do myself the Honor to transmit to Congress, as soon as they can be collected by the Heads of Departments, to which they belong.

Colo. Laurens & the Viscount de Noailles, on the Part of the combined Army, were the Gentlemen who acted as Commissioners for forming & setting the Terms of Capitulation & Surrender herewith transmitted—to whom I am particularly obliged for their Readiness & Attention exhibited on the Occasion.

Colo. Tilghman, one of my Aids de Camp, will have the Honor to deliver these dispatches to your Excellency—he will be able to inform you of every minute Circumstance which is not particularly mentioned in my Letter. His Merits, which are too well known to need any Observations at this Time, have gained my particular Attention—& I could wish that they may be honored by the Notice of your Excellency & Congress.

Your Excellency & Congress will be pleased to accept my Congratulations on this happy Event—& believe me to be With the highest Respect & Esteem sir Your Excellencys Most Obedient and most humble Servant

Go: Washington[23]

1782

AUGUST 15
TO JAMES MCHENRY

The victory at Yorktown did not end the war. Washington spent much of the winter of 1781–1782 in Philadelphia, lobbying Congress—which had become less, not more, effective as the war progressed—for desperately needed reforms in the army. Supplies of food and clothing remained poor, and the soldiers received pay—nearly worthless due to continuing inflation—months after it was due. The British, meanwhile, had withdrawn General Henry Clinton and replaced him with Sir Guy Carleton, who conducted no offensive operations and spoke of impending peace. Washington remained skeptical, as he explained in this letter to future secretary of war James McHenry, who was now serving as Lafayette's aide.

Newburgh [N.Y.] 15th Augt 1782

My dear Doctr

If the Commanders of the Fleets and Armies of our late, *most Gracious Sovereign,* in America; are not guilty of more duplicity than comports with candid Minds; we are now advanced to that critical & important Crisis, when our hands are to be tried at the Arts of Negociation.

In a Letter which I have received and forwarded to Congress, from Sir Guy Carlton & Admiral Digby, are these Words "We are acquainted, Sir, by Authority, that Negociations for a General Peace have already commenced at Paris, and that Mr Grenville is invested with full powers to treat with all Parties at War, and is now at Paris in the execution of his Commission. And we are likewise Sir, further made acquainted, that His Majesty in order to remove all obstacles to that Peace which he so ardently wishes to restore, has Commanded his Ministers to direct Mr Grenville, that the Independency of the thirteen Provences should be proposed by him in the first instance, instead of making it a condition of a general Treaty; however, not without the highest confidence, that the loyalists shall be restored to their possessions, or a full compensation made them for whatever confiscations may have taken place."

Here then, if these expressions are not Intrenched in General Conways Speech (when he threw out an Idea of giving to America the same *kind* of Independency that they were about granting to Ireland) is a solid basis for our Commissioners to raise their Superstructure upon; and things may, & probably soon will, be brought to a speedy and happy Issue. But, if the Ministry mean no more than Genl Conway has hinted at, 'tis plain their only aim is to gain time, that they may become more formidable at Sea—form new Alliances, if possible—or disunite us. Be their object what it may, we, if wise, should push our preparations with vigour; for nothing will hasten Peace more, than to be in a Condition for War—and if the contest is to continue, 'tis indispensably necessary.

One thing however is certain, but how it came to pass is not very well understood; and that is, that the Letter of Carleton & Digby to me, has been published in New York, and has spread universal consternation among all the Tribes of Refugees; who, actuated by different Passions— or the same passion in different degrees & forms; are a mere medley of confused—enraged—& dejected characters. Some it is said are cursing— others Crying—while far the greatest part of them are struck dumb, and do not know what to do.

Adieu—I rejoice to hear of your recovery—It is unnecessary for me to repeat to you, that I am Your sincere friend & Affecte Servt

Go: Washington[1]

OCTOBER 2

TO BENJAMIN LINCOLN

Washington's greatest fear at this juncture of the war was complacency—and he had reason to be afraid. While the politicians in Philadelphia relaxed and spoke of peace and independence, a greater danger to freedom than perhaps any the nation had ever faced—a discontented army—was preparing to remind the United States what it owed them. Washington explained the danger in this letter to the secretary of war.

Head Quarters [Verplanck Point, N.Y.]
Octr 2nd 1782

My dear Sir

Painful as the task is to discribe the dark side of our affairs, it some times becomes a matter of indispensable necessity—Without disguize or palliation, I will inform you candidly of the discontents which, at this moment, prevail universally throughout the Army.

The Complaints of Evils which they suppose almost remediless are, the total want of Money, or the means of existing from One day to another, the heavy debts they have already incurred, the loss of Credit the distress of their Families (ie. such as are Maried) at home, & the prospect of Poverty & Misery before them. It is vain Sir to suppose that Military Men will acquiesce *contentedly* with bare rations, when those in the Civil walk of life (unacquainted with half the hardships they endure) are regularly paid the emoluments of Office—While the human Mind is influenc'd by the same passions, & have the same inclinations to endulge it cannt be. A Military Man has the same turn to sociability, as a person in Civil life—he conceives himself equally called upon to live up to his rank—& his pride is hurt when circumstances restrain him—only conceive then, the mortification they (even the Genl Officers) must suffer when they cannot invite a French Officer—a visiting friend—or travelling acquaintance to a better Repast than stinking whiskey (& not always that) & a bit of Beef without Vegitable, will afford them.

The Officers also complain of other hardships which they think might & ought to be remedied without delay, viz. the stopping Promotions where there have been vacancy's open for a long time, the withholding Commissions from those who are justly entitled to them & have Warrants or Certificates of their Appointments from the Executive of their

States, and particularly the leaving the compensation for their services in a loose equivocal state, without ascertaining their claims upon the public, or making provision for the future payment of them.

While I premise, that tho 'no one that I have seen or heard of appears opposed to the principle of reducing the Army as circumstances may require; Yet I cannot help fearing the Result of the measure in contemplation, under present circumstances, when I see such a number of Men goaded by a thousand stings of reflexion on the past, & of anticipation on the future, about to be turned into the World, soured by penury & what they call the ingratitude of the Public, involved in debts, without one farthing of Money to carry them home, after having spent the flower of their days & many of them their patrimonies in establishing the freedom & Independence of their Country, and suffered every thing human Nature is capable of enduring on this side of death—I repeat it, in these irritable circumstances, without one thing to sooth their feelings, or brighten the gloomy prospects, I cannot avoid apprehending that a train of Evils will follow, of a very serious & distressing Nature—On the other hand could the Officers be placed in as good a situation as when they came into service, the contention, I am persuaded, would be not who should continue in the field, but who should retire to private life.

I wish not to heighten the shades of the picture, so far as the real life would justify me in doing, or I would give Anecdotes of patriotism & distress which have scarcely ever been paralleled, never surpassed in the history of Mankind—but you may rely upon it, the patience & long sufferance of this Army are almost exhausted, and that there never was so great a spirit of Discontent as at this instant; While in the field, I think it may be kept from breaking out into Acts of Outrage, but when we retire into Winter Quarters (unless the Storm is previously dissipated) I cannot be at ease, respecting the consequences—It is high time for a Peace.

To you, my dear Sir, I need not be more particular in discribing my anxiety & the grounds of it—You are too well acquainted, from your own service, with the real sufferings of the Army to require a longer detail; I will therefore only add that exclusive of the common hardships of a Military life, Our Troops have been, & still are obliged to perform more services, foreign to their proper duty, without gratuity or reward, than the Soldiers of any other Army—for example, the immense labours expended in doing the duties of Artificers in erecting Fortifications & Military Works; the fatigue of building themselves Barracks or Huts annually—And of cutting & transporting Wood for the use of all our Posts & Garrisons, without any expence whatever to the Public.

Of this Letter, (which from the tenor of it must be considered in some degree of a private nature) you may make such use as you shall think proper—Since the principal objects of it were, by displaying the Merits, the hardships, the disposition & critical state of the Army, to give information that might eventually be useful, & to convince you with what entire confidence & esteem I am My dear Sir &c.[2]

————

OCTOBER 23
TO WILLIAM GORDON

Washington's concern with present troubles did not prevent him from taking the long view, and pondering how, and with what resources, future generations would judge the Revolutionary War and his role in it.

Verplanks point 23d Oct. 1782

Dear Sir

. . .

It appears to me impracticable for the best Historiographer living, to write a full & correct history of the present revolution who has not free access to the Archives of Congress—those of Individual States—the Papers of the Commander in Chief, & Commanding Officers of seperate departments. Mine—while the War continues—I consider as a species of Public property, sacred in my hands; & of little Service to any Historian who has not that general information which is only to be derived with exactitude from the sources I have mentioned—When Congress then shall open their registers—& say it is proper for the Servants of the public to do so, it will give me much pleasure to afford all the Aid to your labors & laudable undertaking which my Papers can give—'till one of those periods arrive I do not think myself justified in suffering any inspection of, and extracts to be taken from my Records. . .

Go: Washington[3]

DECEMBER 14

TO MAJOR GENERAL CHASTELLUX

The time had come for farewells to Washington's departing French allies.

Newburgh, December 14, 1782.

My dear Chevr

I felt too much to express any thing, the day I parted with you; A Sense of your public Services to this Country, & gratitude for your private friendship, quite overcame me at the moment of our seperation—But I should be wanting to the feelings of my heart, & should do violence to my inclination, was I to suffer you to leave this Country without the warmest assurances of an affectionate regard for your person & character.

Our good friend the Marqs. de la Fayette prepared me (long before I had the honor to see you) for those Impressions of esteem which oppertunities, & your own benevolent Mind has since improved into a deep, & lasting friendship—a friendship which neither time nor distance can ever eradicate.

I can truly say, that never in my life did I part with a Man to whom my soul clave more sincerely than it did to you. My warmest wishes will attend you in your voyage across the Atlantic—to the rewards of a generous Prince—the Arms of Affectionate friends. and be assured that it will be one of my highest gratifications to keep up a regular intercourse with you by Letter.

I regret, exceedingly, that circumstances should withdraw you from this Country before the final accomplishment of that Independence & Peace which the Arms of our good Ally has assisted in placing before us in so agreeable a point of view. Nothing would give me more pleasure than to accompany you in a tour through the Continent of North America at the close of the War, in search of the Natural curiosities with which it abounds, and to view the foundation of a rising Empire. I have the honr to be &ca.

Go: Washington[4]

DECEMBER 14
TO LIEUTENANT GENERAL ROCHAMBEAU

Newburgh Decr 14th 1782

I cannot, my dear Genl, permit you to depart from this Country without repeating to you the high sense I entertain of the Services you have rendered America, by the constant attention which you have paid to the Interests of it. By the exact order and discipline of the Corps under your command—and your readiness, at all times, to give facility to every measure which the force of the combined Armies was competent to.

To this testimony of your Public character, I should be wanting to the feelings of my heart, was I not to add expressions of the happiness I have enjoyed in your private friendship—The remembrance of which will be one of the most pleasing, circumstances of my life.

My best wishes will accompany you to France, where I have no doubt of your meeting the Smiles & rewards of a generous Prince—and the warmest embraces of affectionate friends. I have the honor to be with great personal attachment, respect & regard, Yr Most Obedt & Most Hble Servant

Go: Washington[5]

———

1783

JANUARY 15
TO BUSHROD WASHINGTON

*When Washington's twenty-year-old nephew Bushrod Washington went to Phila-
delphia to begin service as a legal apprentice, the commander in chief was not too
busy with his military duties to offer some words of advice.*

Newburgh 15th Jany 1783

Dear Bushrod,
    You will be surprized perhaps at receiving a letter from me—but if the
end is answered for which it is written, I shall not think my time miss-
spent. Your Father, who seems to entertain a very favourable opinion of
your prudence, & I hope you merit it; in one or two of his letters to me,
speaks of the difficulty he is under to make you remittances. Whether
this arises from the scantiness of his funds, or the extensiveness of your
demands is matter of conjecture, with me—I hope it is not the latter, because common prudence, & every other consideration which ought to have
weight in a reflecting mind is opposed to your requiring more than his
conveniency and a regard to his other Children will enable him to pay
& because he holds up no idea in his Letter, which would support me in
the conclusion. yet when I take a view of the inexperience of youth—the
temptations in, & vices of Cities; and the distresses to which our Virginia

Gentlemen are driven by an accumulation of Taxes & the want of a market; I am almost inclined to ascribe it, in part to both. Therefore, as a friend, I give you the following advice.

Let the object, which carried you to Philadelphia be always before your Eyes—remember, that it is not the *mere* study of the Law, but to become eminent in the profession of it which is to yield honor and profit—the first was your choice; let the second be your ambition. and that dissipation, is incompatible with both.

That the Company in which you will improve most, will be least expensive to you—and yet I am not such a Stoic as to suppose you will, or to think it right that you ought, always to be in Company with Senators & Philosophers; but, of the young and juvenile kind let me advice you to be choice. It is easy to make acquaintances, but very difficult to shake them off, however irksome & unprofitable they are found after we have once committed ourselves to them—the indiscretions, & scrapes which very often they involuntarily lead one into, proves equally distressing & disgraceful.

Be courteous to all, but intimate with few, and let those few be well tried before you give them your confidence—true friendship is a plant of slow growth, and must undergo & withstand the shocks of adversity before it is entitled to the appellation.

Let your *heart* feel for the affliction, & distresses of every one—and let your *hand* give, in proportion to your purse—remembering always, the estimation of the Widows mite. But, that it is not every one who asketh, that deserveth charity; all however are worthy of the enquiry—or the deserving may suffer.

Do not conceive that fine Clothes make fine Men, any more than fine feathers make fine Birds—A plain genteel dress is more admired and obtains more credit than lace & embroidery in the Eyes of the judicious & sensible.

The last thing I shall mention is first of importance. and that is, to avoid Gaming—This is a vice which is productive of every possible evil. equally injurious to the Morals & health of its votaries—It is the child of Avarice—the brother of inequity—& father of Mischief—It has been the ruin of many worthy familys—the loss of many a mans honor—& the cause of Suicide. To all those who enter the lists, it is equally fascinating—the successful gamester, pushes his good fortune till it is overtaken by a reverse—the loosing gamester, in hopes of retrieving past misfortunes, goes on from bad to worse; till grown desperate, he pushes at every thing; and looses his all. In a word, few gain by this abominable practice (the profit, if any, being diffused) while thousands are injured.

Perhaps you will say my conduct has anticipated the advice, & that "not one of these cases apply to me"—I shall be heartily glad of it. It will add not a little to my happiness, to find those, to whom I am so nearly connected, pursuing the right walk of life—it will be the sure road to my favor, & to those honors, & places of profit, which their Country can bestow, as merit rarely goes unrewarded. I am Dr Bushrod Yr Affecte Uncle

Go: Washington[1]

FEBRUARY 6

TO MAJOR GENERAL NATHANAEL GREENE

In moments of leisure, Washington contemplated the nature of the struggle that was drawing to a close, and wondered how victory had been achieved.

Newburgh Feby 6th 1783

My dear Sir,

. . .

It is with a pleasure which friendship only is susceptible of, I congratulate you on the glorious end you have put to hostilities in the Southern States—the honor and advantages of it, I hope, & trust, you will live long to enjoy. when this hemisphere will be equally free is yet in the womb of time to discover—a little while, however 'tis presumed, will disclose the determinations of the British senate with respect to Peace or war as it seems to be agreed on all hands, that the present Primeir (especially if he should find the opposition powerful) intends to submit the decision of these Matters to Parliament. The Speech, the Addresses—and Debates for which we are looking in every direction, will give a data from which the bright rays of the one; or gloomy prospect of the other may be discovered.

If Historiographers should be hardy enough to fill the page of History with the advantages that have been gained with unequal numbers (on the part of America) in the course of this contest, & attempt to relate the distressing circumstances under which they have been obtained, it is more than probable that Posterity will bestow on their labors the epithet & marks of fiction for it will not be believed that such a force as Great Britain has employed for eight years in this Country could be baffled in their plan of Subjugating it by numbers infinitely less—composed of Men oftentimes half starved—always in Rags—without pay—& experiencing, at times, every Species of distress which human nature is capable of undergoing.

. . .

Go: Washington[2]

FEBRUARY 16
TO DAVID RITTENHOUSE

Washington had spent most of his time during the previous nine years not on the battlefield, but at his headquarters desk. Age, and all of the thousands of letters he wrote and read, took a toll on his eyes. His new pair of reading glasses, supplied by David Rittenhouse, would play a surprising role in the crisis that was about to erupt.

Newburgh Feby 16th 83

Sir,

I have been honored with your letter of the 7th, and beg you to accept my sincere thanks for the favor confered on me in the Glasses—which are very fine—but more particularly for the flattering expressions which accompanied the present.

The Spectacles suit my Eyes extremely well—as I am perswaded the reading glasses also will when I get more accustomed to the use of them— At present I find some difficulty in coming at the proper Focus—but when I do obtain it, they magnify properly & shew those objects very distinctly which at first appear like a mist blended together & confused. I send the amount of the Silver Smiths charge—and with great esteem & respect am Sir Yr Most Obt & Hble Servt

G: W——n[3]

MARCH II
GENERAL ORDERS

On March 10, Washington received an anonymous note calling all of the army's officers to a meeting the next day, and enclosing an address to the troops from a "fellow soldier." America, the soldier declared, had become "a country that tramples upon your rights, disdains your cries and insults your distresses." Neither the politicians nor the civilians cared what happened to the troops; and yet, the address darkly warned, "the army has its alternative." If Congress signed a peace treaty with Great Britain, the soldiers could keep the field, march on Philadelphia, and impose their demands by force. And if the British resumed the war, then the soldiers—"courting the auspices, and inviting the direction of your illustrious leader [Washington]"— could withdraw from the field and leave America at Britain's mercy.⁴ A horrified Washington immediately issued general orders condemning the address and calling an "official" meeting for the fifteenth.

Head Quarters Newburgh Tuesday March 11th 1783
The Commander in Chief having heard that a General meeting of the officers of the Army was proposed to be held this day at the Newbuilding in an ananonimous paper which was circulated yesterday by some unknown person conceives (altho he is fully persuaded that the good sense of the officers could induce them to pay very little attention to such an irregular invitation) his duty as well as the reputation and true interest of the Army requires his disapprobation of such disorderly proceedings, at the same time he requests that General & Field officers with one officer from each company and a proper representation of the Staff of the Army will assemble at 12 o'clock on Saturday next at the Newbuilding to hear the report of the Committee of the Army to Congress.

After mature deliberation they will devise what further measures ought to be adopted as most rational and best calculated to attain the just and important object in view. The senior officer in Rank present will be pleased to preside and report the result of the Deliberations to the Commander in Chief. . . .⁵

MARCH 12
TO JOSEPH JONES

On the following day, Washington wrote to the new president of Congress, Elias Boudinot, reporting recent events. He had hardly finished writing the letter when he received a note containing another anonymous address to the troops. Distributed throughout the army in the form of flyers, the address announced that Washington's assent to a meeting indicated that he agreed with its purpose, and also asserted that the commander in chief had privately "sanctified" the soldiers' claims—as indeed he had done in recent correspondence with Congress and fellow officers. If Washington repudiated these claims, the address implied that he would also repudiate the army; if not, he might instigate a military rebellion, with himself—though unwilling—at its head. Jones was a delegate to Congress from Virginia, and one of Washington's old acquaintances.

Newburgh 12th March 1783

Dear Sir,

I have received your letter of the 27th Ulto, & thank you for the information & freedom of your communication. My official letter to Congress of this date will inform you what has happened in this Quarter. In addition to which, it may be necessary it should be known to you & to such others as you may think proper, that the *temper* of the Army, tho 'very irritable on acct of their long protracted sufferings, has been apparently extremely quiet while their business was depending before Congress, untill four days past. in the mean time it should seem, reports have been propagated in Philadelphia that dangerous combinations were forming in the Army, & this at a time when there was not a syllable of the kind in agitation in Camp.

It also appears that upon the arrival of a certain Gentleman from Philadelphia in Camp, whose name I do not at present incline to mention, such sentiments as these were immediately & industriously circulated. That it was universally expected that the Army would not disband untill they had obtained Justice. That the public creditors looked up to them for redress of their grievances, would afford them every aid, and even join them in the field, if necessary. That some Members of Congress wished the measure might take effect, in order to compel the public—particularly the delinquent States, to do justice. with many other suggestions of a similar nature, from whence and a variety of other considerations it is generally believed the scheme was not only planned, but also digested & matured in Philadelphia: and that some people have been playing a double game—spreading at the Camp, & in Philadelphia reports, and raising jealousies equally void of foundation, untill called into being by their vile artifices. for as soon as the Minds of the *Officers* were thought to be prepared for the transaction, an anonymous invitation was circulated requesting a general meeting of the Officers next day—at the same instant, many copies of the Address to the Officers of the Army was circulated in every state line of it.

So soon as I obtained knowledge of these things, I issued the order of the 11th (transmitted to Congress;) in order to rescue the foot that stood wavering on the precipice of despair, from taking those steps which would have led to the abyss of misery, while the passions were inflamed and the mind tremblingly alive with the recollection of past sufferings, and their present feelings. I did this upon the principle that it is easier to divert from a wrong to a right path, than it is to recall the hasty & fatal steps which have been already taken.

It is commonly supposed, if the Officers had met agreeably to the anonymous summons, resolutions might have been formed, the consequences of which may be more easily conceived than expressed. Now, they will have leisure to view the matter more calmly & seriously—It is to be hoped they will be induced to adopt more rational measures, and wait a while longer for the settlement of their Accts; the postponing of which gives more uneasiness in the Army than any other thing. there is not a man in it, who will not acknowledge that Congress have not the means of paying—but why not say they—one & all—liquidate the accts, & certify our dues? Are we to be disbanded & sent home without this? are we afterwards to make individual applications for such settlements at Philadelphia, or at any Auditing Office in our respective States; to be shifted perhaps from one board to another, & dance attendance at all; & finally be postponed till we lose the substance, in pursuit of the shadow. while they are agitated by these considerations there are not wanting invidious characters who tell them "it is neither the wish nor the intention of the public to settle your accounts but to delay them under one pretext or another 'till peace, which we are upon the verge of, and a seperation of the Army takes place; which it is well known, it will be difficult if not impracticable, a general settlement never can be accomplished; and that individual loss *in this instance,* will be a public gain."

However derogatory these ideas are to the dignity, honor, & justice of government; yet in a matter so interesting to the Army, & at the same time so easy to be effected by the public as that of liquidating the accounts is delayed, without any apparent or obvious necessity; they will have their place in a mind that is soured, & has become irritated—Let me entreat you therefore, my good Sir, to push this matter to an issue—and if there are Delegates among you, who are really opposed to doing justice to the Army, scruple not to tell them—if matters do come to extremety—that they must be answerable for all the ineffable horrors which may be occasioned there by. With great truth and sincerity I am—Dear Sir Yr Most Obedt & affecte Servt

Go: Washington[6]

MARCH 15

TO THE OFFICERS OF THE ARMY

At noon on March 15, Washington entered a large building that the soldiers had erected to serve as a combination chapel and dance hall, and addressed his officers. After he finished, Washington looked up and decided that his listeners remained unconvinced. Pulling out a long letter from delegate Joseph Jones on Congress's fiscal difficulties, the commander in chief fumbled for a moment and then pulled out the reading glasses he had recently ordered. No one had seen him wearing them before, and he thought an explanation was in order. "Gentlemen, you must pardon me," he said. "I have grown gray in your service and now find myself growing blind."

The moment was electric. Washington could have drawn his sword and waved it in the air, recalling the heroic deeds they had shared together at Trenton, Monmouth, or Yorktown; or he could have spoken sternly, threatening the officers with punishment if they continued on their wayward course. Instead, Washington had donned his spectacles, deliberately or inadvertently reminding the officers of the long hours he had spent at his desk over the past 3,000 days, writing letters, compiling reports, perusing returns—all to ensure that his officers and men were fed, clothed, equipped, cared for in sickness, paid, and pensioned. Overwhelmed with emotion, the officers listened silently while Washington finished reading Jones's letter. After he turned and left the building, they conferred under the chairmanship of Horatio

Gates—Washington's erstwhile enemy—and unanimously decided to reject the two anonymous addresses, declare their confidence in Congress, and ask Washington to mediate all future negotiations with the government. The last great crisis of the war had ended.

Head Quarters Newburgh 15th of March 1783.

Gentlemen,

By an anonymous summons, an attempt has been made to convene you together—how inconsistent with the rules of propriety! how unmilitary! and how subversive of all order and discipline. let the good sense of the Army decide.

In the moment of this summons, another anonymous production was sent into circulation; addressed more to the feelings & passions, than to the reason & judgment of the Army. The Author of the piece, is entitled to much credit for the goodness of his Pen: and I could wish he had as much credit for the rectitude of his Heart—for, as Men see thro 'different Optics, and are induced by the reflecting faculties of the Mind, to use different means to attain the same end; the Author of the Address, should have had more charity, than to mark for Suspicion, the Man who should recommend moderation and longer forbearance—or, in other words, who should not think as he thinks, and act as he advises. But he had another plan in view, in which candor and liberality of Sentiment, regard to justice, and love of Country, have no part; and he was right, to insinuate the darkest suspicion, to effect the blackest designs.

That the Address is drawn with great art, and is designed to answer the most insidious purposes. That it is calculated to impress the Mind, with an idea of premeditated injustice in the Sovereign power of the United States, and rouse all those resentments which must unavoidably flow from such a belief. That the secret mover of this Scheme (whoever he may be) intended to take advantage of the passions, while they were warmed by the recollection of past distresses, without giving time for cool, deliberative thinking, & that composure of Mind which is so necessary to give dignity & stability to measures, is rendered too obvious, by the mode of conducting the business, to need other proof than a reference to the proceeding.

Thus much, Gentlemen, I have thought it incumbent on me to observe to you, to shew upon what principles I opposed the irregular and hasty meeting which was proposed to have been held on Tuesday last: and not because I wanted a disposition to give you every opportunity, consistent with your own honor, and the dignity of the Army, to make known your grievances. If my conduct heretofore, has not evinced to you, that I have been a faithful friend to the Army; my declaration of it at this time would be equally unavailing & improper. But as I was among the first who embarked in the cause of our common Country—As I have never left your side one moment, but when called from you, on public duty—As I have been the constant companion & witness of your Distresses, and not among the last to feel, & acknowledge your Merits—As I have ever considered my own Military reputation as inseperably connected with that of the Army—As my Heart has ever expanded wth joy, when I have heard its praises—and my indignation has arisen, when the Mouth of detraction has been opened against it—it can *scarcely be supposed,* at this late stage of the War, that I am indifferent to its interests.

But—how are they to be promoted? The way is plain, says the anonymous Addresser—If War continues, remove into the unsettled Country—there establish yourselves, and leave an ungrateful Country to defend itself—But who are they to defend? Our Wives, our Children, our Farms, and other property which we leave behind us. or—in this state of hostile seperation, are we to take the two first (the latter cannot be removed)—to perish in a Wilderness, with hunger cold & nakedness? If Peace takes place, never sheath your Swords says he untill you have obtained full and ample Justice—this dreadful alternative, of either deserting our Country in the extremest hour of her distress, or turning our Army against it, (which is the apparent object, unless Congress can be compelled into an instant compliance) has something so shocking in it, that humanity revolts at the idea. My God! What can this writer have in view, by recommending such measures? Can he be a friend to the Army? Can he be a friend to this Country? Rather, is he not an insidous Foe? Some Emissary, perhaps, from New York, plotting the ruin of both, by sowing the seeds of discord & seperation between the Civil & Military powers of the Continent? And what a Compliment does he pay to our understandings, when he recommends measures in either alternative, impracticable in their nature?

But here, Gentlemen, I will drop the curtain; because it would be as imprudent in me to assign my reasons for this opinion, as it would be insulting to your conception, to suppose you stood in need of them. a moments reflection will convince every dispassionate Mind of the physical impossiblity of carrying either proposal into execution.

There might, Gentlemen, be an impropriety in my taking notice, in this Address to you, of an anonymous production—but the manner in which that performance has been introduced to the Army—the effect it was intended to have, together with some other circumstances, will amply justify my observations on the tendency of that Writing. With respect to the advice given by the Author—to suspect the Man, who shall recommend moderate measures and longer forbearance—I spurn it—as every man, who regards that liberty, & reveres that justice for which we contend, undoubtedly must—for if Men are to be precluded from offering their sentiments on a matter, which may involve the most serious and alarming consequences, that can invite the consideration of Mankind; reason is of no use to us—the freedom of Speech may be taken away—and, dumb & silent we may be led, like sheep, to the Slaughter.

I cannot, in justice to my own belief, & what I have great reason to conceive is the intention of Congress, conclude this Address, without giving it as my decided opinion; that that Honorable Body, entertain exalted sentiments of the Services of the Army; and, from a full conviction of its merits & sufferings, will do it compleat Justice: That their endeavors, to discover & establish funds for this purpose, have been unwearied, and will not cease, till they have succeeded, I have not a doubt. But, like all other large Bodies, where there is a variety of different Interests to reconcile, their deliberations are slow. Why then should we distrust them? and, in consequence of that distrust, adopt measures, which may cast a shade over that glory which, has been so justly acquired; and tarnish the reputation of an Army which is celebrated thro 'all Europe, for its fortitude and Patriotism? and for what is this done? to bring the object we seek for nearer? No! most certainly, in my opinion, it will cast it at a greater distance.

For myself (and I take no merit in giving the assurance, being induced to it from principles of gratitude, veracity & justice)—a grateful sence of the confidence you have ever placed in me—a recollection of the chearful assistance, & prompt obedience I have experienced from you, under every vicisitude of Fortune, and the sincere affection I feel for an Army, I have so long had the honor to Command, will oblige me to declare, in this public & solemn manner, that, in the attainment of compleat justice for all your toils & dangers, and in the gratification of every wish, so far as may be done consistently with the great duty I owe my Country, and those powers we are bound to respect, you may freely command my services to the utmost of my abilities.

While I give you these assurances, and pledge my self in the most unequivocal manner, to exert whatever ability I am possesed of, in your favor—let me entreat you, Gentlemen, on your part, not to take any measures, which, viewed in the calm light of reason, will lessen the dignity, & sully the glory you have hitherto maintained—let me request you to rely on the plighted faith of your Country, and place a full confidence in the purity of the intentions of Congress; that, previous to your dissolution as an Army they will cause all your Accts to be fairly liquidated, as directed in their resolutions, which were published to you two days ago—and that they will adopt the most effectual measures in their power, to render ample justice to you, for your faithful and meritorious Services. And let me conjure you, in the name of our common Country—as you value your own sacred honor—as you respect the rights of humanity, & as you regard the Military & National character of America, to express your utmost horror & detestation of the Man who wishes, under any specious pretences, to overturn the liberties of our Country, & who wickedly attempts to open the flood Gates of Civil discord, & deluge our rising Empire in Blood.

By thus determining—& thus acting, you will pursue the plain & direct road to the attainment of your wishes. You will defeat the insidious designs of our Enemies, who are compelled to resort from open force to secret Artifice. You will give one more distinguished proof of unexampled patriotism & patient virtue, rising superior to the pressure of the most complicated sufferings; And you will, by the dignity of your Conduct, afford occasion for Posterity to say, when speaking of the glorious example you have exhibited to man kind, "had this day been wanting, the World had never seen the last stage of perfection to which human nature is capable of attaining."

Go: Washington[7]

MARCH 18

TO ELIAS BOUDINOT

Washington, knowing that he and the country owed much to the officers and soldiers for their continued fidelity and patriotism, became their fierce advocate with Congress, refusing to rest until all of their grievances had been addressed satisfactorily.

Head Quarters Newburgh 18th March 1783.

Sir,

The result of the proceedings of the grand Convention of the Officers, which I have the honor of enclosing to your Excellency for the inspection of Congress, will, I flatter myself, be considered as the last glorious proof of Patriotism which could have been given by Men who aspired to the distinction of a patriot Army; and will not only confirm their claim to the justice, but will encrease their title to the gratitude of their Country.

Having seen the proceedings on the part of the Army terminate with perfect unanimity, and in a manner entirely consonant to my wishes; being impressed with the liveliest sentiments of affection for those who have so long, so patiently, and so chearfully suffered & fought under my immediate direction; having from motives of justice, duty & gratitude, spontaneously offered myself as an advocate for their rights; and having been requested to write to your Excellency earnestly entreating the most speedy decision of Congress upon the subjects of the late address from the Army to that Honorable Body—it now only remains for me to perform the task I have assumed—and to intercede in their behalf, as I now do, that the Sovereign Power will be pleased to verify the predictions I have pronounced of, and the confidence the Army have reposed in the justice of their Country.

And here, I humbly conceive it is altogether unnecessary—(while I am pleading the cause of an Army which have done & suffered more than any other Army ever did in the defence of the rights & liberties of human nature—) to expatiate on their *Claims* to the most ample compensation for their meritorious Services—because they are perfectly known to the whole World—and because, (altho 'the topics are inexhaustible) enough has already been said on the subject.

To prove these assertions, to evince that my sentiments have ever been uniform, and to shew what my ideas of the rewards in question have always been, I appeal to the Archives of Congress, and call on those sacred deposits to witness for me. And in order that my observations and arguments in favor of a future adequate provision for the Officers of the Army may be brought to remembrance again, and considered in a single point of view without giving Congress the trouble of having recourse to their files, I will beg leave to transmit herewith an Extract from a representation made by me to a Committee of Congress so long ago as the 29th of January 1778—and also the transcript, of a Letter to the President of Congress—dated near Passaic Falls Octr 11th 1780.

That in the critical & perilous moment when the last mentioned communication was made, there was the utmost danger a dissolution of the Army would have taken place unless measures similar to those recommended had been adopted, will not admit a doubt. That the adoption of the resolution granting half-pay for life has been attended with all the happy consequences I had foretold so far as respected the good of the service—let the astonishing contrast between the State of the Army at this instant, and at the former period determine. And that the establishment of funds, and security of the payment of all the just demands of the Army will be the most certain means of preserving the National faith & future tranquillity of this extensive Continent, is my decided opinion.

By the preceeding remarks it will readily be imagined that instead of retracting and reprehending—(from farther experience and reflection—) the mode of compensation so strenuously urged in the Inclosures, I am more & more confirmed in the Sentiment—and if in the wrong suffer me to please myself with the grateful delusion.

For if, besides the simple payment of their Wages, a farther compensation is not due to the sufferings & sacrafices of the Officers, then have I been mistaken indeed. If the whole Army have not merited whatever a grateful people can bestow, then have I been beguiled by prejudice & built opinion on the basis of error—If this Country should not in the event perform every thing which has been requested in the late Memorial to Congress, then will my belief become vain, and the hope that has been excited void of foundation—And "if"—(as has been suggested for the purpose of inflaming their passions) "the Officers of the Army are to be the only sufferers by this *revolution:* if retiring from the Field they are to grow old in poverty wretchedness and contempt—If they are to wade thro 'the vile mire of dependency and owe the miserable remnant of that life to charity, which has hitherto been spent in honor," then shall I have learned what ingratitude is, then shall I have realized a tale, which will imbitter every moment of my future life.

But I am under no such apprehensions, a Country rescued by their Arms from impending ruin, will never leave unpaid the debt of gratitude.

Should any intemperate or improper warmth have mingled itself amongst the foregoing observations, I must entreat your Excellency & Congress it may be attributed to the effusion of an honest zeal in the best of Causes, and that my peculiar situation may be my apology—And I hope I need not on this momentous occasion make any new protestations of personal disinterestedness, having ever renounced for myself the idea of pecuniary reward. The consciousness of having attempted faithfully to discharge my duty, and the approbation of my Country will be a sufficient recompense for my Services. I have the honor to be With perfect respect Yr Excellencys Most Obedt Servt

Go: Washington[8]

MARCH 31

TO MAJOR GENERAL NATHANAEL GREENE

Almost simultaneously with the conclusion of the crisis at Newburgh, news arrived in camp that a treaty signed in Paris had suspended hostilities between the United States and Great Britain.

Head Quarters March 31, 1783

Dear Sir

I have the pleasure to inclose to you a letter from the Marquis de la fayette, which came under cover to me, by the Packet Triumph, dispatched by the Marquis and the Count de Estaing from Cadiz to Phila.

All the Accounts which this Vessel has bro't, of a Conclusion of a General Peace, you will receive before this can reach you.

You will give the highest credit to my Sincerity, when I beg you to accept my warmest Congratulations on this glorious & happy Event, an Event which crowns all our Labors, and will sweeten the Toils which we have experienced in the course of an Eight Years distressing War.

The Army here, universally participate in the general Joy which this Event has diffused, and, from this Consideration, together with the late Resolutions of Congress, for the Commutation of the Half pay, and for a Liquidation of all their Accounts, their Minds are filled with the highest Satisfaction. I am sure you will join with me in this additional occasion of joy.

It remains only for the States to be Wise, and to establish their Independence on that Basis of inviolable efficacious Union, and firm Confederation, which may prevent their being made the Sport of European Policy—May Heaven give them Wisdom to adopt the Measures still necessary for this important Purpose. With the warmest Sentiments Esteem & Regard, I have the honor to be My Dear Sir Your most Obedient Servant

Go: Washington[9]

APRIL 5

TO MAJOR GENERAL LAFAYETTE

Head Qrs Newburgh 5th Apl 1783

My dear Marqs,

It is easier for you to conceive than for me to express the sensibility of my Heart at the communications in your letter of the 5th of Feby from Cadiz. It is to these communications we are indebted for the only account yet received of a general Pacification. My Mind upon the receipt of this news was instantly assailed by a thousand ideas—all of them contending for pre-eminence, but beleive me my dear friend none could supplant, or ever will eradicate that gratitude, which has arisen from a lively sense of the conduct of your Nation; from my obligations to many illustrious characters of it, among whom (I do not mean to flatter, when) I place you at the head of them; And from my admiration of the Virtues of your August Soverign; who at the same time that he stands confessed the Father of his own people, & defender of American rights has given the most exalted example of moderation in treating with his Enemies.

We now stand an Independent People, and have yet to learn political

Tactics. We are placed among the Nations of the Earth, and have a character to establish; but how we shall acquit our selves time must discover—the
probability, at least I fear it is, that local, or state Politics will interfere
too much with that more liberal & extensive plan of Government which
wisdom & foresight—freed from the mist of prejudice—would dictate;
and that we shall be guilty of many blunders in treading this boundless
theatre before we shall have arrived at any perfection in this Art—In a
word that the experience which is purchased at the price of difficulties
and distress, will alone convince us that the honor, power, & true Interest
of this Country must be measured by a Continental Scale; & that every
departure therefrom weakens the Union, & may ultimately break the band,
which holds us together. To avert these evils—to form a Constitution that
will give consistency, stability & dignity to the Union; & sufficient powers
to the great Council of the Nation for general purposes is a duty which
is incumbent upon every Man who wishes well to his Country—and will
meet with my aid as far as it can be rendered in the private walks of life;
for henceforward my Mind shall be unbent; & I will endeavor to glide
down the stream of life 'till I come to that abyss, from whence no traveller
is permitted to return.

. . .

The scheme, my dear Marquis which you propose as a precedent, to
encourage the emancipation of the black people of this Country from that
state of Bondage in which they are held, is a striking evidence of the
benevolence of your Heart. I shall be happy to join you in so laudable
a work; but will defer going into a detail of the business, 'till I have the
pleasure of seeing you. . . . It only remains for me now, My dear Marquis,
to make a tender of my respectful Compliments in which Mrs Washington
unites, to Madame La Fayette: & to wish you, her, & your little offspring,
all the happiness this life can afford—I will extend my Compliments to
the Gentlemen, with whom I have the honor of an Acquaintance, in your
circle. I need not add how happy I shall be to see you in America—& more
particularly at Mount Vernon—or with what truth and warmth of Affection I am Yr Most Obedt & faithful friend

Go: Washington[10]

APRIL 18
GENERAL ORDERS

Friday April 18th 1783

. . .

The Commander in Chief orders the Cessation of Hostilities between the United States of America and the King of Great Britain to be publickly proclaimed tomorrow at 12 o'clock at the Newbuilding, and that the Proclamation which will be communicated herewith, be read tomorrow evening at the head of every regiment & corps of the army—After which the Chaplains with the several Brigades will render thanks to almighty God for all his mercies, particularly for his over ruling the wrath of man to his own glory, and causing the rage of war to cease amongst the nations.

Altho the proclamation before alluded to, intends only to the prohibition of hostilities and not to the annunciation of a general peace, yet it must afford the most rational and sincere satisfaction to every benevolent mind—as it puts a period to a long and doubtful contest, stops the effusion of human blood, opens the prospect to a more splended scene, and like another morning star, promises the approach of a brighter day than hath hitherto illuminated the Western Hemisphere—on such a happy day, a day which is the harbinger of Peace, a day which compleats the eighth year of the war, it would be ingratitude not to rejoice! it would be insensibility not to participate in the general felicity!

The Commander in Chief far from endeavouring to stifle the feelings of Joy in his own bosom, offers his most cordial Congratulations on the occasion to all the Officers of every denomination, to all the Troops of the United States in General, and in particular to those gallant and persevering men who had resolved to defend the rights of their invaded country so long as the war should continue—For these are the men who ought to be considered as the pride and boast of the American Army; And, who crowned with well earned laurels, may soon withdraw from the field of Glory, to the more tranquil walks of civil life.

While the General recollects the almost infinite variety of Scenes thro which we have passed, with a mixture of pleasure, astonishment, and gratitude; while he contemplates the prospects before us with rapture; he can not help wishing that all the brave men (of whatever condition they may be) who have shared in the toils and dangers of effecting this glorious revolution, of rescuing Millions from the hand of oppression, and of laying the foundation of a great Empire, might be impressed with a proper idea of the dignifyed part they have been called to act (under the Smiles of providence) on the stage of human affairs: for, happy; thrice happy shall they be pronounced hereafter, who have contributed any thing, who have performed the meanest office in creating this steubendous [sic] *fabrick of Freedom* and *Empire* on the broad basis of Indipendency! who have assisted in protecting the rights of humane nature and establishing an Asylum for the poor and oppressed of all nations of religions. The glorius task for which we first flew to Arms being thus accomplished the liberties of our Country being fully acknowledged, and firmly secured by the smiles of heaven, on the purity of our cause, and the honest exertions of a feeble people (determined to be free) against a powerfull Nation (disposed to oppress them) and the Character of those who have persevered, through every extremity of hardship; suffering and danger being immortalized by the illustrious appellation of the *patriot Army*—Nothing more remains but for the actors of this mighty Scene to preserve a perfect unvarying consistency of character through the very last act; to close the Drama with applause; and to retire from the Military Theatre with the same approbation of Angells and men which have crowned all their former virtuous Actions. For this purpose no disorder or licentiousness must be tolerated—every considerate and well disposed soldier must remember it will be absolutely necessary to wait with patience untill peace shall be declared or Congress shall be enabled to take proper measures for the security of the public stores &ca—as soon as these Arrangements shall be made the General is confident there will be no delay in discharging with every mark of distinction & honor all the men enlisted for the war who will then have faithfully performed their engagements with the public. The General has already interested himself in their behalf; and he thinks he need not repeat the assurances of his disposition to be useful to them on the present, and every other proper occasion. In the mean time he is determined that no Military neglects or excesses shall go unpunished while he retains the command of the Army.

. . .

An extra ration of liquor to be issued to *every* man tomorrow, to drink Perpetual Peace, Independence & Happiness to the United States of America. . . .[11]

JUNE 17

TO ELIAS BOUDINOT

Washington's suggestion of bounty land as a fitting reward for military service reflected his understanding of America's future potential—and boded ill for Native Americans.

Head Quarters Newburgh June 17th 1783

Sir

I have the honor of transmitting to your Excellency for the consideration of Congress, a Petition from a large number of Officers of the Army in behalf of themselves, and such other Officers and Soldiers of the Continental Army as are entitled to rewards in lands, and may choose to avail themselves of any Previledges and Grants which shall be obtained in consequence of the present solicitation—I enclose also the Copy of a Letter from Brigr General Rufus Putnam in which the sentiments and expectations of the Petitioners are more fully explained; and in which the ideas of occupying the Posts in the western Country will be found to correspond very nearly with those I have some time since communicated to a Committee of Congress, in treating of the subject of a Peace Establishment. I will beg leave to make a few more observations on the general benifits of the Location and Settlement now proposed; and then submit the justice & policy of the measure to the wisdom of Congress.

Altho 'I pretend not myself to determine, how far the district of unsettled Country which is described in the Petition is free from the claim of every State, or how far this disposal of it may interfere with the views of Congress—yet it appears to me this is the Tract which from its local position and peculiar advantages ought to be first settled in preference to any other whatever, and I am perfectly convinced that it cannot be so advantageously settled, by any other Class of Men as by the disbanded Officers and Soldiers of the Army—to whom the faith of Government hath long since been pledged, that lands should be granted at the expiration of the War, in certain proportions, agreeably to their respective grades.

I am induced to give my sentiments thus freely on the advantages to be expected from this plan of Colonization—because it would connect our Government with the frontiers—extend our Settlements progressively—and plant a brave, a hardy & respectable Race of People, as our advanced

Post, who would be always ready & willing (in case of hostility) to combat the Savages, and check their incursions—A Settlement formed by such Men would give security to our frontiers—the very name of it would awe the Indians, and more than probably prevent the murder of many innocent Families, which frequently, in the usual mode of extending our Settlements & Encroachments on the hunting grounds of the Natives, fall the hapless Victims to savage barbarity—Besides the emoluments which might be derived from the Peltry Trade at our Factories, if such should be established; The appearance of so formidable a Settlement in the vicinity of their Towns (to say nothing of the barrier it would form against our other Neighbours) would be the most likely means to enable us to purchase upon equitable terms of the Aborigines their right of preoccupancy and to induce them to relinquish our Territories, and to remove into the illimitable regions of the West.

Much more might be said of the public utility of such a Location, as well as of the private felicity it would afford to the Individuals concerned in it—I will venture to say it is the most rational & practicable Scheme which can be adopted by a great proportion of the Officers & Soldiers of our Army, and promises them more happiness than they can expect in any other way. The Settlers, being in the prime of life, inured to hardship, & taught by experience to accomodate themselves in every situation—going in a considerable body, and under the patronage of Government, would enjoy in the first instance *advantages* in procuring subsistence, and all the necessaries for a comfortable beginning, superior to any common class of Emigrants, & quite unknown to those who have heretofore extended themselves beyond the Apalachian Mountains—they may expect after a little perseverance, *Competence & Independence* for themselves—a pleasant retreat in old age—and the fairest prospects for their Children. I have the honor to be Your Excellency's Most Obedt Servant

Go: Washington[12]

JULY 8

TO WILLIAM GORDON

The vision with which Washington beheld the new country's political future is set out at length in in this letter to his longtime friend, William Gordon.

Head Qrs Newburgh 8th July 1783

Dear Sir,

. . .

I now thank you for your kind congratulations on this event—I feel sensibly the flattering expressions, & fervent wishes with which you have accompanied them—and make a tender of mine, with much cordiality, in return. It now rests with the Confederated Powers, by the line of conduct they mean to adopt, to make this Country great, happy, & respectable; or to sink it into littleness—worse perhaps—into Anarchy & Confusion; for certain I am, that unless adequate Powers are given to Congress for the *general* purposes of the Federal Union that we shall soon moulder into dust and become contemptable in the Eyes of Europe, if we are not made the sport of their Politicks—to suppose that the general concerns of this Country can be directed by thirteen heads, or one head without competent powers, is a solecism, the bad effects of which every Man who has had the practical knowledge to judge from, that I have, is fully convinced of; tho 'none perhaps has felt them in so forcible, & distressing a degree. The People at large, and at a distance from the theatre of Action, who only know that the Machine was kept in motion, and that they are at last arrived at the first object of their wishes are satisfied with the event, without investigating the causes of the slow progress to it, or of the Expences which have accrued & which they now seem unwilling to pay—great part of which has arisen from the want of energy in the Federal Constitution which I am complaining of, and which I wish to see given to it by a Convention of the People, instead of hearing it remarked that as we have worked through an arduous contest with the Powers Congress already have (but which, by the by, have been gradually diminishing) why should they be invested with more?

To say nothing of the invisible workings of Providence, which has conducted us through difficulties where no human foresight could point the way; it will appear evident to a close Examiner, that there has been a concatenation of causes to produce this Event; which in all probability at no time, or under any other Circumstances, will combine again—We deceive ourselves therefore by the mode of reasoning, and what would be much worse, we may bring ruin upon ourselves by attempting to carry it into practice.

We are known by no other character among Nations than as the United States—Massachusetts or Virginia is no better defined, nor any more thought of by Foreign Powers than the County of Worcester in Massachusetts is by Virginia, or Gloucester County in Virginia is by Massachusetts (respectable as they are); and yet these Counties, with as much propriety might oppose themselves to the Laws of the State in which they are, as an Individual State can oppose itself to the Federal Government, by which it is, or ought to be bound. Each of these Counties has, no doubt, its local polity & Interests. these should be attended to, & brought before their respective legislatures with all the force their importance merits; but when they come in contact with the general Interest of the State—when superior considerations preponderate in favor of the whole—their Voices should be heard no more—so should it be with individual States when compared to the Union—Otherwise I think it may properly be asked for what purpose do we farcically pretend to be United? Why do Congress spend Months together in deliberating upon, debating, & digesting plans, which are made as palatable, & as wholesome to the Constitution of this Country as the nature of things will admit of, when some States will pay no attention to them, & others regard them but partially; by which means all those evils which proceed from delay, unfelt by the whole; while the compliant States are not only suffering by these neglects, but in many instances are injured most capitolly by their own exertions, which are wasted for want of the United effort. A hundred thousand men coming one after another cannot move a Ten weight—but the united strength of 50 would transport it with ease. So has it been with great part of the expence which has been incurred this war. In a word, I think the blood & treasure, which has been spent in it has been lavished to little purpose, unless we can be better Cemented; and that is not to be effected while so little attention is paid to the recommendations of the Soverign Power.

To me it would seem not more absurd, to hear a traveller, who was setting out on a long journey, declare he would take no money in his pocket
to defray the Expences of it but rather depend upon chance & charity
lest he should misapply it than are the expressions of so much fear of the
powers and means of Congress—For Heavens sake who are Congress?
are they not the Creatures of the People, amenable to them for their Conduct, and dependant from day to day on their bread? Where then can be
the danger of giving them such Powers as are adequate to the great ends
of Government, and to all the general purposes of the Confederation (I
repeat the word *general,* because I am no advocate for their having to do
with the particular policy of any state, further than it concerns the Union
at large)—What may be the consequences if they have not these Powers
I am at no loss to guess; and deprecate the worst; for sure I am, we shall,
in a little time, become as contemptable in the great Scale of Politicks as
we now have it in our power to be respectable—and that, when the band
of Union gets once broken, everything ruinous to our future prospects is
to be apprehended—the best that can come of it, in my humble opinion
is, that we shall sink into obscurity, unless our Civil broils should keep us
in remembrance & fill the page of history with the direful consequences
of them.

You say that, Congress loose time by pressing a mode that does
not accord with the genius of the People, & will thereby endanger the
Union—And that it is the quantum they want—Permit me to ask if the
quantum has not already been demanded? whether it has been obtained?
and whence proceed the accumulated evils—& poignant distresses of
many of the public Creditors. particularly in the Army? For my own part
I hesitate not a moment to confess, that I see nothing wherein the Union
is endangered by the late requisition of that body, but a prospect of much
good, justice, & propriety from the compliance with it. I know of no Tax
more convenient—none so agreeable, as that which every man may pay,
or let it alone as his convenience, abilities, or Inclination shall prompt—I
am therefore a warm friend to the Impost . . . Mrs Washington joins me in
Compliments to Mrs Gordon. and I am Dr Sir—Yr Most Obedt & Most
Hble Servt

Go: Washington[13]

SEPTEMBER 2

TO ANNIS BOUDINOT STOCKTON

Annis Boudinot Stockton (1736–1801), sister of Elias Boudinot, was one of America's first important female poets. Her poems in praise of Washington elicited his admiration and gratitude—along with a dose of flirtatious levity.

Rocky Hill [N.J.] Septr 2nd 1783

You apply to me, My dear Madam, for absolution as tho 'I was your father Confessor; and as tho 'you had committed a crime, great in itself, yet of the venial class—You have reason good—for I find myself strangely disposed to be a very indulgent ghostly adviser on this occasion and, notwithstanding "you are the most offending Soul alive" (that is if it is a crime to write elegant Poetry) yet if you will come & dine with me on Thursday, and go thro 'the proper course of penetence which shall be prescribed, I will strive hard to assist you in expiating these Poetical Trespasses on this side of Purgatory—Nay more, if it rests with me to direct your future lucubrations, I shall certainly urge you to a repetition of the same conduct, on purpose to shew what an admirable knack you have at confession & reformation—and so without more hesitation I shall venture to command the Muse not to be restrained by its grounded timidity, but to go on and prosper.

You see Madam, when once the Woman has tempted us, & we have tasted the forbidden fruit, there is no such thing as checking our appetites, whatever the consequences may be. You will, I dare say, recognize our being the genuine descendents of those who are reputed to be our great Progenitors.

Before I come to the more serious conclusion of my letter—I must beg leave to say a word or two about these fine things you have been telling in such harmonious & beautiful numbers—Fiction is to be sure the very life & Soul of Poetry—All Poets & Poetesses have been endulged in the free and indisputable use of it, time out of Mind—and to oblige you to make such an excellent Poem, on such a Subject, without any materials but those of simple reality, would be as cruel as the Edict of Pharoah which compelled the Children of Israel to manufacture Bricks without the necessary Ingredients.

Thus are you sheltered under the Authority of prescription, and I will not dare to charge you with an intentional breach of the Rules of the Decalogue in giving so bright a colouring to the Services I have been enabled to render my Country; tho 'I am not conscious of deserving any thing more at your hands, than what the purest & most disinterested friendship has a right to claim; actuated by which you will permit me, to thank you in the most affectionate manner for the kind wishes you have so happily expressed for me & the partner of all my Domestic enjoyments—Be assured we can never forget our friend at Morven; and that I am, My dear Madam, with every sentiment of friendship & esteem Your Most Obedt & obliged Servt

Go: Washington[14]

NOVEMBER 2

FAREWELL ADDRESS TO THE ARMY

The Treaty of Paris, officially ending the war and establishing American independence, was signed on September 3. News of it reached North America at the end of October. The time had come to disband the army, and for Washington to say farewell to the officers and men who had served with him during the past nine years.

Genll Washington's Farewell Orders issued to the Armies of the United States of America the 2d day of Novr 1783—*Rocky Hill,* near Princeton

The United States in Congress assembled, after giving the most honorable testimony to the Merits of the Federal Armies, and presenting them with the thanks of their Country for their long, eminent and Faithful Services, having thought proper, by their Proclamation bearing date the 18th day of October last, to discharge such part of the Troops, as were engaged for the War, and to permit the Officers on Furlough to retire from Service from and after tomorrow, which Proclamation having been communicated in the public papers for the information and government of all concerned, it only remains for the Commander in Chief to address himself once more, and that for the last time, to the Armies of the United States (however widely dispersed the Individuals who composed them may be) and to bid them an affectionate—a long farewell.

But before the Commander in Chief takes his final leave of those he holds most dear, he wishes to indulge himself a few moments in calling to mind a slight review of the past, He will then take the liberty of exploring with his Military friends their future prospects, of advising the general line of conduct which in his opinion ought to be persued, and he will conclude the Address, by expressing the obligations he feels himself under for the spirited and able assistance he has experienced from them, in the performance of an arduous office.

A contemplation of the compleat attainment (at a period earlier than could have been expected) of the object for which we contended, against so formidable a power, cannot but inspire us with astonishment and gratitude—The disadvantageous circumstances on our part, under which the War was undertaken, can never be forgotten—The singular interpositions of Providence in our feeble condition were such, as could scarcely escape the attention of the most unobserving, while the unparallelled perseverence of the Armies of the United States, through almost every possible suffering and discouragement, for the space of eight long years, was little short of a standing Miracle.

It is not the meaning nor within the compass of this Address, to detail the hardships peculiarly incident to our Service, or to discribe the distresses which in several instances have resulted from the extremes of hunger and nakedness, combined with the rigors of an inclement season. Nor is it necessary to dwell on the dark side of our past affairs. Every American Officer and Soldier must now console himself for any unpleasant circumstances which may have occurred, by a recollection of the uncommon scenes in which he has been called to act, no inglorious part; and the astonishing Events of which he has been a witness—Events which have seldom, if ever before, taken place on the stage of human action, nor can they probably ever happen again. For who has before seen a disciplined Army formed at once from such raw materials? Who that was not a witness could imagine, that the most violent local prejudices would cease so soon, and that Men who came from the different parts of the Continent, strongly disposed by the habits of education, to despise and quarrel with each other, would instantly become but one patriotic band of Brothers? Or who that was not on the spot can trace the steps by which such a wonderful Revolution has been effected, and such a glorious period put to all our Warlike toils?

It is universally acknowledged that the enlarged prospect of happiness, opened by the confirmation of our Independence and Sovereignty, almost exceeds the power of description. And shall not the brave Men who have

contributed so essentially to these inestimable acquisitions, retiring victorious from the Field of War, to the Field of Agriculture, participate in all the
blessings which have been obtained? In such a Republic, who will exclude
them from the rights of Citizens and the fruits of their labours? In such a
Country, so happily circumstanced, the persuits of Commerce and the cultivation of the Soil, will unfold to industry the certain road to competence.
To those hardy Soldiers, who are actuated by the spirit of adventure, the
Fisheries will afford ample and profitable employment, and the extensive
and fertile Regions of the West, will yield a most happy Asylum to those,
who fond of domestic enjoyment, are seeking for personal independence.
Nor is it possible to conceive that any one of the United States will prefer a
National Bankrupcy and a dissolution of the Union, to a compliance with
the requisitions of Congress and the payment of its just debts, so that the
Officers and Soldiers may expect considerable assistance in recommencing
their civil occupations, from the sums due to them from the Public, which
must and will most inevitably be paid.

In order to effect this desireable purpose, and to remove the prejudices which may have taken possession of the Minds of any of the good
People of the States, it is earnestly recommended to all the Troops that,
with strong attachments to the Union, they should carry with them into
civil Society the most conciliating dispositions; and that they should prove
themselves not less virtuous and usefull as Citizens, than they have been
persevering and victorious as Soldiers. What tho 'there should be some
envious Individuals who are unwilling to pay the Debt the public has
contracted, or to yield the tribute due to Merit, yet let such unworthy treatment produce no invective, or any instance of intemperate conduct, let it
be remembered that the unbiased voice of the Free Citizens of the United
States has promised the just reward, and given the merited applause; let it
be known and remembered that the reputation of the Federal Armies is established beyond the reach of Malevolence, and let a conciousness of their
atchievements and fame, still incite the Men who composed them to honorable Actions; under the persuasion that the private virtues of œconomy,
prudence and industry, will not be less amiable in civil life, than the more
splendid qualities of valour, perseverance and enterprise, were in the Field:
Every one may rest assured that much, very much of the future happiness
of the Officers and Men, will depend upon the wise and manly conduct
which shall be adopted by them, when they are mingled with the great

body of the Community. And altho', the General has so frequently given it as his opinion in the most public and explicit manner, that unless the principles of the Federal Government were properly supported, and the Powers of the Union encreased, the honor, dignity, and justice of the Nation would be lost for ever; yet he cannot help repeating on this occasion, so interesting a sentiment, and leaving it as his last injunction to every Officer and every Soldier, who may view the subject in the same serious point of light, to add his best endeavours to those of his worthy fellow Citizens towards effecting these great and valuable purposes, on which our very existence as a Nation so materially depends.

The Commander in Chief conceives little is now wanting to enable the Soldier to change the Military character into that of the Citizen, but that steady and decent tenor of behaviour which has generally distinguished, not only the Army under his immediate Command, but the different Detachments and seperate Armies, through the course of the War; from their good sense and prudence he anticipates the happiest consequences; And while he congratulates them on the glorious occasion which renders their Services in the Field no longer necessary, he wishes to express the strong obligations he feels himself under, for the assistance he has received from every Class—and in every instance. He presents his thanks in the most serious and affectionate manner to the General Officers, as well for their Counsel on many interesting occasions, as for their ardor in promoting the success of the plans he had adopted—To the Commandants of Regiments and Corps, and to the other Officers for their great Zeal and attention in carrying his orders promptly into execution—To the Staff for their alacrity and exactness in performing the duties of their several Departments—And to the Non-commissioned officers and private Soldiers, for their extraordinary patience in suffering, as well as their invincible fortitude in Action—To the various branches of the Army, the General takes this last and solemn oppertunity of professing his inviolable attachment & friendship—He wishes more than bare professions were in his power, that he was really able to be usefull to them all in future life; He flatters himself however, they will do him the justice to believe, that whatever could with propriety be attempted by him, has been done. And being now to conclude these his last public Orders, to take his ultimate leave, in a short time, of the Military Character, and to bid a final adieu to the Armies he has so long had the honor to Command—he can only again offer in their behalf his recommendations to their grateful Country, and his prayers to the God of Armies. May ample justice be done them here; and may the choicest of Heaven's favors both here and hereafter attend those, who under the divine auspices have secured innumerable blessings for others: With these Wishes, and this benediction, the Commander in Chief is about to retire from service—The Curtain of seperation will soon be drawn—and the Military Scene to him will be closed for ever.[15]

––––––––––

DECEMBER 23
RESIGNATION ADDRESS TO THE CONTINENTAL CONGRESS

The British evacuated New York on November 25. After a final, emotional leavetaking with his general officers at Fraunces Tavern on December 4, Washington rode south toward Annapolis, Maryland, where he would present his resignation to Congress. Passing through Philadelphia on the eighth and Baltimore on the seventeenth, he arrived at Annapolis on the twenty-third. He was eager to get home to Mount Vernon by Christmas, but one final formality remained. Washington read his resignation address with trembling hands, and tears in his eyes.

The great events on which my resignation depended having at length taken place; I have now the honor of offering my sincere Congratulations to Congress & of presenting myself before them to surrender into their hands the trust committed to me, and to claim the indulgence of retiring from the Service of my Country.

Happy in the confirmation of our Independence and Sovereignty, and pleased with the oppertunity afforded the United States of becoming a respectable Nation, I resign with satisfaction the Appointment I accepted with diffidence—A diffidence in my abilities to accomplish so arduous a task, which however was superseded by a confidence in the rectitude of our Cause, the support of the Supreme Power of the Union, and the patronage of Heaven.

The successful termination of the War has verified the most sanguine expectations—and my gratitude for the interposition of Providence, and the assistance I have received from my Countrymen encreases with every review of the momentous Contest.

While I repeat my obligations to the Army in general, I should do injustice to my own feelings not to acknowledge in this place the peculiar Services and distinguished merits of the Gentlemen who have been attached to my person during the War. It was impossible the choice of confidential Officers to compose my family should have been more fortunate. Permit me Sir, to recommend in particular those, who have continued in Service to the present moment, as worthy of the favorable notice & patronage of Congress.

I consider it an indispensable duty to close this last solemn act of my Official life, by commending the Interests of our dearest Country to the protection of Almighty God, and those who have the superintendence of them, to his holy keeping.

Having now finished the work assigned me, I retire from the great theatre of Action—and bidding an Affectionate farewell to this August body under whose orders I have so long acted, I here offer my Commission, and take my leave of all the employments of public life.[16]

Amid awed silence, Washington handed his commission and address to Thomas Mifflin, who read a brief note of thanks. The delegates then removed their hats, and Washington, a private citizen, left the room. He reached Mount Vernon, and the embraces of Martha and his grandchildren, on Christmas Eve.

———

Notes

Guide to Repository Symbols

CLjJC   Copley Newspapers Incorporated, James S. Copley Library, La Jolla, Calif.

CSmH   Huntington Library, San Marino, Calif.

Ct   Connecticut State Library, Hartford

CtHi   Connecticut Historical Society, Hartford

CtY   Yale University, Sterling Memorial Library, New Haven, Conn.

DeHi   Historical Society of Delaware, Wilmington

DLC   Library of Congress, Washington, D.C.

DLC:GW   Library of Congress: Papers of George Washington

DNA:PCC   National Archives: Papers of the Continental Congress

DTP   Tudor Place Foundation, Washington, D.C.

Ford, *Writings*   Worthington Chauncey Ford, ed., *The Writings of George Washington,* 14
  vols., New York, 1889–93

MHi   Massachusetts Historical Society, Boston

MiU-C   University of Michigan, William L. Clements Library, Ann Arbor

N   New York State Library, Albany, N.Y.

NhD   Dartmouth College, Hanover, N.H.

NHi   New-York Historical Society

NjHi   New Jersey Historical Society, Newark

NjMoNP   Morristown National Historical Park, N.J.

NjP   Princeton University, Princeton, N.J.

NN   New York Public Library

NNGL   Gilder Lehrman Collection, on deposit at the New-York Historical Society

NNPM   Pierpont Morgan Library, New York, N.Y.

OkTG   Thomas Gilcrease Institute of American History and Art, Tulsa, Okla.

PGW   Theodore J. Crackel, ed., *The Papers of George Washington*: *Revolutionary War
  Series.*, 17 vols. to date., Charlottesville, Va., 1985–

PHC   Haverford College, Haverford, Pa.

PHi   Historical Society of Pennsylvania, Philadelphia

Powell, *Leven Powell*   Robert C. Powell, ed., *A Biographical Sketch of Col. Leven Powell*, Alexandria, Va., 1877

PPAmP   American Philosophical Society, Philadelphia

PPRF   Rosenbach Museum and Library, Philadelphia

P.R.O.   Public Record Office, London

PVFNHiP   Valley Forge National Historical Park, Pa.

PWacD   David Library of the American Revolution, Washington Crossing, Pa.

R-Ar   Rhode Island State Archives, Providence

RPJCB   John Carter Brown Library, Providence, R.I.

ScHi   South Carolina Historical Society, Charleston

Sparks, *Writings*   Jared Sparks, ed., *The Writings of George Washington*, 12 vols., Boston, 1833–1837

Van Rensselaer, *Annals of the Van Rensselaers*   Maunsell Van Rensselaer, *Annals of the Van Rensselaers in the United States.*, Albany, N.Y., 1888

ViHi   Virginia Historical Society, Richmond

ViMtV   Mount Vernon Ladies' Association, Mount Vernon, Va.

1775

1. Benjamin Rush, *The Autobiography of Benjamin Rush: His "Travels Through Life" Together with His Commonplace Book for 1789–1813,* edited by George W. Corner (Princeton: Princeton University Press, 1948), 113.
2. DNA:PCC, item 152.
3. DTP.
4. DLC:GW.
5. ViMtV.
6. ViMtV.
7. DLC:GW.
8. DLC:GW.
9. MHi: John Thomas Papers.
10. MiU-C: Gage Papers.
11. NN: Schuyler Papers.
12. NN: Emmet Collection.
13. NNPM.
14. CLjJC.
15. DLC:GW.
16. Sparks, *Writings,* 3:151–154.
17. RPJCB.

1776

1. DLC:GW.
2. RPJCB.
3. DLC:GW.
4. NN: Schuyler Papers.
5. RPJCB.
6. RPJCB. The portraits appear in PGW, 3:226–7.
7. RPJCB.
8. RPJCB.

9. DNA:PCC, item 152.
10. NhD: Wheelock Papers.
11. DLC:GW.
12. DNA:PCC, item 152
13. DLC:GW.
14. DNA:PCC, item 152.
15. NjP: Armstrong Collection.
16. DLC:GW.
17. DNA:PCC, item 152.
18. DLC:GW.
19. DNA:PCC, item 152.
20. DNA:PCC, item 152.
21. DLC:GW.
22. DLC:GW.
23. DNA:PCC, item 152.
24. DLC:GW.
25. DLC:GW.
26. CtHi: Hoadly Collection.
27. DLC:GW.
28. DNA:PCC, item 152.
29. DNA:PCC, item 152.
30. DNA:PCC, item 152.
31. CtY: Washington Family Papers.
32. DNA:PCC, item 152.
33. DNA:PCC, item 152.
34. Ford, *Writings*, 4:456–60.
35. DNA:PCC, item 152.
36. DNA:PCC, item 152.
37. DLC:GW.
38. DNA:PCC, item 152.
39. RPJCB.
40. NNGL: Knox Papers.
41. Powell, *Leven Powell*, 44–45.
42. DNA:PCC, item 152.
43. DNA:PCC, item 152.

1777

1. DNA:PCC, item 152.
2. DNA:PCC, item 152.
3. N: New York Provincial Congress Revolutionary Papers.
4. DLC:GW.
5. NjMoNP.
6. DLC:GW.
7. Phi: Gratz Collection.
8. DLC:GW.
9. DLC:GW.

10. DLC:GW.
11. DLC:GW.
12. DNA:PCC, item 152.
13. DNA:PCC, item 152.
14. DNA:PCC, item 152.
15. DLC:GW.
16. DLC:GW.
17. DLC:GW.
18. NNGL.
19. NHi: Gates Papers.
20. *Continental Journal* (Boston), April 8, 1779.
21. DLC: GW.
22. DLC: GW.
23. DLC:GW.
24. PVFNHiP.
25. DLC:GW.

1778

1. DLC:GW.
2. R-Ar.
3. PGW, 13:78–79.
4. DNA:PCC, item 152.
5. NHi: Gates Papers.
6. DLC:GW.
7. Monthly Magazine (London), 9 (1800), 545–46.
8. Ct: Trumbull Papers.
9. PHC.
10. Phi: Washington-Biddle correspondence.
11. DLC:GW.
12. DLC: Digges-L'Enfant-Morgan Papers.
13. DLC:GW.
14. ViHi.
15. ViMtV.
16. DLC:GW.
17. DNA:PCC, item 152.
18. DLC:GW.
19. DNA:PCC, item 152.
20. DNA:PCC, item 152.
21. Van Rensselaer, *Annals of the Van Rensselaers*, facing p.147.
22. DLC:GW.
23. *United States Gazette* (Philadelphia), October 25, 1826.
24. MHi: Heath Papers.
25. DLC:GW.
26. DLC:GW.
27. ScHi: Laurens Papers.
28. DLC:GW.

1779

1. ScHi: Laurens Papers.
2. DeHi.
3. OkTG.
4. DLC:GW.
5. DLC:GW.
6. Phi: Wayne Mss.
7. RPJCB.
8. NHi: George and Martha Washington Letters.
9. DLC:GW.
10. DLC:GW.
11. Privately owned.
12. DLC:GW.
13. NjMoNp.

1780

1. PWacD: Sol Feinstone Collection, on deposit PPAmP.
2. DLC:GW.
3. RPJCB.
4. MHi: Bowdoin-Temple Letters [Note: Privately owned].
5. Privately owned.
6. DLC:GW.
7. DNA:PCC, item 152.
8. Facsimile published in *This Month at Goodspeeds*, March 1941.
9. DNA:PCC, item 152.
10. P.R.O. 30/35, Carlton Papers, no. 3030.
11. NjHi.
12. Phi: Conarroe Collection.
13. DNA:PCC, item 152.

1781

1. NjMoNP.
2. Privately owned.
3. Phi: Wayne MSS.
4. Privately owned.
5. DLC:GW.
6. DLC:GW.
7. DLC:GW.
8. MHi: Heath Papers.
9. PWacD: Sol Feinstone Collection, on deposit PPAmP.
10. DLC:GW.
11. Privately owned.
12. Privately owned.
13. DLC:GW.
14. DLC:GW.

15. Privately owned.
16. DLC:GW.
17. DLC:GW.
18. DLC:GW.
19. DLC:GW.
20. DLC:GW.
21. DLC:GW.
22. P.R.O.: Cornwallis Papers, London.
23. DNA:PCC, item 152.

1782

1. PWaC: Sol Feinstone Collection, on deposit PPAmP.
2. DLC:GW.
3. DLC:GW.
4. DLC:GW.
5. DLC: Rochambeau Papers.

1783

1. DLC:GW.
2. DLC:GW.
3. DLC:GW.
4. Worthington Chauncey Ford, Journals of the Continental Congress (Washington, D.C.: Government Printing Office, 1904–37), 24:295–97.
5. DLC:GW.
6. CSmH.
7. MHi.
8. DNA:PCC, item 152.
9. NjMoNP.
10. DLC:GW.
11. DLC:GW.
12. DNA:PCC, item 152.
13. DLC:GW.
14. PWacD: Sol Feinstone Collection, on deposit PPAmP.
15. DLC:GW.
16. NN: Emmet Collection.

Index

Adams, John, 3–4
African-Americans
    as slaves, 226, 230
    GW's views on, 42–43, 175
    in Continental Army, 136
    plans for emancipation of, 275
Albany (N.Y.), 103
Alexandria (Va.), 5, 18
Alexandria (N.J.), 78
Allen, Mr., 113
Allentown (Pa.), 157
André, John, 209–12, 214
Annapolis (Md.), 288
Appalachian Mountains, 279
Armstrong, John, 109, 112
Arnold, Benedict, 27, 230–31
    in Canada, 16, 34
    at Saratoga, 115
    attacks Virginia, 224–25
    letters to, 21–22
    treason of, 209–12, 214
Assunpink Creek (N.J.), 95

Baltimore (Md.), 80, 288
Basking Ridge (N.J.), 78
Bassett, Anna Maria Dandridge, 8
Bassett, Burwell
    letters to, 7–8
Baum, Friedrich, 107
Baylor, George, 36
Beall, Rezin, 77
Bennington (Vt.), 107
Bergen County (N.J.), 213
Billingsport (N.J.), 112
Blaine, Ephraim, 141
Blair, John, 165
Bland, Humphrey, 25
Bloomingdale (N.Y.), 67
Board of War
    letters to, 135
Bordentown (N.J.), 88, 94–95

Boston, 24, 164
    evacuation of, 47–49
    siege of, 3, 9–10, 40–41,
        43–46
Boudinot, Elias, 264
    letters to, 271–73, 278–79
Bowdoin, James
    letters to, 204–5
Bradley, Philip Burr, 86
Brandywine Creek (Pa.), 144
    battle of, 109–111, 117
Brant, Joseph, 182, 189
Bristol (Pa.), 88, 221
Brooklyn Heights (N.Y.), 59–60
Brown, Roger, 235
Brunswick (N.J.), 94, 97
Bucks County (Pa.), 107
Bunker Hill (Mass.), 47
    battle of, 18, 20, 39, 46
Bunner, Rudolph, 160
Burgoyne, John, 103, 107, 114–16,
        118–19, 122, 129
Burlington (N.J.), 96–97
Butler, John, 182, 189
Butler, Richard, 158, 220
Butler, Walter, 189

Cadwalader, John, 88, 94–95
Cadwalader, Lambert, 76–77
Calvert, Benedict, 18
Cambridge (Mass.), 9–10, 50
Camden (S.C.)
    battle of, 208
Camden, Lord, 148
Campbell, Alexander, 36
Canada, 103
GW's address to inhabitants, 22–24
    invasion of, 16–17, 21–22, 27, 34, 37,
        165–68
Carleton, Guy, 17, 249–50
Carroll, Daniel, 111

297